DOWNSIZING THE U.S.A.

Downsizing the U.S.A.

Thomas H. Naylor
and
William H. Willimon

William B. Eerdmans Publishing Company
Grand Rapids, Michigan / Cambridge, U.K.

© 1997 Wm. B. Eerdmans Publishing Co.
255 Jefferson Ave. S.E., Grand Rapids, Michigan 49503 /
P.O. Box 163, Cambridge CB3 9PU U.K.

Printed in the United States of America

02 01 00 99 98 97   7 6 5 4 3 2 1

Library of Congress Cataloging-in-Publication Data

Naylor, Thomas H., 1936-
    Downsizing the U.S.A., / Thomas H. Naylor and William H. Willimon.
        p.   cm.
    Includes bibliographical references.
    ISBN 0-8028-4330-1 (paper : alk. paper)
    1. United States — Social conditions — 1980- 2. United States — Economic
    conditions — 1981- 3. United States — Social policy — 1993-I. Willimon,
    William H. II. Title.
    HN59.2.N394 1997
    306'.0973 — dc21   97-8919
                                                                CIP

Contents

In the Beginning

It is a glorious sight, rendered in exact detail. A large, sixteenth-century warship sails upon rolling waves. Cannon bristle from every opening. There must be two hundred of them protruding on all sides of the vessel. The ship's many sails billow in the strong wind. Each sail is held by scores of ropes, ladders, all sorts of pulleys and wheels. A lone sailor peers from the crow's nest toward the distant shore.

In his engraving *Man-of-War with Fall of Icarus*, Pieter Bruegel depicts a wondrous sight, homage to the summit of technological achievement, the cultural complexity, the powers of invention and organization in that day.[1] His drawing of a warship underway would be the equivalent of a photograph of a B-2 stealth bomber or a pictorial representation of President Reagan's Strategic Defense Initiative in our own day. Was there ever anything more grand and glorious than this ship, product of our own hands, fierce, powerful, indomitable?

Look more closely. Up in the right-hand corner of the etching, high in the sunlit sky, two figures plummet toward earth. Their arms bear wings, but the wings are falling apart; feathers fly. They are Daedalus and Icarus of Greek mythology, the father and son who tried to fashion wings and soar toward heaven. Flying too close to the sun, their wax wings melted and they perished. Not even the huge ship can save them from doom.

See? Bruegel has drawn a critique of our nascent technology and

---

1. Pieter Bruegel, *Man-of-War with Fall of Icarus*, ca. 1565, London, British Museum.

1

our obsession with bigness. The glorious ship is sailing into oblivion. Size and technological complexity are not risk-free. Daedalus and Icarus remind us of the price of our uncritical affirmation of bigness and modern complexification. This book is about that.

Henry David Thoreau on the Internet

We are in great haste to construct a magnetic telegraph from Maine to Texas, but Maine and Texas, it may be, have nothing important to communicate. . . . We are eager to tunnel under the Atlantic and bring the Old World some weeks nearer to the New, but perchance the first news that will leak through into the broad, flapping American ear will be that the Princess Adelaide has the whooping cough.

Henry David Thoreau
Walden

Another ancient image comes to our minds as we begin this book — a story, a Bible story from our beginnings. In the beginning, according to Genesis, the first book of the Bible, there was one human community. There was "one language and few words" (Genesis 11:1, RSV). This is the world as God created it to be — unified, simple, communal. People are able to communicate. Linguistic comprehension is no problem with one language and few words.

> Now the whole earth had one language and the same words. And as they migrated from the east, they came upon a plain in the land of Shinar and settled there. And they said to one another, "Come, let us make bricks, and burn them thoroughly." And they had brick for stone, and bitumen for mortar. Then they said, "Come, let us build ourselves a city, and a tower with its top in the heavens, and let us make a name for ourselves; otherwise we shall be scattered abroad upon the face of the whole earth." The LORD came down to see the city and the tower, which mortals had built. And the LORD said, "Look, they are one people, and they have all one language; and this is only the beginning of what they will do; nothing that they propose to do will now be impossible for them. Come, let us go down, and confuse their language there, so that they will not

understand one another's speech." So the Lord scattered them abroad from there over the face of all the earth, and they left off building the city. Therefore it was called Babel, because there the Lord confused the language of all the earth; and from there the Lord scattered them abroad over the face of all the earth.

Genesis 11:1-9, NRSV

" 'Come! Let us bake bricks, firing them with fire.' They had brick instead of stone and pitch instead of mortar." Technology is born. Among the Israelites, stone would be the natural building material, for there is plenty of stone to be had everywhere. But these people decided to follow the Babylonian practice of using brick.

Bruegel also painted this episode. In his rendering of the Babel story, a great, elaborate tower reaches into the heavens. At the bottom of the picture, barely noticeable, a king in royal robes is visiting the building site.[2] The builder bows before him, showing his plans. The scene is rather silly, knowing as we do, how the story of the great tower will end.

And what are they creating with their bricks? "Come, let us build ourselves a city, and a tower with its top in the sky, in order that we may make for ourselves a name, lest we be scattered abroad upon the face of the whole earth." Note the excessive use of the first-person pronoun. "Let *us* build *ourselves* . . ." They build for themselves, for their own glory, to protect themselves from being "spread abroad upon the face of the whole earth." They build out of fear of human vulnerability. This project is in direct disobedience to the command of God, for God told the first man and woman to "be fruitful and multiply," to "fill the earth" (Genesis 1:28, RSV), to scatter abroad over the earth.

But scattered abroad, humankind feels vulnerable. There is strength in numbers. So we huddle together. We build big cities and big states and erect walls. Now, on the plain of Shinar, we "build ourselves a city, and a tower with its top in the sky."

Now God enters the story. "And the Lord God came down to see the city and the tower which human beings had built." There is delightful humor here. The builders of the great city and tower sought to build such a big structure that its top would reach to the very heavens. Yet, for all their efforts, God has to come down even to see

---

2. Pieter Bruegel, *The Tower of Babel*, Vienna, Kunsthistorisches Museum.

the tower! The impressiveness of their human engineering is far less impressive when seen from a divine perspective.

God says, "Behold! They are one people, with one language. This is only the beginning of what they will do; nothing that they decide to do will be impossible for them." It is not so much that the great God is threatened by these presumptuous humans, it is that, if they have tried to be gods unto themselves, with their tower in the heavens, what else might they try?

God now descends a second time, this time to confuse their speech. Now, "God scattered them." Once, God wanted the whole earth populated with people, being fruitful and multiplying. Now, there will be scattering, but not due to the fulfillment of God's plans. Rather, this scattering is the confused, cacophonous babble of different languages. The writer ends the story by saying, "That is why its name is Babel, because there the Lord confused the language of all the earth."

The story begins with the self-confident human declaration, "Let us make a name for ourselves. Let us organize! Let us build!"

The story ends with the babbling confusion of tongues.

The people who told this story had seen the great Babylonian ziggurat temple-towers. Those technological marvels are here interpreted as the embodiment of human pride and the lust for power, self-sufficiency, autonomy. The city, which is built for human protection, is here interpreted as a sign of human rebellion and disobedience of God.

Images of Babel, eerie echoes of an ancient tale, are evoked by this revealing statement by Walter Gropius, founder of the Bauhaus architectural school in early twentieth-century Germany:

> Together let us design, conceive, and create the new structure of the future, which will embrace architecture and sculpture and painting in one unity and which will one day rise toward heaven from the hands of a million workers like the crystal symbol of a new faith.[3]

3. Quoted by Stanley J. Grenz, *A Primer on Postmodernism* (Grand Rapids: Eerdmans, 1996), p. 23. A curious revival of architectural fascination with Babel is Rem Koolhaas and Bruce Moe, *S, M, L, XL: Small, Medium, Large, Extra-Large* (New York: Monacelli Press, 1996). Koolhaas exalts extra-large cities because their size renders them ungovernable and therefore immune to centralized state control. Koolhaas adores "Babel-like multilevel car parks" as a glory of modern architecture.

It is the Tower of Babel — done this time in glass and steel, paid for by Seagrams, Donald Trump, or the Rockefellers in Manhattan — all over again. Modernity's "new faith" may not be so new.

The Bible story suggests that our human desire for unity and coherence ought to be evaluated critically. Isn't human unity a good thing, in and of itself? Not so, suggests the story of Babel. Unity for what purpose? Unity on what basis? Fearful humanity attempts to deal with its vulnerability in a variety of ways, one of which is organizing and producing, "making a name for ourselves."

This book is "postmodern" in the sense that herein we acknowledge the shadow side of modernity's lust for universal solutions to problems, dehumanizing uniformity, and standardized mass production. We choose a certain amount of social disorder over state-imposed order, diversity of groups over national unity, a decentered willingness to risk the diffusion of power among a variety of groups, and an abiding trust in the local, the specific, and the small as opposed to the universal, the general, and the large.

The very form of this book embodies our political convictions. The book is a communal construct — two writers rather than one. We have deliberately avoided the temptation to speak with one voice or to smooth the rough edges of our interaction with one another. Our text is frequently broken by a collage of other voices. Jacques Derrida has called the collage the primary form of discourse in a postmodern world which has become reticent to impose unity, order, and meaning upon the rich diversity of reality and which attempts to hear those voices modernity has hitherto suppressed. The collage quite naturally draws you, the reader, into our conversation, requiring you to fill in the gaps and to deal with the discrepancies. The collage demonstrates that we have forsaken the quest for top-down imposition of order or meaning by "experts." Our "voice" in this book is neither univocal nor stable. We believe that we must get over modernity's fear of disunity and conflict, that the local community (i.e., *you*) must become involved in the production of a better future.

Our book is the fruit of a decade of collaboration between an economist and a theologian, further elaboration of themes begun in earlier collaborative works like *The Search for Meaning, The Search for Meaning in the Workplace,* and *The Abandoned Generation.* Thomas has done most of the research and writing for this book.[4] For Thomas, this

4. Some of the ideas contained in this book first appeared in the following articles by Thomas H. Naylor: "Downsizing the United States of America," *Chal-*

book is not only an intellectual project, it is also the result of a deliberate move he and his family made a few years ago from urban America to rural Vermont.

Will has come after Thomas to an interest in these themes. As a campus pastor, Will developed an interest in the search for community and the effects of organizational size upon human life. After Will collaborated on a book on denominational downsizing (*A New Connection: Reforming the United Methodist Church*, Abingdon, 1996, with Andy Langford), Thomas invited Will to join him in his continuing thought on how the size and complexity of institutions affect the quality of life therein. From the beginning of this project, we decided that we would not demand complete agreement among ourselves in order to put forth an idea for reform. Therefore, although we believe that all of the proposals herein are worthy of debate in our various communities, each of us is not equally invested in all of the proposals. What we need is not caution and uniform consensus, but lively, courageous debate.

We include many quotes within the text — quotes from persons as diverse as Stokely Carmichael and John Stuart Mill. By these quotes we indicate that we are in dialogue with a diverse community of thinkers who are thinking it is time for fundamental change in our institutions, though there is much disagreement among us as to the means and the ends of these changes.

The American Angst

I think we need to find out why the citizens of the world's wealthiest, most envied, most powerful country are so cynical, so distressed, so angry, so ticked off about so many things.

William J. Bennett
Former Secretary of Education

---

lenge, November-December 1994, pp. 55-58; "Toward a More Perfect Disunion," *Journal of Commerce*, July 3, 1995; "America Small and Beautiful," *Resurgence*, November-December 1995, pp. 20-21; "Is What's Good for AT&T Good for America?" *Across the Board*, March 1996.

In this book we take a critical look at many of the unification schemes wrought in modernity — our nation, our states, our cities, our corporations, our schools, our universities, our churches, our military, and our social welfare system. Too often unity is achieved through coercion, collectivism, the military. In the process of perverted human attempts to unify and secure ourselves, we end up destroying community, scattering ourselves, fracturing into a thousand different voices, falling to earth in disaster. Meltdown. Is it possible that America has become a metaphor for life after Babel? What, if anything, can be done about it? These are the questions to which we turn our attention.

THOMAS H. NAYLOR
WILLIAM H. WILLIMON

1 The State of the Union

There seems only one cause behind all forms of social misery: *bigness*. It appears to be the one and only problem permeating all creation. Wherever something is wrong, something is too big.[1]

Throughout the early 1990s, hardly a month went by without some major American company announcing layoffs of several thousand employees. The list of premier companies engaged in downsizing includes AT&T, General Electric, General Motors, IBM, and Xerox, to mention only a few. There is an increasing realization that bigger is no longer better. The so-called law of increasing returns to scale, which misled us into believing that average costs would decrease with increases in company size, turns out to be a myth. If output continues to grow for a firm, there is some point beyond which additional increments in production result in reduced efficiency, higher costs, and lower profits. The firm may become unmanageable. As the size of the firm increases, problems of alienation, motivation, coordination, communication, and control become more acute. The combined effect of increased global competition and decreasing returns to scale has forced hundreds of large corporations to restructure.

1. Leopold Kohr, *The Breakdown of Nations* (New York: E. P. Dutton, 1978), p. xvii.

The Nation

When the Soviet Union collapsed in December 1991, it was due in part to the failure of socialism to meet the needs of the Soviet people. But it was also because the Soviet Union — not unlike many large American companies — had become fundamentally unmanageable. There was no way 285 million people could be managed from one central bureau in Moscow. The Soviet Union was too big and contained too many hetero-geneous republics, ethnic minorities, religions, and nationalities to be run by Kremlin bureaucrats.

Aristotle on State Size

To the size of states there is a limit, as there is to other things, plants, animals, implements; for none of these retain their natural power when they are too large or too small, but they either wholly lose their nature, or are spoiled.

Aristotle
Politics

If one examines the per capita incomes of the ten most populous countries in the world, one finds that eight of them are poor. Indeed, Bangladesh, China, India, Indonesia, Nigeria, and Pakistan are among the world's poorest countries. Of these ten nations, only Japan and the United States are not poor. On the other hand, seven of the ten richest countries in the world are tiny European states. Luxembourg, Switzer-land, Denmark, and Norway have higher per capita incomes than the United States. All seven have lower incidences of poverty, homeless-ness, drug abuse, violence, and crime than the United States. They also have less pollution, less traffic congestion, and less urban sprawl. These countries work because they are tiny, hardworking, and democratic with a strong sense of community. Five of them are smaller than Que-bec, two smaller than Vermont.

Like China, Japan, India, Brazil, and the former Soviet Union, the United States is also unmanageable in its present form. Just as Mikhail S. Gorbachev found it impossible to manage the Soviet Union from Moscow, so too have the White House and Congress found it equally futile to impose top-down, Washington-based solutions on such

The Ten Largest Countries

Country	Population[a]	Per Capita Income[b]
1. China	1,190,918,000	$530
2. India	913,600,000	310
3. USA	260,529,000	25,860
4. Indonesia	189,907,000	880
5. Brazil	159,143,000	3,370
6. Russia	148,366,000	2,650
7. Pakistan	126,284,000	440
8. Japan	124,782,000	34,630
9. Bangladesh	117,787,000	230
10. Nigeria	107,900,000	280

a. 1994 population — *U.S. Statistical Abstract,* 1994.
b. 1994 GNP Per Capita (dollars) — *World Bank Atlas,* 1996.

The Ten Richest Countries

Country	Population[a]	Per Capita Income[b]
1. Luxembourg	401,000	$39,850
2. Switzerland	7,127,000	37,180
3. Japan	124,782,000	34,630
4. Denmark	5,173,000	28,110
5. Norway	4,318,000	26,480
6. USA	260,529,000	25,860
7. Germany	81,141,000	25,580
8. Austria	7,915,000	24,950
9. Iceland	266,000	24,590
10. Sweden	8,735,000	23,630

a. 1994 population — *U.S. Statistical Abstract,* 1994.
b. 1994 GNP Per Capita (dollars) — *World Bank Atlas,* 1996.

problems as poverty, homelessness, racism, drug abuse, violent crime, child abuse, and a failing education system. The problems of the poor, the underprivileged, and the disfranchised are not amenable to solutions imposed from above. Solutions require the bottom-up participation of those affected, as well as a sense of community that connects those who have been victimized with those in a position to influence the results.

> The era of big government is over.
>
> President Bill Clinton
> State of the Union Address
> January 23, 1996

So apathetic were American voters to the 1996 presidential election that fewer than 49 percent of them actually voted — the lowest voter turnout since 1924.

Neither the Democrats nor the Republicans have a clue as to how to go about solving most of our serious domestic problems. The big-government, tax-and-spend policies of the Democrats have done little to slow the death spiral of our cities or to allay rural poverty. By usurping the power of state and local governments, the federal government has suppressed local community initiative and sense of social responsibility. The Republicans, on the other hand, would have us believe that the only solution to our problems lies in reducing federal taxes, gutting the federal government, and abolishing most Democratically supported programs. Curiously, many Republicans have come to believe that the family, sexuality, and human reproduction are government problems. Neither party talks about local responsibility for the solution of neighborhood, village, or farm community problems. The Democrats want the government to assume too much responsibility; the Republicans hardly any at all, except in the bedroom. Regardless of which party is in power, the results are much the same. It matters not whether one believes that the federal government has reneged on its guarantee of a republican form of government for every state or whether the states have merely abdicated their responsibility to Washington.

The United States is so large and so diverse that the problems of Los Angeles and Chicago bear little resemblance to those of Vermont

> ## The 1996 Presidential Election:
> ## The Nonevent of the Century

or the Mississippi Delta. People living in Richmond, Virginia, could care less about the problems of Harlem. And vice versa.

Is it any wonder that Congress has such difficulty reaching a consensus on anything? It is unrealistic for one legislative body to try to represent so many heterogeneous states, ethnic minorities, political ideologies, and religious sects. Thus gridlock is the rule on Capitol Hill.

Is it possible that congressional budget battles have far more to do with sheer size than with political ideology? Could it be that Washington has simply become impotent to deal with the unwieldy combination of big government, big cities, big business, big labor, big military, and big social welfare?

In the words of University of Vermont political scientist Frank Bryan, "America's federal arrangement has been replaced by a confederation of special interests that have less in common than the former colonies — or even, perhaps, than the states that comprise the United Nations. America resembles more a League of Interests than it does a nation."

What is conspicuously absent in the United States these days is a well-defined sense of connectedness linking our fifty disjointed states. This is in sharp contrast to such tiny countries as Austria, Finland, Norway, Sweden, and Switzerland, which not only enjoy a very high standard of living but a real sense of community.

> ## The Longing for Community
>
> What America hungers for is not more goods or greater power, but a manner of life, restoration of the bonds between people that we call community, a philosophy which values the individual rather than his possessions, and a sense of belonging, of shared purpose and enterprise.[2]

2. Richard N. Goodwin, "The End of Reconstruction," in *You Can't Eat Magnolias*, ed. H. Brandt Ayers and Thomas H. Naylor (New York: McGraw-Hill, 1972), pp. 57-58.

Corporate America

Since the end of World War II, large American corporations have provided their employees with job security, increased income, social status, health insurance, and other fringe benefits. Unfortunately, the restructuring of corporate America has shattered the illusion of life-time employment with any corporation. According to an analysis by the *New York Times* of data compiled by the U.S. Bureau of Labor Statistics, more than 43 million jobs, including many high-paying manufacturing jobs, were extinguished in the United States between 1979 and 1995. Although 27 million new jobs were created during this same period, many of these jobs are low-paying service jobs with no benefits, such as those provided by fast-food establishments like McDonald's and Kentucky Fried Chicken.[3] As evidence of this trend, average per capita income adjusted for inflation has remained essentially flat over the last two decades. The income gap between the rich and the poor which began to increase during the 1980s continues to widen as the rich get richer at the expense of the poor, who get poorer. The distribution of wealth has followed a similar pattern. Personal bankruptcies are at an all-time high, and credit card delinquencies have reached a record level.

There has been a significant increase in the percentage of people who work full time yet cannot lift their family out of poverty without outside assistance. This problem is particularly acute among unskilled workers. A number of social ills are adversely affected by this trend, including rates of welfare dependency, out-of-wedlock birth, child poverty, child abuse, and general social disaffection.

Twenty years ago a family of four could easily be supported by the income of only one family member. Today, even though both part-ners are working harder than ever, they are hardly holding their own financially. How will they send their kids to college? Will their children be able to find middle-class jobs and keep them? Increasingly the Amer-ican dream of "a better life for our kids" is just that — a dream.

Many of the high-wage manufacturing jobs lost through cor-porate downsizing may be lost forever to countries such as Mexico, Taiwan, and South Korea. Is it possible that our industrial future lies not with corporate giants such as IBM, General Electric, and General Motors, but rather with small, homegrown, entrepreneurial-driven

---

3. "The Downsizing of America," *New York Times*, March 3, 1996, p. 27.

firms such as those found in Vermont — Ben & Jerry's, Green Mountain Coffee, and Vermont Teddy Bear, to mention only a few?

We believe that the downsizing of corporate America is a necessary evil. Painful though it may be to those who lose their jobs, many companies are still too big. The way further to reduce the negative economic, social, political, and environmental effects of big businesses is to scale them back even further. However, our primary concern is in extending the concept of downsizing to include virtually every important institution in America. Our government, our schools, our churches, our social welfare system, and our military all suffer from excessive bigness.

Urban America

In many sections of Los Angeles, Miami, New York, and Richmond, Virginia, one cannot walk the streets at night without the real possibility of being mugged, raped, or even murdered. However, since violent crime has decreased in some cities, such as New York, urban problems were given short shrift in the 1996 presidential campaign. But indigence, dehumanization, substance abuse, teenage violence, traffic congestion, urban sprawl, floundering public schools, and deteriorating infrastructure continue without letup in most cities.

Some cities are disintegrating before our eyes. They have become unmanageable towers of Babel which are too big, too crowded, and too unjust with regard to the distribution of income, wealth, jobs, educational services, and political power.

Chicago Crime

If we want to eliminate the Chicago rate of crime, we must not educate Chicago or populate it with members of the Salvation Army. We must eliminate communities the *size* of Chicago.[4]

There is no sense of community in our big cities anymore — not even in some of the Irish, Italian, and Jewish neighborhoods, which

4. Kohr, p. 35.

once solved most of their own social problems internally without calling upon the power of the state.

In Robert Kennedy's words,

> Great cities are too huge to provide the values of community. Community demands a place where people can see and know each other, where children can play and adults work together and join in the pleasures and responsibilities of the place where they live.

There are no top-down, quick-fix solutions to the problems of urban America. These problems don't lend themselves to solutions imposed by bureaucrats sitting in Washington, the statehouse, or city hall. Downsizing may be the only game in town.

Rural America

While the sixty-year exodus of small farmers to American cities continues, the family farm remains a cherished tradition in Western Europe. The European Union supports ten times the number of farmers found in our country. Unlike in the United States, small farms are still a valued way of life. Reflecting the low priority Americans place on the family farm, traditional farming is being devoured, replaced by huge, corporate-owned megafarms. Over half of the food in America is now produced by only 4 percent of our farms. Corporate farms are increasingly dependent on chemicals, pesticides, and energy-guzzling methods of raising crops and transporting them long distances to market. Corporate farmers are obsessed with high crop yields which destroy rather than nurture the soil. As family farms fade away, so too do rural communities and their businesses, schools, and hospitals.

African Americans were not motivated to remain on the exploitive tenant farms to which they were relegated after the Civil War. Anything Chicago, Cleveland, or Detroit had to offer was better than life in the Mississippi Delta. The quality of education, medical care, cultural life, transportation, and public utilities available throughout rural America in the 1940s and 1950s provided little incentive for white farmers to remain in the countryside either. There was an arrogant attitude among our increasingly urban population that life on the farm was not worth preserving.

The American Way

The cause of many of our problems lies in the surrender by smaller communities to untrammeled central national government; followed by the consumerist-driven abdication by national government of power to an unelected corporate authority of no fixed abode, to the point where there has ceased to be any effective political control in the social interest.[5]

We have paid dearly for our myopic views and policies toward rural America. Many of our worst urban social and economic problems are directly attributable to our inability to create a more balanced approach to urban and rural development since World War II.

Unlike the case in the United States, agricultural subsidies in Europe protect small farmers. While it is true that European farms are smaller and less efficient than American farms, and food costs in Europe are higher, there are many compensating benefits. Since small European farms use fewer nitrates, pesticides, and herbicides, wells and streams are much less likely to be contaminated than in the United States. Because the quality of life has remained high in small European towns and villages, one does not find the urban poverty, crime, homelessness, and despair in European cities which one finds in New York, Washington, Los Angeles, and Detroit.

The Family Farm

We believe the survival of the family farm is vital — and not just to us as a business making ice cream from fresh Vermont milk. Family farming is crucial to all of us. It's the historic, living foundation of our food supply, our values, and the rural communities from which our country has always drawn strength, character and economic security.

Ben & Jerry's

---

5. Peter Cruttwell, "History out of Control," *Resurgence,* January/February 1996, p. 5.

We have managed over the past half-century to transfer the alienation, poverty, and despair of the small family farmer from the countryside to the inner-city ghettos of our large metropolitan areas — a subject rarely mentioned by our politicians.

Public Education

Both public education and higher education are troubled American institutions whose problems are rooted in size. Excessive federal, state, and local education bureaucracies as well as school consolidation have contributed to the demise of public education in America. Neighborhood schools in which parents, teachers, and students work together in a community are truly exceptions to the rule these days. In most cities, towns, and even villages there is little sense of community surrounding the local school. Bigger schools are not necessarily better schools.

Small Schools

For the last century, rural parents have been told that sending their progeny to small, nearby schools is a form of child abuse. Only large centralized education factories run by parchment collectors can produce a thoroughly modern kiddie: technology-literate, properly socialized, able and willing to serve as fodder in whatever wars (World, Cold, global economic) Uncle Sam is fighting this week.[6]

Higher Education

In our book *The Abandoned Generation: Rethinking Higher Education*[7] we provided considerable evidence to support the proposition that:

> Few parents realize what they are doing to their children by sending them to some of our most prestigious institutions of higher educa-

---

6. Bill Kauffman, "The Miseducation of America, Part II," *Family in America*, April 1996, p. 2.

7. William H. Willimon and Thomas H. Naylor, *The Abandoned Generation: Rethinking Higher Education* (Grand Rapids: Eerdmans, 1995).

tion. All too many of our colleges and universities charge too much and teach too little to too many students. In this unfriendly, permissive, anti-intellectual environment, students take too few courses, drink too much, party too much, and learn too little from faculties concerned more with political correctness than truth.

American universities have tried unsuccessfully to be all things to all people. Paraphrasing the *Economist*, to undergraduates they are landlords and liberal-arts colleges, to scholars they are multidisciplinary research institutes, to entrepreneurs they are science parks, to state government officials they are engines of economic growth, and to gung-ho alumni they are the sponsors of professional football and basketball teams disguised as college teams. Is it any wonder that the cost of higher education is out of control and the mission of most universities appears to be garbled and inconsistent? Many large universities have become inefficient, dehumanized, bureaucratic agglomerations of unrelated activities. This is a far cry from the 1950s and 1960s when universities were viewed by American conservatives as economic growth engines, by liberals as agents of social change, and by taxpayers as avenues of social mobility.

Religion

All large mainstream religious denominations in America are losing membership. Big religious institutions are no different from big government, big business, big cities, or big universities. They are into *having* — owning, possessing, manipulating, and controlling people, power, and things. They violate one of the most powerful aspects of the Christian faith — its ability to empower ordinary people to do extraordinary things.

Few religious congregations in America ever evolve into real communities, despite their spiritual claims. By evoking the authority of God, rabbis, priests, and ministers set themselves apart from the rest of the congregation. In United Methodist and Roman Catholic churches, local congregations have little to say about the choice of their priest or minister. A clergyperson is simply assigned to the local congregation by the hierarchy of the denomination with too little evaluation of local concerns.

Is it any wonder that so many young people are turned off by organized religion in America? Denominations are burdened by yesterday's mode of organization. The gap between the congregation and the clergy is so great in most religious congregations that community is illusory. The inherited organizational structure of many of our churches disempowers the laity.

The Welfare State

No American institution has been the subject of more political rhetoric and until recently so little action than our ill-conceived social welfare system. Ralph Segalman has characterized the American way of welfare as follows:

> A social policy that either weakens the institutions of the intact family and the effective community or serves to provide weak incompetent substitutes for them would have to be seriously questioned. A welfare system that makes dropping out of school easier, that makes nonpreparation for employment and career routine, that makes irresponsible fathering of illegitimate children normative, that makes unmarried motherhood an accepted rite of passage, and that turns hundreds of thousands of children onto the ghetto and suburban streets for rearing by their premoral peers surely requires revision.[8]

Two other American social institutions which suffer from excessive complexity and size include our virtually unmanageable health care system and many large nonprofit charitable organizations, some of which are accountable to no one.

Military Might

Where is the glue that binds our fifty states together? Throughout the twentieth century, four principal threats helped keep our nation intact — World War I, the Great Depression, World War II, and the Soviet Union. For more than forty-five years our national sense of meaning

8. Ralph Segalman, *The Swiss Way of Welfare* (New York: Praeger, 1986), pp. 196-97.

The Age of Bigness

On a small scale, everything becomes flexible, healthy, manageable, and delightful, even a baby's ferocious bite. On a large scale everything becomes unstable and assumes the proportions of terror, even the good. Love turns into possessiveness; freedom into tyranny. Harmony, based on the interplay of countless different, little, and vivacious individual actions, is replaced by unity, based on magnetized rigidity and maintained by laborious co-ordination and organization. This is why the great hero of the age of bigness is neither the artist, nor the philosopher, nor the lover. It is the great organizer.[9]

---

was based almost entirely on anticommunism. Throughout the cold war, we knew what we were against — godless communism and the Soviet Union. But now that the cold war is finally over, we don't have the foggiest idea what we are for.

The Military-Industrial Complex

In the councils of Government, we must guard against the acquisition of unwarranted influence, whether sought or unsought, by the military-industrial complex. The potential for the disastrous rise of misplaced power exists and will persist.

We must never let the weight of this combination endanger our liberties or democratic processes. We should take nothing for granted. Only an alert and knowledgeable citizenry can compel the proper meshing of a huge industrial and military machinery of defense with our peaceful methods and goals, so that security and liberty may prosper together.

President Dwight D. Eisenhower
Farewell Address
January 16, 1961

---

9. Kohr, p. 95.

War

The danger of aggression arises spontaneously, irrespective of nationality or disposition, the moment the power of a nation becomes so great that, in the *estimate* of its leaders, it has outgrown the power of its prospective adversaries.[10]

The made-for-television Persian Gulf drama precipitated by Saddam Hussein's invasion of Kuwait contained all the essential ingredients for a Tom Clancy post–cold war thriller — a demonic enemy, suspense, political intrigue, high-tech military heroics, and Middle East oil. The action-packed TV series became an instantaneous success with American viewers in need of a new demon to replace the Soviet Union. What if no new Saddam Hussein were to emerge over the next five years?

The demise of communism and the collapse of the Soviet Union have unmistakably exposed our psychological vulnerability. What do

---

Something's Missing

Isn't America searching for something? Despite all of the wealth and grandness that is so apparent, . . . something's missing. There's no hero, no heroine, no great cause, no soaring ideology. We are riddled with political answers that seem too shallow, too short-sighted, too explosive, too harsh.

We need something real to believe in, to hold onto. Something deeper, stronger, grander that can help us deal with our problems by making us better than we are — instead of meaner. That can lift our aspirations instead of lowering them.

Mario Cuomo
Former Governor of New York

---

10. Kohr, p. 37.

we want to be now that the cold war is over? Our nation has lost its way. We suffer from meaninglessness, which in turn leads to separation, alienation, and ultimately to despair. Our political, spiritual, academic, and business leaders have no vision of the future. We have no sense of connectedness. The specter of nihilism looms over us, as evidenced by the Los Angeles riots, the bombings in Oklahoma City and Atlanta, the Unabomber, the O. J. Simpson trials, and the Heaven's Gate cult.

Our States

For at least three decades, conservative politicians have been calling for the decentralization of political power from the federal government back to the states. Only recently have both the Democratic and Republican parties begun calling for the devolution of power to state and local governments. Many Americans seem to be rethinking their views about states' rights.

Downsizing

This then is the great American challenge of the twenty-first century: saving the center by shoring up its parts, preserving union by emphasizing disunion, making cosmopolitanism possible by making parochialism necessary, restoring the representative republic by rebuilding direct democracy, strengthening the national character through the rebirth of local citizenship.[11]

For example, with the elimination of the Soviet threat, some states may conclude that it's no longer in their interest to finance their share of the nation's $5 trillion debt. Vermont's pro rata share of the $500 billion savings-and-loan bailout was $1.1 billion, even though it had no saving-and-loan bank failures whatsoever. Over half of the federal funds went to Texas depositors, with most of the rest going to a handful of Sun Belt states. Idaho and Washington have expressed

11. Frank Bryan and John McClaughry, *The Vermont Papers* (Post Mills, Vt.: Chelsea Green, 1989), p. 3.

outrage that they may be forced to supply water to Los Angeles. What if states started asking tough questions about the cost-benefit ratio of federal programs aimed at reducing poverty? What would be the reaction of Congress and the White House if a state like Vermont were to secede?

State-enforced segregation in the South was truly evil; but is state-imposed integration any better? Not unlike the Soviet Union's attempt to impose communism on the Baltic republics and Eastern Europe, no form of government has been less effective than court-ordered desegregation and busing. This top-down attempt to impose community on unwilling subjects has resulted in our nation's schools being more segregated than they have been in over twenty-five years. Forced integration has snuffed out neither segregation nor racism.

Minority States

Switzerland solved the problems of minorities by means of creating minority *states* rather than minority *rights*.[12]

While there are many more African American elected officials in the South than ever, most of the public schools in southern cities are predominantly African American — the whites having fled to private segregation academies and lily-white suburban public schools. Although there are some affluent African Americans living in the urban South, parts of Alabama, Louisiana, Mississippi, and South Carolina still resemble Third World countries. Most of the African Americans living in the rural South today are not only poor, but they are very poor.

Megastates such as California with a population of 31.4 million, Texas with 18.4 million, and New York with 18.2 million may not only be candidates for secession but downsizing as well. There is a small but very vocal group in California calling for the division of California into three independent states.

12. Kohr, p. 59.

Dissolution

We believe that both political conservatives and political liberals have erred in assuming that the individual is the basic unit of society, the end result by which all social arrangements must be measured. The "individual" is a social construct who is dependent upon some community for values, identity, and direction. If people want more courageous, better-functioning individuals, they ought not to work for greater expansion of rights and entitlements (the devastating results of *that* project are all around us). They ought to join with us in working for a polity which permits a plethora of diverse groups to flourish. The powerful, intrusive megastate is not the hope of individual freedom. Only a state which gives room for a variety of communities can foster individuals with the narratives, values, and sense of meaning necessary to make their way well in the world.

The United States has become too big, too authoritarian, and too undemocratic. Its states assume too little responsibility for the solution of their own social, economic, and political problems. So starved for revenue are our states that they are all too willing to abdicate to the federal government their responsibilities for public education, criminal justice, employment, and environmental protection. Fine tuning or patching our badly crippled political system will do little to turn the situation around. *There is only one solution to the problems of America — peaceful dissolution, not piecemeal devolution.*

As Thomas Jefferson pointed out in the Declaration of Independence, "Whenever any form of government becomes destructive, it is the right of the people to alter or abolish it, and to institute a new government." Just as a group has a right to form, does it not also have a right to disband, to subdivide itself, or to secede from a larger unit?

In the divisive 1860s the Confederate States of America tried unsuccessfully to lead our nation into disunion for all the wrong reasons — preservation of slavery, racism, and the "Southern way of life." After military defeat, occupation, and Reconstruction, they were dragged kicking and screaming back into the Union. Maybe it's high time the South and the rest of the nation reconsidered secession. This time for the right reasons.

Few words invoke more negative feelings among many Americans than "secession." But in Eastern Europe, the former Soviet Union, and Quebec secession is associated with freedom, democracy, and the aspirations of the oppressed — as was the case when the United States was founded in 1776.

Lincoln on Secession

No state, upon its own mere motion, can lawfully get out of the Union.

Plainly, the central idea of secession, is the essence of anarchy.

Abraham Lincoln

Our government encouraged the secession of six Eastern European countries from the Soviet bloc in 1989 and the breakup of the Soviet Union two years later. When Yugoslavia first began unraveling, America blinked. The split between the Czechs and the Slovaks was a nonevent.

Pushed to its limits, states' rights leads not to devolution but to secession. If a state truly wants to be independent of Washington, then it should be free to leave the Union — an act which is clearly not prohibited by our Constitution. Few political conservatives seem to realize that by weakening the control the federal government has over the states, forces will be set loose which not only encourage competition among states but will lead to renewed interest in secession.

Brilliant though the crafters of the American Constitution may have been, they could not have anticipated the size and diversity of the United States today. We have created an unworkable meganation which defies central management and control. The time has come to begin planning the rational downsizing of America. States such as Alaska, Hawaii, Oregon, and Vermont should be allowed to secede. Big cities should have the right to break up or become independent city-states.

How much worse must our domestic problems — particularly our urban problems — become before we consider radical alternatives to the "bigger is better" syndrome? Would our government's reaction to secession be any different from Moscow's heavy-handed response to Chechnya's ill-fated attempt to secede from Russia?

Vermont may lead the way. Vermont is smaller, more rural, more democratic, less violent, and more egalitarian than most of the other states. It shares a number of common values with the Swiss — independence, democracy, hard work, and a strong sense of community. Can Vermont provide a communitarian alternative to the dehumanized, mass production, mass consumption, narcissistic lifestyle which pervades most of the United States? Is it possible that by invoking its own motto — Freedom and Unity — Vermont might help save our nation from the debiliating effects of big government and big business by providing an independent role model for the other states to follow?

2 The Meltdown of Corporate America

The complexity of trying to manage these different businesses began to overwhelm the advantages of our integration. The world has changed. Markets have changed. Conflicts have arisen, and each of our businesses has to react more quickly.[1]

AT&T is reinventing itself once again. This restructuring is the next logical turn in our journey since divestiture. In recent months it's become clear that for AT&T's businesses to take advantage of the incredible growth opportunities in every part of the information industry it has to separate into smaller and more focused businesses.[2]

Corporate Dinosaurs

AT&T, the fifth-largest industrial company in the United States with annual sales of $75 billion and a workforce of 304,500, split into a $50

1. Robert E. Allen, chairman of AT&T, as quoted in John J. Keller, "Defying Merger Trends, AT&T Plans to Split into Three Companies," *Wall Street Journal*, September 21, 1995, p. 1.
2. Robert E. Allen, chairman of AT&T, as quoted in Evan Ramstad, "AT&T Will Split into Three Firms," *Burlington Free Press*, September 21, 1995, p. 9A.

billion communication service company, a $20 billion communication hardware company, and an $8 billion computer systems company — the largest corporate breakup in history. This followed on the heels of its 1984 court-ordered divestiture of seven separate local telephone companies. So large was AT&T before its breakup that its annual revenues exceeded the gross national product (GNP) of 127 of the 159 countries for which the World Bank tracks GNP.

Even though some think AT&T is still too big, its management, in a complete strategy reversal, is now trying to engineer the largest merger ever — a $50 billion deal with SBC Communications.

Corporate Control

There is one modern belief that has enabled managers to take over much of our society, to direct our lives and even to manipulate our goals. It is the belief in control. The widespread idea that we are or ought to be in total control of the world and of our own destinies within the world is familiar to most of us, as is the accompanying idea that anything we don't control now, we will tomorrow or the next day.[3]

Since the days of Henry Ford and Alfred P. Sloan Jr., many Americans have subscribed to the view that not only are big companies good for consumers, employees, and investors, but they do little damage to the environment. Former GM CEO Charles E. Wilson said it all: "What's good for General Motors is good for our country."

I want to see what it's like to be big!

Ted Turner

In a *New York Times* piece appropriately entitled "What My Ego Wants, My Ego Gets," New York real estate tycoon Donald J. Trump

3. David Ehrenfeld, "The Management Explosion and the Next Environmental Crisis," *Tenth Annual E. F. Schumacher Lectures* (Great Barrington, Mass., October 1990), pp. 2-3.

may have effectively captured the essence of what drives him and many other corporate high rollers such as CNN's Ted Turner, Disney's Michael D. Eisner, Microsoft's Bill Gates, IBM's Louis Gerstner Jr., and media mogul Rupert Murdoch:

> Almost every deal I have ever done has been at least partly for my ego — and I have made a great deal of money and have had both fun and artistic enjoyment because of this.[4]

When Wal-Mart, the Arkansas-based retailing Goliath with annual sales of over $100 billion, finally bullied its way into picturesque Bennington, Vermont, it was a major defeat for thousands of Vermonters, many of whom had fought its entry into the Green Mountain State tooth and nail. Vermont was the last state to succumb to the heavy-handed retailer thought by some to be the Great Satan — the enemy of small towns and small merchants everywhere. Ultimately, tiny Vermont was no match for the 3,000-store Wal-Mart empire. With its seductive low prices, and 130,000-square-feet stores filled with tantalizing plastic yuck, Wal-Mart has successfully muscled its way into Bennington, Rutland, and Williston. Already inundated by fast-food chains, Bennington will soon look like every other American strip mall.

Has Wal-Mart become a metaphor for America? Or is America a metaphor for Wal-Mart?

Not only are small businesses everywhere being forced out of business by megabusinesses like Wal-Mart, but they also face fierce competition from the $60 billion mail-order catalogue industry. Over 100 million people make purchases from catalogue companies each year.

Much of our highly touted freedom is illusory. Conservatives rail against — and rightly so — our loss of freedom to big government. But through sophisticated media manipulation, the high priests of corporate America tell us what to buy, when to buy it, where to buy, how much to pay for it, and when to replace it. This is called free enterprise.

The Federal Trade Commission, the Justice Department, and the Environmental Protection Agency are concerned more with protecting corporate America from consumers rather than the other way around.

Drug addiction is illegal. But addiction to beer, cigarettes, junk

---

4. Donald J. Trump, "What My Ego Wants, My Ego Gets," *New York Times*, September 17, 1995, p. F13.

foods, TV, video games, automobiles, personal computers, shopping malls, and credit cards is encouraged by every form of advertising. We have laws against child seduction and molestation. Yet what child manipulators like Toys "R" Us, with "more than a million toys in stock," do to the psyches of children is unconscionable. How many kids have been drawn to McDonald's by the attraction of a free plastic toy or a Michael Jordan slam-dunk? With 20,000 restaurants serving 33 million people daily in 101 countries, the McDonaldization of the world continues unabated. What if home-cooked food prepared in a family-owned restaurant were suddenly to become popular again?

As government influence wanes throughout the world, the tie that increasingly binds countries together is huge multinational corporations. To whom are they accountable? "We answer to the world," International Paper Company proudly proclaims in its advertisements. Whom can we trust in such a world? Therein lies one source of our angst.

And according to Czech Republic president Václav Havel, the behavior of large, privately owned, multinational corporations differs little from their state-owned counterparts:

> It is well known, for instance, that enormous private multinational corporations are curiously like socialist states. With industrialization, centralization, specialization, monopolization, and finally with automation and computerization, the elements of depersonalization and the loss of meaning in work become more and more profound everywhere.[5]

Although the number of shareholders in some of these corporate giants is substantial, the percentage of shareholders who have a voice in corporate management is usually minuscule. Before it broke up, AT&T had 2.3 million shareholders — the largest number of any American company. Yet the plan for splitting the company into three parts was one of the best-kept secrets in corporate history. How many AT&T shareholders knew about the breakup plans before the surprise announcement? Only a handful of senior executives who also happened to own AT&T shares.

Not unlike the hierarchical Roman Catholic Church and the former Communist Party in Moscow, large American companies are among the least-democratic institutions in the world. As was the case

5. Václav Havel, "Work, by Any Other Name," *Columbia*, fall 1990, p. 40.

with AT&T, only a handful of people have any significant influence over the answers to such fundamental strategic questions as:

1. In which businesses should we be?
2. What should be our level of commitment to each business?
3. How should we finance our businesses?
4. In which countries should we operate?
5. How should we organize?
6. What should we research and develop?
7. What should we produce?
8. How should we produce?
9. To whom should we sell?
10. How should we sell?

While espousing a philosophy based on individualism, democracy, and freedom of choice, most large American companies do everything possible to silence dissent and quell any form of behavior which differs significantly from the corporate norm. CEOs are the high priests of the corporate faith and enforcers of sacred business dogmas. Conformity and compliance are the twin pillars on which corporate America rests.

The typical employee has little input into decisions related to such matters as hiring and firing, salaries and wages, fringe benefits, working conditions, mergers, acquisitions, divestitures, and plant closings. There are no rights to freedom of speech, freedom of assembly, freedom of the press, or due process. One can be fired on the spot at the whim of one's superior without questions or legal recourse.

Not surprisingly, the labor unions representing the employees of big companies have emulated the strategies of their corporate adversaries. However, the number of American industrial workers belonging to labor unions has dropped to 16 percent of the workforce in contrast to 60 percent for Austria and 85 percent for Sweden. It is unlikely that the newly created two-million-member union of automobile workers, steelworkers, and machinists will have any more clout than its three separate predecessors in dealing with corporate America. There is little evidence to suggest that bigger labor unions in America have proven to be any more effective than small ones.

Not unrelated to big corporations are big factories, big machines, big computers, big telecommunications networks, big air traffic control systems, and big science and technology.

Technological Sublime

Each day crowds visit the Kennedy Space Center, ascend St. Louis's Gateway Arch, and visit the observation decks of prominent skyscrapers in New York, Chicago, Boston, Minneapolis, and other major cities. For almost two centuries the American public has repeatedly paid homage to railways, bridges, skyscrapers, factories, dams, airplanes, and space vehicles.

The sublime underlies this enthusiasm for technology. One of the most powerful human emotions, when experienced by large groups the sublime can weld society together. In moments of sublimity, human beings temporarily disregard divisions among elements of the community. The sublime taps into fundamental hopes and fears. It is not a social residue, created by economic and political forces, though both can inflect its meaning. Rather, it is an essentially religious feeling, aroused by the confrontation with impressive objects, such as Niagara Falls, the Grand Canyon, the New York skyline, the Golden Gate Bridge, or the earth-shaking launch of a space shuttle.[6]

Many of our politicians in Washington have been mesmerized by big high-technology projects — particularly nuclear energy projects. Among the high-tech nuclear projects which failed in the 1980s and cost American taxpayers billions of dollars were the Clinch River Breeder Reactor ($1.5 billion), the Hanford Fast Flux Test Facility ($540 million), the Rocky Flats Plutonium Processing Building ($225 million), the Portsmouth Gas Centrifuge Uranium Enrichment Plant ($3.5 billion), the Brookhaven High Energy Physics Atomic Particle Accelerator ($172 million), the Hanford Nuclear Reactor ($110 million), and the Savannah River Fuel Materials Facility ($176 million).[7] Although these projects were financed almost entirely by the federal government, they were vigorously promoted by large energy-related companies that reaped substantial profits from them. The Apollo moonwalks, the space shuttle, the B-1 bomber, the stealth bomber, the Trident II missile system,

6. David E. Nye, *American Technological Sublime* (Cambridge: MIT Press, 1994), p. xiii.

7. "Energy Projects That Failed," *New York Times*, December 12, 1988.

and President Reagan's Strategic Defense Initiative were more of the same. The recent discovery of the possibility of life on Mars may provide windfall gains to space scientists in search of new sources of government funding.

In response to the repeated failures of the aging air traffic control computer system in Chicago, no one considered the possibility of limiting the number of flights in and out of Chicago. The only alternative proposed was a bigger, faster, more sophisticated, more expensive computer so the sky over Chicago could become even more crowded.

The Capitalist Threat

Although I have made a fortune in the financial markets, I now fear that the untrammeled intensification of laissez-faire capitalism and the spread of market values into all areas of life is endangering our open and democratic society. The main enemy of the open society, I believe, is no longer the communist but the capitalist threat.[8]

George Soros
The Atlantic Monthly

Closely correlated with the bigger-is-better syndrome espoused by corporate America is the "winner take all" syndrome described by economists Robert H. Frank and Philip J. Cook in their provocative book, *The Winner-Take-All Society.*[9] Chicago Bulls basketball superstar Michael Jordan receives $25 million a year to play basketball, not to mention the additional tens of millions he makes each year hawking commercial products on television — $20 million for Nike alone. Jordan makes more money in a year than all the workers in all the Nike factories in Indonesia. When Washington Bullets forward Juwan Howard threatened to jump ship and head south to the Miami Heat in 1996, the Bullets countered with a $100 million offer. The twenty-three-

8. George Soros, "The Capitalist Threat," *The Atlantic Monthly*, February 1997, p. 45.
9. Robert H. Frank and Philip J. Cook, *The Winner-Take-All Society* (New York: Martin Kessler Books, 1995).

year-old idol of Washington kids decided to stick around for another seven years. When Orlando Magic center Shaquille O'Neal was purchased by the Los Angeles Lakers for $120 million over seven years, the Lakers had to raise the price of their cheapest seats from $9.50 a game to $21.00. Atlanta Braves pitcher John Smoltz makes $8 million annually.

Although the idea of high-paid celebrities began in Hollywood and spread to big-league professional sports and entertainment, the star system is now pervasive in such diverse fields as law, medicine, business, finance, and even academia. How many kids expect to be the next Michael Jordan or Michael Jackson? How many law students or business students respectively aspire to the fame and fortune of high-profile attorney F. Lee Bailey or billionaire George Soros? Most of the high-paid superstars are men. However, Oprah Winfrey, the highest paid celebrity in America, earns $171 million each year.

Nothing better illustrates the winner-take-all syndrome than the compensation for senior executives in the United States. In 1996 the Standard & Poor's 500-stock index rose by an impressive 23 percent, corporate profits by a more modest 11 percent. But in a cover story article entitled "Executive Pay, It's Out of Control," *Business Week* reported that average total compensation (including salary, bonus, retirement benefits, incentive plans, and stock option gains) for the CEOs of the 365 largest American companies increased by a whopping 54 percent to $5,781,300.[10] The average CEO's compensation was 209 times that of an average factory worker whose wages increased by a paltry 3 percent. Junk-bond king Michael Milken once received $550 million from Drexel Burnham Lambert in a single year. When Sam Walton, founder of Wal-Mart stores, died in 1992, he was the wealthiest person in America — the shares of Wal-Mart stock held collectively by his family were valued at $23 billion. According to *Forbes* magazine, Bill Gates is the wealthiest American today with a net worth of $18.5 billion.

Is it possible that megacompanies such as McDonald's, Wal-Mart, IBM, and AT&T may someday become extinct not unlike the dinosaurs? Have they become too big, too powerful, too insular, and too self-serving for the good of their stockholders, their customers, their employees, their local communities, and the global environment?

10. "Executive Pay, It's Out of Control," *Business Week*, April 21, 1997, p. 59.

Downsizing Corporate America

Long before AT&T announced it was splitting into three separate companies, hundreds of large American companies were splitting off divisions and reducing the size of their workforces. IBM and General Electric had already shed nearly two hundred thousand jobs. Sears Roebuck and AT&T itself had previously eliminated over one hundred thousand jobs each before the AT&T breakup. A few months earlier ITT had announced it was breaking up into insurance, industrial products, and resorts and recreation. Sears Roebuck had spun off Allstate insurance and its stock brokerage business, Dean Witter. General Motors had unloaded EDS, its huge computer system business.

The Breakup of AT&T

Rejecting the notion that bigger is better, the company thinks its parts are worth more sundered than together: each business would be more nimble, better able to respond to changing market conditions and unshackled from the financial or regulatory pressures of other units.[11]

By splitting itself into three companies and dropping out of the personal computer business, AT&T abandoned its once-grand vision of combining communication and computers into a single corporate empire. In the end, that vision proved to be a costly illusion. So much for "synergy" — the ungainly term used for decades to justify all manner of mergers, and most recently to explain the wave of media-industry deals. AT&T's retreat may hold lessons for companies pursuing visions of synergy.[12]

In every case these huge companies had become unfocused and too unwieldy to manage. The so-called law of returns to scale about which we spoke in chapter 1 had turned against them. As they became bigger and bigger, they became less efficient, their costs began to rise, their profit margins declined, and the price of their stock reacted accordingly.

11. "Directory Assistance," *New York Times*, September 21, 1995, p. D1.
12. Steve Lohr, "Going against the Grain," *New York Times*, September 21, 1995, p. 1.

Among the other megacompanies thought to be serious candidates for further downsizing, if not outright breakup, are AlliedSignal, Ford, General Electric, General Motors, IBM, Philip Morris, Raytheon, RJR Nabisco, and Tenneco.

Most large American companies employ the same authoritarian management philosophy and hierarchical organizational structures today which worked so well for them in the 1950s and 1960s. However, the typical employee in the 1950s was often a child of poverty, relatively poorly educated, and not uncomfortable with military authority. Today's workers and managers alike are well educated, affluent, and resentful of heavy-handed authority. This mismatch between today's employees and obsolete organizational development strategies gives rise to feelings of separation, alienation, detachment, ambivalence, and complete disaffection — feelings which are widespread throughout corporate America. Many employees are alienated from their work, their boss, their family, their government, and their basic beliefs. Alienation in the workplace is the result of an individual being transformed into a dehumanized thing or object through work itself. This incongruity between modern workers and the business environment contributes to the explanation of such work-related problems as substance abuse, absenteeism, declining productivity, and reduced competitiveness.[13]

Is it any wonder that so many Americans who work for these corporate giants find themselves alienated? They work longer and harder for wages that buy less, in jobs which provide poorer health insurance, fewer fringe benefits, more risk, and less job security than was the case a decade ago.

In our factories, corporate offices, and shopping malls, there is a widespread feeling of detachment and disconnectedness — a longing for community. We are haunted by the yearning for connectedness, an irresistible need for communication, engagement, and friendship with other human beings in the workplace.

The Return of Merger Mania

While hundreds of large American companies were downsizing over the past ten years, over a hundred multibillion-dollar mergers

13. See Thomas H. Naylor, William H. Willimon, and Rolf Österberg, *The Search for Meaning in the Workplace* (Nashville: Abingdon, 1996).

Corporate America's Challenge

The number one managerial challenge facing corporate America is balancing the expectations of investors against those of employees.

Robert M. Phillips
Director
Unilever, North America

---

were simultaneously taking place. Many companies were shrinking in size, but others were growing even larger. Among the most notable of these megamergers were the $24.9 billion acquisition of RJR Nabisco by Kohlberg Kravis Roberts, the $19 billion acquisition of ABC television network by Walt Disney, and the $15 billion acquisition of Burroughs Wellcome by Glaxo, both British pharmaceutical companies.

The three mergers that got the most attention in 1995 all involved major national television networks — the Time Warner–Turner Broadcasting merger, the Disney-ABC merger, and the Westinghouse-CBS merger. Also consummated in 1995 was the $10 billion merger of Chase Manhattan with Chemical Bank with combined assets of $295 billion, thus surpassing Citicorp as the nation's largest bank.

In addition to the Glaxo-Wellcome merger, there was also the $13 billion merger of Upjohn and Sweden's Pharmacia, resulting in the creation of the world's ninth-largest pharmaceutical company. Only a few months after the AT&T breakup, two large regional telephone companies, Bell Atlantic and NYNEX, announced their plans to create the second-largest telephone company in the United States after AT&T. With a stock-market value of $51 billion, the proposed new company is expected to have annual sales of $27 billion, 127,600 employees, and over 36 million customers in twelve states.[14]

Not content with having only 70 to 80 percent of the computer-operating systems market share, Microsoft formed a new software company to produce multimedia programs with Hollywood producer Steven Spielberg and introduced its new, widely publicized product Windows 95. On its cover page, the *New York Times Magazine*

---

14. Mark Landler, "NYNEX and Bell Atlantic Reach Accord," *New York Times*, April 22, 1996, p. 1.

depicted Microsoft as an eight-hundred-pound gorilla characterized as follows:

> If the software giant has its way, it will soon be in a position to collect a charge from every airline ticket you buy, every credit card purchase you make, every fax you send, every picture you download, every Web site you visit. It's time to draw the line. But where?[15]

Consistent with his cyber-ego and his global high-tech image, Microsoft's Bill Gates built himself a $30 million, 45,000-square-foot techno-dwelling featuring a reception hall lined with twenty-four video monitors, each with a forty-inch picture tube. Several other Microsoft executives have similar abodes in the neighborhood.

While all of this was happening, neither the benign antitrust division of the U.S. Justice Department nor the Federal Trade Commission uttered hardly a peep.

			Megamergers
Year	Company	Acquirer	Acquisition Cost (Billions)
1984	Gulf Oil	Chevron	13.3
1988	Kraft	Philip Morris	13.1
1988	RJR Nabisco	Kohlberg Kravis Roberts	24.9
1989	Squibb	Bristol-Myers	11.5
1990	Warner	Time	13.9
1994	Lockheed	Martin Marietta	10.0
1995	ABC	Disney	19.0
1995	Chemical Bank	Chase Manhattan	10.0
1995	Wellcome	Glaxo	15.0
1996	Bell Atlantic	NYNEX	20.8
1996	MCI	British Telecom	21.8
1997	McDonnell Douglas	Boeing	13.0

15. James Gleik, "The Microsoft Monopoly," *New York Times Magazine*, November 5, 1995.

So commonly do large newspaper chains like Gannett, Knight-Ridder, and Newhouse swallow up locally owned daily newspapers that when Gannett *(USA Today)* acquired eleven daily and forty-nine other newspapers as well as five television stations from Multimedia for only $1.7 billion, no one hardly noticed. About the diminished role of newspapers in American society William Glaberson said, "With chain-owned newspapers in most cities looking more and more alike, as though stamped from some giant corporate cookie cutter, many no longer play the vibrant role they played when there were more of them and they answered to more different kinds of owners."[16]

Major Newspaper Chains		
Company	*Daily Circulation*[a]	*Daily Newspapers*
1. Gannett	5.8 million	82
2. Knight-Ridder	3.6 million	27
3. Newhouse	3.0 million	26
4. Times Mirror	2.6 million	11
5. New York Times	2.4 million	25
6. Dow Jones	2.4 million	22

a. Average daily circulation as of September 30, 1994 for all the newspapers owned by each company on July 30, 1995.

Source: Newspaper Association of America

Despite the media hype over the recent rash of megamergers, one should not forget the fate of some other large companies that resulted from mergers. For example, the 1968 dream merger of the Pennsylvania and New York Central Railroads ended in bankruptcy. Not only did ITT not take over the world as many liberals thought would surely be the case in the 1960s, but it, too, recently split into three separate companies. Whatever happened to Eastern Air Lines, "the largest airline in the free world"; Pan American World Airways, America's flagship international carrier; or Aeroflot, the biggest airline in the nonfree world? Eastern and Pan Am both went belly-up and Aeroflot

16. William Glaberson, "The Press: Bought and Sold and Gray All Over," *New York Times,* July 30, 1995.

struggles to stay afloat in a free market. And the $15 billion Eurotunnel connecting England and France could turn out to be one of the greatest white elephants of all time.

Pepsico never found the synergy with KFC, Pizza Hut, and Taco Bell. Can Ted Turner ever be vice chairman of anything? Is bigger health care either better health care or lower cost health care?

Sustainable Business

When IBM, Digital Equipment, Simmonds Precision, and St. Johnsbury Trucking began laying off hundreds of employees in response to a soft economy and corporate "restructuring," the knee-jerk reaction of Vermont's governor, economic development officials, chambers of commerce, and utility executives was a clarion call for action. But their proposal to save Vermont jobs and attract industry differed little from strategies employed by low-wage states such as Arkansas, Mississippi, and North Carolina.

> ### Diversified Portfolio
>
> I tend to favor an economic system based on the maximum possible plurality of many decentralized, structurally varied, and preferably small enterprises that respect the specific nature of different localities and different traditions, and that resist the pressures of uniformity by maintaining a plurality of modes of ownership and economic decision-making, from private enterprises, through various types of cooperative and shareholding ventures, right up to state ownership.[17]

Influenced by financially strapped Alabama, which put together a $300 million incentive package to entice Mercedes-Benz there, Vermont strategists call for tax breaks, discounted electric rates, and government subsidies and financing to attract manufacturing firms. But this strategy is fundamentally flawed, for it overlooks the fact that

17. Havel, p. 41.

relatively few of the tens of thousands of manufacturing jobs lost recently in the Northeast have ended up in low-cost, nonunion states. Most of the jobs lost by Vermont have gone to countries such as Mexico, Taiwan, China, and South Korea. Tiny Vermont has little influence over the downsizing of corporate America.

Sustainability

Sustainability is a community's control and prudent use of capital — all forms of capital: natural capital, human capital, human-created capital, social capital, and cultural capital — to ensure, to the degree possible, that present and future generations can attain a high degree of economic security and achieve democracy while maintaining the integrity of the ecological systems upon which all life and all production depends.

Stephen Viederman
Jessie Smith Noyes Foundation

The industrial future of Vermont and many other states lies not with corporate giants, but rather with small, homegrown, entrepreneurial-driven companies. Thriving in the bucolic Green Mountain State are dozens of small, socially responsible, sustainable businesses such as Ben & Jerry's, Autumn Harp, Otter Creek Brewing, and Vermont

---

Green Mountain Strategies

1. Entrepreneurial driven
2. Niche market
3. Premium quality
4. High value added
5. Upscale pricing
6. Community based
7. Participatory management
8. Socially aware
9. Environmentally responsible
10. Vermont oriented

Teddy Bear. Without exception, these high-performance companies trade heavily on Vermont's uniqueness — its tiny size, its rural nature, its tradition of freedom and democracy, and its strong sense of community. These small firms account for 95 percent of Vermont's businesses, and employ 85 percent of the private workforce.

Sustainable businesses are small, profitable, unregulated, market-oriented businesses which reduce the consumption of energy and natural resources; provide safe, stable, and meaningful employment; produce useful goods and services; reduce waste and damage to the biosphere; and restore degraded habitats and ecosystems.

Keynes on Homespun Goods

I sympathize therefore, with those who would minimize, rather than those who would maximize, economic entanglement between nations. Ideas, knowledge, art, hospitality, travel — these are the things which should of their nature be international. But let goods be homespun whenever it is reasonably and conveniently possible; and, above all, let finance be primarily national.

John Maynard Keynes

Small niche-market Vermont businesses such as Green Mountain Coffee, Rhino Foods, Danforth Pewterers, Vermont Butter & Cheese, and Catamount Brewing produce high-quality, high value added products which sell for premium prices. Not unlike Switzerland, the label "made in Vermont" has become synonymous with quality. Consider Vermont free-range turkeys which sell for twice the price of ordinary turkeys — and are worth every cent. Other Vermont agricultural products with upscale prices include organic vegetables, nonplastic tomatoes, drug-free beef, maple syrup, and a wide variety of specialty foods such as pasta, bread, and salsa. Vermont is the home of fourteen different salsa firms. Just as oil companies discovered they could increase their profits in the 1960s by going into the petrochemical business, so too did Vermont's Cabot Creamery increase its profits by the further processing of milk into cheeses, butter, yogurt, and other dairy products.

The Vermont Department of Agriculture has found that the word

> ## Work of the Future
>
> The work of the future will be friendly toward the environment and will accept the environment's friendliness toward us; it will be interdependent rather than competitive and bellicose toward other humans; it will not exaggerate individualism or jingoism, sectarianism, or nationalism but will have a planetary worldview about it; it will not be about controlling the environment; it will not fall into the fallacy of an infinitely expanding mode of thinking about a finite reality, namely the Earth and its gifts to us; it will not succumb to economic determinism; it will look for its values and its creativity beyond technology alone.[18]

"Vermont" on a product's label yields 10 percent greater sales than might otherwise be the case. A product which has been given the so-called Vermont Seal of Quality will on the average experience yet an additional 10 percent sales increase. No one trades more heavily on the Vermont image and sells it more effectively than Ben & Jerry's.

Many small Vermont companies have a high degree of environmental integrity, engage in participatory management practices, and maintain a high level of social consciousness. You would not mind having some of them in your own backyard. Over three hundred Vermont businesses belong to an organization called Vermont Businesses for Social Responsibility, whose mission is:

> To foster a business ethic in Vermont that recognizes the opportunity and the responsibility of the business community to set high standards for protecting the natural, human, and economic environments of our citizens.

With its avowed policy of "caring capitalism," Ben & Jerry's stands at the forefront of enlightened, socially responsible American businesses. Its parnerships located in low-income areas are joint ventures with nonprofit, community-minded organizations aimed at creat-

18. Matthew Fox, *The Reinvention of Work* (San Francisco: Harper San Francisco, 1994), pp. 75-76.

ing employment opportunities, helping revitalize poor neighborhoods, and empowering neighborhood residents. When dairy prices plummeted in 1991, Ben & Jerry's paid Vermont farmers premium prices for dairy products, reflecting what the company called its determination to support family farmers. Ben & Jerry's has one of the most liberal employee benefit programs in the United States.

Sustainable Business Strategies

1. Replace nationally and internationally produced items with products created locally and regionally.
2. Take responsibility for the effects they have on the natural world.
3. Do not require exotic sources of capital in order to develop and grow.
4. Engage in production processes that are human, worthy, dignified, and intrinsically satisfying.
5. Create objects of durability and long-term utility whose ultimate use or disposition will not be harmful to future generations.
6. Change consumers to customers through education.

Paul Hawken
The Ecology of Commerce

In 1993 when Ben & Jerry's informed its sole supplier of chocolate chip cookie dough, Rhino Foods, that it would not need any more cookie dough for at least three months, Rhino's employees came up with an uncommon solution to a common problem — overstaffing. Rather than laying off the surplus employees, Rhino entered into an innovative employee exchange program with Gardener's Supply of Burlington, a national mail-order company with a temporary influx of catalogue orders, and nearby Ben & Jerry's. The exchange program lasted for six weeks at Gardener's and for about two months at Ben & Jerry's. The host companies paid the salaries of guest employees and Rhino covered their fringe benefits. When Rhino's flow of orders returned to normal, the employees reclaimed their old jobs.

Not surprisingly, Vermont's industries have one of the best track records in the nation in terms of release of toxic chemicals to the air and water.

> ### Sense of Place
>
> Large corporations, once rooted in place, no longer have any com-
> mitment to place. This in turn is reflected by a lack of commitment
> to the social and ecological infrastructure of the place. What is good
> for Eastman Kodak when it lays off 10,000 workers in Rochester, is
> not good for Rochester.
>
> Capital's search for the cheapest place destroys community and
> ecology, because neither play any role in the definition of economic
> value in the global economic system.
>
> If we define citizenship as love and commitment to place, there
> can be no real community nor citizenship in a capital mobile world.
> Nor, as a result, can there be sustainability.
>
> Stephen Viederman
> Jessie Smith Noyes Foundation

The presence of IBM, a state-of-the-art telecommunications switching network, and a well-educated workforce contribute to an environment conducive to high-tech entrepreneurial activity in microprocessors, computer software, information processing, robotics, avionics, and high-tech equipment in Vermont. Burlington has attracted a large number of computer programmers, design engineers, word processors, and high-tech consultants who operate out of their homes.

In Vermont small firms work in harmony rather than in conflict with the local environment — a kinder, gentler approach to economic development rather than the "bigger is better" urban industrial paradigm. Business and government consciously cooperate to preserve a strong sense of community.

Ultimately, corporate America marches to the beat of a single drummer — the marketplace. As millions of people lose their high-paying industrial jobs through corporate downsizing and are forced to accept lower-paying jobs, who will be able to afford to buy all of the stuff produced by big American companies? In his book *One World, Ready or Not,* William Greider expresses concern that excess industrial capacity throughout the world could precipitate a global market cor-

---

Strategies to Encourage Business Downsizing

1. Abolish the U.S. Departments of Commerce and Labor.
2. Repeal all federal government regulations which promote corporate bigness.
3. Encourage corporate downsizing through the use of local market power rather than state-imposed regulatory power.
4. Buy locally and regionally produced products from small local merchants and family farmers.
5. Avoid large national chains such as Wal-Mart, Toys "R" Us, McDonald's, Pizza Hut, Sheraton, and Hilton.
6. Invest in small, sustainable, local and regionally owned businesses.
7. Bank with small local and regionally owned banks, not large national banks.
8. Boycott local newspapers owned by national chains.
9. Avoid all catalogue purchases from faraway mail-order companies.
10. Patronize local concerts, museums, theaters, art galleries, and sports events.
11. Make a concerted effort to spend your money so that it remains in the town, village, or neighborhood in which you reside. Follow the same practice whenever you travel to another town.

---

rection.[19] Could we be on the brink of a major market shift in which consumers, employees, neighborhoods, and villages alike demand an end to the "bigger is better" paradigm? Are we witnessing the beginning of the end — the meltdown of corporate America?

19. William Greider, *One World, Ready or Not: The Manic Logic of Global Capitalism* (New York: Simon & Schuster, 1997).

3 Urban America:
Modern-Day Tower of Babel

"Come, let us build ourselves a city, with a tower that reaches to the heavens, so that we may make a name for ourselves and not be scattered over the face of the whole earth."

But the LORD came down to see the city and the tower that the men were building. The LORD said, "If as one people speaking the same language they have begun to do this, then nothing they plan to do will be impossible for them. Come, let us go down and confuse their language so they will not understand each other."

So the LORD scattered them from there over all the earth, and they stopped building the city. That is why it was called Babel — because there the LORD confused the language of the whole world. From there the LORD scattered them over the face of the whole earth.

Genesis 11:4-9, NIV

Urban Angst

So common were homicides in Richmond, Virginia — 160 for a city of two hundred thousand in one year — that when a young African American male was murdered by another, it was virtually a nonevent — usually given only one or two column-inches on page three of the metro

48

section of the *Richmond Times-Dispatch*. But when seventeen-year-old Patricio "Pach" Torres was shot four times in the back in front of the Coliseum on Good Friday, it was quite a different story. His slaying was the front-page headline the following day. Not only was Pach a white high school honor student, but his father was one of the most prominent and caring psychiatrists in Richmond. He was a musician, a poet — a kind and gentle person loved by his family and many friends — and a close friend of the Naylors.

In response to a phone call from a friend who had become ill at the Naughty by Nature Hip Hop Hooray rap show, Pach and his girl-friend drove to the Coliseum around 11:00 P.M. As he left his car he was attacked and brutally beaten by several unknown male teenagers. When he tried to escape from his assailants, he was shot dead execution-style. Pach was but one of three of Magdalena Naylor's friends murdered independently during the Naylors' last year in Richmond.

Pach's murder, an escalating pattern of violence including ran-dom drive-by shootings, and the complete breakdown of any sem-blance of community literally drove our family out of Richmond. Mo-tivated by a longing for spiritual and emotional connectedness and increasing concerns about the safety and education of our six-year-old son, Alexander, three months later we moved to Charlotte, Vermont. Even though the move to Vermont reduced our annual family income by two-thirds, and we took a $20,000 hit on the sale of our Richmond house, we found what we were looking for in Vermont — a real sense of community whether it be on the farm or in the village, the town, the school, the church, or the workplace. People in Vermont actually seem to care about each other's mind, body, heart, and soul and are com-mitted to nurturing this connectedness through town meetings, small community schools, active religious congregations, and participatory management in the workplace.

When we first moved to Richmond in 1989, the city was expe-riencing a miniboom. A plethora of new buildings, including a coliseum, a convention center, high-rise hotels, and several modern skyscrapers, created the illusion that all was well in the seat of the Old Confederacy. Virginia had a progressive black governor and every local television station had an African American coanchor reading the eve-ning news. It was a facade. Richmond was in a death spiral — which few Richmonders were prepared to admit.

While the wealthy whites living in the posh West End were reaping the economic benefits of the Reagan era, the poor blacks in East

Richmond were becoming more desperate. The meandering James River and the clever design of Richmond's system of interstate highways help preserve the long-standing economic and racial caste system. The combined effects of the river and the expressways further isolate the elitist West End from the rest of the city. For many young black males, living in the isolated housing projects, drug dealing is the only way out of the ghetto. Thirty years of top-down federal, state, and local government programs have done little to assuage the feeling of detachment and disconnectedness among Richmond blacks, giving rise to separation, alienation, and eventually to despair.

It's Drugs, Stupid

For 30 years, America has tried to curb crime with more judges, tougher punishments and bigger prisons. We have tried to rein in health costs by manipulating payments to doctors and hospitals. We've fought poverty with welfare systems that offer little incentive to work. All the while, we have undermined these efforts with our personal and national denial about the sinister dimension drug abuse and addiction have added to our society.

If a mainstream disease like diabetes or cancer affected as many individuals and families as drug and alcohol abuse and addiction do, this nation would mount an effort on the scale of the Manhattan Project to deal with it.[1]

The upscale, all-white Saint Stephen's Episcopal Church where we attended services appeared to us more like the spiritual annex of the Country Club of Virginia conveniently located across the street. Not only was there little sense of community in the church, but it had little connection to the rest of the city — particularly the predominantly African American inner city. Members seemed to be uncommitted to anyone other than themselves.

When forced school integration became a fact of life in the early 1970s, the state legislature passed a bill making it virtually impossible for the City of Richmond to annex any additional territory in the ad-

---

1. Joseph A. Califano Jr., "Its Drugs, Stupid," *New York Times Magazine,* January 29, 1995, pp. 40-41.

joining counties. As a result of this racial chicanery, those whites who could afford it fled either to the white county schools or the expensive private schools. Since we lived within the City of Richmond, Alexander's options were either a rapidly deteriorating public school system, which was becoming increasingly dangerous, or elitist private schools. We opted for Vermont. Others — nearly 4 million Americans — have chosen exclusive, private, upscale, closed-off, crime-free, gated communities, some of which not only have their own security guards but their own private schools as well.[2]

Privatopia

Millions of affluent homeowners are encouraged to secede from urban America, with its endless flux and ferment, its spontaneity and diversity and its unpredictable rewards and hazards. They are beckoned to a privatized artificial, utopian environment I call "Privatopia," where master-planning, homogeneous populations, and private governments offer the affluent a chance to escape from urban realty.[3]

There were virtually no children in our upper-middle-income neighborhood — just elderly couples living in their isolated, air-conditioned, burglar-proof, split-level homes enclosed by protective fences. Nothing was within walking distance of our neighborhood — the school, the church, the bank, the shopping center, or even a restaurant. Glitzy suburban shopping malls filled with plastic yuck drove downtown Richmond's two elegant department stores out of business, further accelerating the city's decline. Broad Street and the Midlothian Turnpike are two of the ugliest strip malls in America — miles of nonstop auto dealerships, fast-food restaurants, and huge discount stores.

These problems were further aggravated by a daily newspaper, the *Richmond Times-Dispatch*, which reads like the *Jackson (Miss.) Daily News* did back in the 1950s. The smug Chamber of Commerce proposed

2. Timothy Egan, "Many Seek Security in Private Communities," *New York Times*, September 3, 1995, p. 1.
3. Evan McKenzie, "Trouble in Privatopia," *Progressive*, October 1993, pp. 30-33.

three top-down strategies to "fix" Richmond's problems. First, erect a giant football stadium so as to attract a National Football League franchise. Second, sometime in the next ten years construct a mega regional airport between Richmond and Norfolk. Third, develop a research park similar to the Research Triangle Park in North Carolina, which only took thirty years to mature fully. "What's in it for us?" must surely have been the response of young African Americans living in Richmond.

For Thomas Naylor, who had spent fifty-two of his fifty-seven years in the South, the journey to the Green Mountain State was the painful acknowledgment that the "New South" about which he had dreamed since the 1950s was an illusion. The urban South had not managed to avoid the mistakes of the North — its socioeconomic problems confounded by the never-ending politics of race. The legacy of slavery, the plantation mentality, and racial injustice had all taken their toll, rendering real community a virtual impossibility in most Southern cities.

But the problems of crime, violence, public schools, traffic congestion, environmental pollution, and urban decay of Richmond pale in comparison to those of megacities such as New York, Los Angeles, Chicago, Houston, and Philadelphia. Even comparatively small cities like Richmond appear to be unmanageable.

The Problem of Size

> When we get piled upon one another in large cities, as in
> Europe, we shall become as corrupt as Europe.
>
> Thomas Jefferson

There is considerable evidence to suggest that sheer size alone is an important determinant of the long-term viability of a community, whether it be a neighborhood, town, or city. Urban poverty, homelessness, crime, congestion, sprawl, overcrowding, traffic jams, pollution, and absence of community are all firmly rooted in size.

In his book *Human Scale*, Kirkpatrick Sale suggests optimum size limits for a *neighborhood* and a *town*. A neighborhood is a group of between four hundred and one thousand people — a face-to-face community such as a Swiss Alpine village or a section of a large city: Chinatown, Little Italy, or the French Quarter.

In Sale's view the optimum size for a neighborhood is only five hundred people. A town, on the other hand, is an extended group of from five thousand to ten thousand people. In *Small Is Beautiful*, E. F. Schumacher asserts that "the upper limit of what is desirable for the size of a city is probably something of the order of half a million inhabitants. It is quite clear that above such a size nothing is added to the virtue of the city."[4]

Population of Ten Largest U.S. Cities

City	Population[a]
1. New York	14,625,000
2. Los Angeles	10,130,000
3. Chicago	6,529,000
4. Philadelphia	4,003,000
5. San Francisco	3,986,000
6. Miami	3,471,000
7. Detroit	2,969,000
8. Dallas	2,787,000
9. Washington, D.C.	2,565,000
10. Boston	2,476,000

a. 1991 metropolitan area population — U.S. Census Bureau

Big Cities

As cities get bigger they have increases in crime rates, traffic congestion, commuting time, pollution, income inequality, physical illness, personal expenses, municipal costs, taxes, crowding, stress, social disorder, and personal hostility. Moreover, as cities get bigger they generally have less parking space, poorer school systems, worse recreation facilities, proportionately fewer hospital beds, and less money per capita for garbage removal, libraries, and fire protection. And in general, the bigger the city the worse the performance, with the very biggest cities almost uniformly ranked at the bottom.[5]

---

4. E. F. Schumacher, *Small Is Beautiful* (New York: Harper & Row, 1973), p. 71.
5. Kirkpatrick Sale, *Human Scale* (New York: Coward, McCann, & Geoghegan, 1980), p. 92.

Population of the World's Ten Largest Cities

City	Population[a]
1. Tokyo	27,245,000
2. Mexico City	20,899,000
3. São Paulo	18,701,000
4. Seoul	16,792,000
5. New York	14,625,000
6. Osaka	13,872,000
7. Bombay	12,101,000
8. Calcutta	11,898,000
9. Rio de Janeiro	11,688,000
10. Buenos Aires	11,657,000

a. 1991 metropolitan area population — U.S. Census Bureau

A 1995 study of the quality of life of 118 cities throughout the world by the prestigious, Geneva-based business organization, the Corporate Resources Group (CRG), named the following as the ten best cities in which to live:[6]

The Ten Best Cities in Which to Live

City	Quality of Life Index[a]	Population[b]
1. Geneva	106.00	378,000
2. Vancouver	105.29	1,603,000
3. Vienna	105.24	2,344,000
4. Toronto	105.20	3,145,000
5. Luxembourg	105.19	401,000
6. Zurich	105.09	834,000
7. Montreal	104.97	2,916,000
8. Dusseldorf	104.78	576,000
9. Singapore	104.76	2,719,000
10. Auckland	104.51	856,000

a. The index assumes a New York base of 100.
b. 1991 population estimates

6. "Geneva Found Global Top in Life Quality," *Swiss American News*, January 25, 1995, p. 1.

The findings of the CRG study were based on the level of security, public services, health care, and political and social stability in the cities surveyed. No American city was ranked in the top ten. The highest-ranked U.S. city was Boston, which was ranked thirtieth, followed by San Francisco, Seattle, and Chicago, which were ranked thirty-first, thirty-third, and thirty-fourth. New York, the largest American city, came in forty-fourth in the survey. Five relatively small West European cities were in the top ten — Geneva, Vienna, Luxembourg, Zurich, and Dusseldorf. Paris came in at only twenty-fourth. Of the sixty largest cities in the world, none were in the top ten. Of the cities ranked in the top ten, five have populations of under 1 million.

In the bottom ten under all four quality-of-life indicators were the three major crime centers of the former Soviet Union — Moscow, Kiev, and Saint Petersburg. The Chinese cities of Beijing, Shanghai, and Guangzhou were also among the ten worst cities, largely because of low availability of consumer goods, medical services, and housing, as well as high pollution levels and poor public services.

Montreal, Singapore, Sydney, Toronto, Vancouver, and Vienna are among the handful of large cities which still seem to work well.

Throwing Out the Baby with the Bathwater

Since the end of World War II, our nation has been so preoccupied with the "bigger is better" economic boosterism model of urban development that we turned our back on rural America — the family farm, sustainable agriculture, and the small country town or village. While pursuing the illusive dream of always bigger and more prosperous industrial-based cities at the expense of our agrarian roots, we have literally "thrown out the baby with the bathwater."

In the 1930s a group of twelve influential Southern writers known collectively as the "Agrarians" tried unsuccessfully to steer the South away from the urban industrial model promoted by Henry Grady and other proponents of the so-called New South. The Agrarians called for the preservation of the rural South, the family farm, and the South's sense of community. As the South enthusiastically embraced the Northern industrial development paradigm, they urged caution, admonishing the South to avoid replicating Northern mistakes in a Southern setting. But that was not to be.

In the divisive 1960s and 1970s Southern liberals dismissed the

The Urban-Rural Imbalance

The all-pervading disease of the modern world is the total imbalance between city and countryside, an imbalance in terms of wealth, power, culture, attraction, and hope. The former has become over-extended and the latter has atrophied. The city has become the universal magnet, while rural life has lost its savor. Yet it remains an unalterable truth that, just as a sound mind depends on a sound body, so the health of the cities depends on the health of the rural areas. The cities, with all their wealth, are merely secondary pro-ducers, while primary production, the precondition of all economic life, takes place in the countryside. The prevailing lack of balance, based on the age-old exploitation of countryman and raw material producer, today threatens all countries throughout the world, the rich even more than the poor. To restore a proper balance between city and rural life is perhaps the greatest task in front of modern man. It is not simply a matter of raising agricultural yields so as to avoid world hunger. There is no answer to the evils of mass unem-ployment and mass migration into cities, unless the whole level of rural life can be raised, and this requires the development of an agro-industrial culture, so that each district, each community, can offer a colourful variety of occupations to its members.[7]

Agrarians and their book *I'll Take My Stand* as romantic and nostalgic. Today, if one travels to Atlanta, Charlotte, Birmingham, Memphis, or New Orleans, one finds all the examples of Northern mistakes which the South replicated. The Americanization of the urban South is almost complete, and it is not a pretty sight.

Houston, Texas, with its crazy-quilted hodgepodge of beautiful residential neighborhoods, churches, schools, and universities laced with unsightly oil refineries, petrochemical plants, strip malls, and convenience stores, is the quintessential example of the result of a combination of unlimited growth, no zoning laws, and a Pollyanna "anything goes" attitude — uncontrollable, dehumanized, concrete-and-steel chaos.

7. Schumacher, pp. 215-16.

The Agrarian Model

Opposed to the industrial society is the agrarian, which does not stand in particular need of definition. An agrarian society is hardly one that has no use at all for industries, for professional vocations, for scholars and artists, and for the life of cities. Technically, perhaps, an agrarian society is one in which agriculture is the leading vocation, whether for wealth, for pleasure, or for prestige — a form of labor that is pursued with intelligence and leisure, and that becomes the model to which the other forms approach as well as they may. But an agrarian regime will be secured readily enough where the superfluous industries are not allowed to rise against it. The theory of agrarianism is that the culture of the soil is the best and most sensitive of vocations, and that therefore it should have the economic preference and enlist the maximum number of workers.[8]

Sun Belt Faith

Unbridled growth — anywhere, anytime — is a good thing.[9]

The Politics of Race

At the crux of many of our urban problems lies the highly divisive politics of race. Fourteen American cities with populations over one hundred thousand have black majorities and another dozen have Hispanic majorities. Since the 1960s the official policy of the U.S. government has been the forced racial integration of public schools, colleges and universities, public accommodations, restaurants, stores, and more recently the workplace. Although this commitment to racial integration once enjoyed broad-based public support, today an increasing number

8. Twelve Southerners, *I'll Take My Stand* (Baton Rouge: LSU Press, 1977), p. xlvi.
9. Sam Howe Verhovek, "'Anything Goes' Houston May Go the Limit: Zoning," *New York Times*, October 27, 1993, p. A14.

of whites, blacks, and Hispanics have either become ambivalent or hostile to forced integration.

At best, the socioeconomic effects of racial integration appear to be mixed. On the positive side, the percentage of black families earning over $50,000 annually (in 1992 dollars) increased from 10.2 percent in 1970 to 16 percent in 1992. However, during the same time period, the proportion of white families with comparable incomes rose from 24.5 percent to 35.7 percent. At the same time the percentage of blacks in professional or managerial jobs increased from 10 percent to 16.8 percent. Meanwhile the percentage of blacks who had completed at least four years of college more than doubled from 6 percent to 12.7 percent.

But median household income for blacks compared to whites changed little over twenty years, with black households earning the same percent of white income in 1992 as in 1972 — 58 percent. And a Harvard University study found that in the 1991-92 school year, 66 percent of the 6.9 million black students in the nation's public schools attended predominantly minority schools — the highest percentage since 1968. Furthermore, in integrated schools and colleges, students often do not interact across racial lines in the classroom or otherwise.[10]

The simple truth is that after thirty years of top-down policies aimed at forcing blacks and whites to be in community with each other, racism and de facto segregation are still alive and well in urban America and elsewhere. Although there is increasing evidence that the quality of life has improved for many African Americans in the 1990s, on balance blacks are still poorer, less well educated, less healthy, and more likely to end up in jail than their white neighbors. Is it realistic to assume that it is possible for our government to force community on blacks and whites, given the history of the relationship between these two races in America — slavery, emancipation, forced segregation, economic discrimination, and thirty years of paternalistic, top-down government programs? More creative solutions are needed. Has integration disempowered minorities, diluting their influence over their communities and implying that every solution to their problems always lies in the hands of the majority-backed government?

10. Charisse Jones, "Years on Integration Road: New Views of an Old Goal," *New York Times*, April 10, 1994, p. 1.

The Mall of America

An integral part of the white flight to the suburbs has been the abandonment of the central-city business district in favor of paved over, dehumanized suburban shopping malls. Today there are more shopping malls than high schools in the United States — over thirty-five thousand. As we previously noted, there are over 3,000 Wal-Mart megastores which function as self-contained minimalls and drive small merchants out of business everywhere.

Meet Me at the Mall

America's thousands of shopping malls are the centerpieces of the most environmentally destructive way of life yet devised. In combination, the suburbs that surround them, the cars that stream into them, the packaged throwaways that stream out of them, and the fast-food outlets and convenience franchises that mimic them cause more harm to the biosphere than anything else except perhaps rapid population growth.[11]

Minneapolis now has the Mall of America, which contains 2.5 million square feet of retail floor space. It covers seventy-eight acres, is four stories tall, and has four major department stores, up to four hundred specialty shops, a fourteen-screen movie theater, dozens of restaurants, several nightclubs, a split-level, high-tech miniature golf course, and a seven-acre indoor amusement park. It employs ten thousand people and generates over 40 million visits annually.

Shopping malls have replaced the town squares and village greens of our past, and their brand names and high-tech gadgets have become the icons of our popular culture.[12] A whole new cult of teenagers, known as "mall rats," has emerged in shopping malls throughout the country; they seem to live only to go to the mall. So unruly is the behavior of some teenagers in shopping malls that they have had curfews imposed on them. Has America itself become a mall?

11. Alan Thein Durning, "Too Many Shoppers: What Malls and Materialism Are Doing to the Planet," *Washington Post,* August 24, 1992.
12. Durning.

Theme Cities

Walt Disney has announced plans to renovate one of New York's 42nd Street's most romantic and decrepit theaters into a 1,900-seat showcase for live Broadway productions. The $34 million project, heavily subsidized with low-interest state and city government loans, will anchor a whole new entertainment district, housing two more theaters, a 25-screen multiplex cinema, theme restaurants — including ESPN sports spa — and a branch of Madame Tussaud's wax museum. Planned for one key corner is a flamboyant 10-story hotel designed by the Miami firm Arquitectonica in which Sega will create an entertainment complex and Disney has the option to set up a vacation club. On the other end of the block, next to Times Square, Disney is planning an 18,000-square-foot memorabilia store.[13]

Obsolete Infrastructures

Although our cities never seem to have a problem raising money to build new convention centers, coliseums, professional football stadiums, airports, and expressways, there is rarely enough money to build new schools, parks, museums, water-sewer systems, public health facilities, and rapid transit systems or to maintain existing streets, highways, bridges, railroad stations, and social service centers. Who knows how many billions of dollars were spent converting Atlanta into a glass and concrete showcase suitable for hosting the 1996 Summer Olympics?

In Nashville the governor supported the building of a shopping mall just north of the state capital building to improve the view of tourists for the 1996 Tennessee Bicentennial Celebration. The mayor raised taxes to build a sports arena several blocks away. Nearby stands the moldering, vacant, magnificent Union Railroad Station Shed, the longest single-span gabled arch structure ever built when it was erected in 1900. Nashville's lone Amtrak passenger train stops at its own inauspicious shed on the edge of town.

When one travels from Boston to Washington, D.C., on Amtrak, one sees some of the least-attractive real estate in the entire nation.

13. Jerry Adler, "Theme Cities," *Newsweek*, September 11, 1995, p. 68.

The Atlanta Olympics

On July 19, 1996, over 85,000 spectators and nearly 3.5 billion television viewers worldwide watched former heavyweight boxing champion Muhammad Ali light the flame at the spectacular opening ceremony at the Atlanta Olympic Games — the global capitalism extravaganza of the century. The megaevent included a cast and crew of 8,250 members and featured a parade of 11,000 athletes from 197 countries. Supporting the Games were a 45,000-volunteer army and a 30,000-deep security force — not to mention a press corps of 15,000.

Sports Illustrated described the Atlanta money-making machine as "a pantheon of disposable corporate monuments, totems to the gods who are footing the bill." Nineteen multinational companies including AT&T, Coca-Cola, IBM, and McDonald's paid $40 million each for exclusive marketing rights at the Games. Anheuser-Busch's contribution was a 17,300-square-foot beer garden called Bud World, and for the nonimbibers Coca-Cola built a twelve-acre downtown amusement park called the Coca-Cola Olympic City where the price of a Coke was $2.50. The Atlanta-based soft-drink giant spent close to $300 million on the Olympics.

NBC paid $456 million for the television broadcast rights for the Atlanta Games, and European television had to cough up another $250 million.

Six days into the competition the highly touted internal information system developed by IBM, "Info 96," still did not work properly. The complex computer system was said to suffer from "start-up" problems. IBM spent $80 million to be the worldwide "technology integrator" for the Games. While the media was reporting the failures of Info 96, IBM continued to run television advertisements promoting the virtues of Info 96.

A pipe bomb exploded in Centennial Olympic Park, resulting in one death and injuries to over a hundred. Atlanta was also plagued by massive traffic jams, an overloaded public transportation system, and crass commercialism. What was supposed to have enhanced Atlanta's global image turned into a public relations nightmare.

(continued on page 62)

(continued from page 61)

The $194 million Olympic Village located on the campus of Georgia Tech housed all of the athletes plus 4,500 officials. It featured an 88,000-square-foot dining hall with seats for 3,400 and a 25,000-square-foot kitchen. Also included were a night club, a video game center, swimming pool, health club and spa, and five McDonald's restaurants.

The sports team attracting the most attention was the National Basketball Association's subsidiary team, the "Dream Team," made up of high-paid, high-profile professional basketball players hoping to become even richer from the international exposure they receive by participating in the Summer Olympics.

The Olympics provides a good example of where bigger truly is better, if better is defined by the number of medals won by a country. The four biggest winners in Atlanta were the United States, Germany, Russia, and China.

The total tab for the City of Atlanta for the seventeen-day commercial orgy was $1.7 billion — most of which was financed by private corporations.

Miles and miles of railroad right-of-way wind their way through a collection of towns and cities which resemble a never-ending war zone — vacant, burned-out factories and apartments; piles of garbage and debris; abandoned automobiles and appliances; and the feeling that surely one must be traveling in a Third World country — not the United States of America. With few exceptions along the way, the railroad stations are dilapidated, dark dumps which few would feel safe entering after dark.

The area surrounding the Amtrak station at the foot of Capitol Street in Jackson, Mississippi, can only be described as grim. The ten-story King Edward Hotel, once the pride of Jackson, has been vacant for over twenty years, inhabited only by rats, pigeons, and an occasional homeless drunk who breaks into the spooky structure. Across the street are two other, smaller hotels, both of which were well-known houses of ill-repute during their day. They too are vacant. And the railroad station, not unlike most American railroad stations everywhere, is in shambles. The City of Jackson seems to be completely powerless to do anything about this disgraceful scene.

With the help of significant amounts of federal funding, many an American city opted first to bulldoze unsightly poor neighborhoods which were giving the downtown area a bad image. Once the neighborhoods were completely destroyed, they were paved over by concrete and steel bridges and expressways — all in the name of progress. Richmond, Charlotte, Jackson, New Orleans, and Atlanta are among countless cities which have engaged in this abominable practice.

As for the private sector, the sky is the limit when it comes to financing new skyscrapers, shopping centers, theme parks, exclusive private colleges and universities, upscale churches and synagogues, and for-profit parks and entertainment centers.

As recently as 1988, only Nevada and New Jersey had legalized casino gambling. In search of new sources of state and local government revenue which avoid additional taxation, forty-eight states now permit some form of gambling, twenty-four of which have casinos. Annual legal-gambling revenues increased by 50 percent to $40 billion nationally in just six years.

Hoping to replicate the financial success of Las Vegas and Atlantic City, several dozen towns and cities — particularly along the Mississippi Gulf Coast — have embraced dockside casino gambling expecting to fill their town coffers with gold. By far the most dramatic example of dockside gambling development is near Biloxi, Mississippi, where there are now no fewer than fifteen large casinos, including five one-thousand-room hotels. Although Mississippi did not issue its first casino license until 1992, it now has the third-highest gambling revenues in the nation behind Nevada and New Jersey.

But as New Orleans learned, casino gambling is not risk-free. Harrah's Jazz, a giant new gambling palace heavily subsidized by the City of New Orleans and mired in incompetence and corruption, filed for bankruptcy before it was half completed. Other new gambling towns have discovered that while legalized gambling may boost tax revenues, there are significant offsetting costs, including higher rates of personal bankruptcy, divorce, crime, and substance abuse, as well as increased traffic and law enforcement expenses.

The City Dweller

Modern man is confined and often crippled by the world he lives in. A city dweller, he is cut off from sustaining contact with nature. It is almost impossible for the individual to escape the vast and frenzied throng of strangers, stripping him at once of isolation and a place in the community. The dissolution of family and neighborhood and community deprive him of those worlds within a world where he once could find a liberating sense of importance and shared enterprise as well as the security of friends.[14]

Separation and Alienation

The Los Angeles riots, the bombings of the World Trade Center in New York and the government building in Oklahoma City, inner-city drug wars, the mob, racism, teenage pregnancies and violence, and homelessness are all evidence that urban America is engulfed in meaninglessness. Those living in big cities have no sense of connectedness to themselves, to others, to nature, to their history, or to the ground of their being. Their lives lack purpose and are grounded in nothingness.

A few hours after an all-white Simi Valley jury acquitted four policemen of the use of excessive force in the widely publicized, videotaped arrest and beating of Rodney King, South Central Los Angeles was ablaze. The two-day riot left fifty-three persons dead, injured twenty-three hundred, and resulted in the arrest of more than ten thousand. Ten thousand buildings were either damaged or destroyed by fire and looting. More than forty thousand people lost their jobs, thousands were left homeless, and property damage alone was estimated to be well in excess of $1 billion.

Political pundits were quick to blame almost everyone for what happened in Los Angeles — white racists, black racists, Koreans, Rodney King, the jury, the L.A. mayor, the police chief, Lyndon Johnson, George Bush, black killer-rapist Willie Horton, liberals, conservatives, and the media, to mention only a few. Others pointed to capitalism,

---

14. Richard N. Goodwin, "The End of Reconstruction," in *You Can't Eat Magnolias,* ed. H. Brandt Ayers and Thomas H. Naylor (New York: McGraw-Hill, 1972), p. 65.

social welfare programs, teenage mothers, food stamps, rap music, and television violence. Nobody considered meaninglessness as the underlying cause of the violence — the meaningless lives of alcohol abuser Rodney King, the policemen who beat him up, the policemen who stood by watching, the jury that acquitted them, impoverished African Americans living in Los Angeles, alienated whites, and opportunistic politicians.

Senator Bill Bradley on American Cities

Urban America has a crisis of meaning. Without meaning there can be no hope; without hope there can be no struggle; without struggle there can be no personal betterment. Absence of meaning, influenced by overt and subtle attacks from racist quarters over many years, as well as increasing pessimism about the possibility of justice, fosters a context for chaos and irresponsibility. Meaning develops from birth. Yet, more than forty percent of all births in the twenty largest cities of America are to women living alone; among Black women, more than sixty-five percent.

For kids who have no family outside the gang, no connection to religion, no sense of place outside the territory, and no imagination beyond the violence on TV, our claims that government is on their side ring hollow. To them, government is at best, incompetent, and at worst corrupt. Instead of being rooted in values such as commitment and community service, their desires, like commodities, become rooted in the shallow ground of immediate gratification. TV bombards these kids with messages of conspicuous consumption. They want it now. They become trapped in the quick-sands of American materialism, surfeited with images of sex, violence, and drugs.

The physical condition of American cities, in the absence of meaning in more and more lives, comes together at the barrel of a gun. If you were to select one thing that has changed in cities since the 1970s, it would be fear. Fear covers the streets like a sheet of ice. The number of murders and violent crimes has doubled in the twenty largest cities since 1978. Ninety percent of all violence is committed by males, and they are its predominant victims. Indeed, murder is the leading cause of death among young Black males.

What happened in Los Angeles could easily happen in dozens of other large cities throughout the United States. What was the purpose of the rioting? Did it have any meaning? What have we learned from the experience? Probably nothing. Meaninglessness breeds powerlessness and more meaninglessness, and the cycle of narcissism and irresponsibility goes on.

We expect our urban public schools to solve all our social, economic, and political problems, and then are disappointed when they fail to meet our expectations. Children who grow up in impoverished, broken homes where there is no sense of meaning have their work cut out for them, even if they are bused to shiny, new, upscale schools in the more affluent suburbs. Unfortunately, neither our underfinanced public schools nor our well-heeled private schools seem to be able to solve the problems of alienation and meaninglessness.

Nothing has contributed more to the breakdown of community in America than television and the automobile. One keeps us glued to the privacy of our living room, the other draws us to the road. Neither does much to build community. When we want to go to the bakery, the bank, the grocery store, or our child's school, we hop in the car and drive. There are few places left where neighbors meet — whether it be in the town, the village, or the neighborhood — just to talk, have coffee, and pass the time. Suburban shopping malls with their pretentious plastic glitter and their moribund parking lots are evidence of our inhumanity and loss of community.

Crime and Punishment

A U.S. Justice Department study estimates that crime costs Americans $450 billion annually, including legal costs, lost work time, police work, mental health care costs, reduced quality of life, and intangibles such as the affection lost for a murder victim's family.

We have the world's highest homicide rate and second highest incarceration rate — over 1.5 million people in prison. "Despite an incarceration rate of five times that of the United Kingdom and 14 times that of Japan, the United States has a level of criminal violence unrivaled in any advanced country, except perhaps that found in the near-anarchy of post-Communist Russia — with nearly 2,000 people murdered in New York City in 1993 alone, compared with just over 3,000 in Northern Ireland during the entire quarter-century since civil order broke down there in 1969."[15] However, to New York City's credit, in 1996 the number of homicides in the city dropped from a 1990 high of 2,245 to below 1,000, a threshold last reached in 1968.

Since the U.S. Supreme Court cleared the way in 1976, thirty-eight states have restored capital punishment. Most of the state-imposed executions have taken place in western states and former slaveholding southern states and have been carried out with disproportionate frequency against African Americans who have killed whites. In 1995 we executed fifty-six prisoners, and the number is expected to reach two hundred by the year 2000. Over three thousand defendants await elec-trocution, hanging, shooting, and lethal injections. Does our blood-thirsty lust for revenge buy us reduced crime and violence?

From a very early age Americans are bombarded with television violence, beginning with the Saturday morning cartoons. The average sixteen-year-old has seen more than one hundred thousand acts of violence on TV. Children who witnessed the Ringling Brothers and Barnum & Bailey Circus several years ago were treated to a particu-larly heavy dose of violence, including a double-barreled human can-non, the Wheel of Death, the Globe of Death motorcycle act, and David Larible — the knife-throwing clown. The Eliminator TS-7, a toy weapon sold by F. A. O. Schwarz for ages five and up, was advertised as "the ultimate sound-and-light defense system." This awesome seven-in-one weapon includes a power dagger, a power sword, a laser sword, an army machine gun, a cyber-gun, and a super eliminator. Trading cards that depict well-known killers and gangsters instead of sports stars have also become popular. Among the criminals whose pictures appear on such cards are California's Zodiac killer, New York's "Son of Sam," Ted Bundy, and Milwaukee's Jeffrey Dahmer, who was convicted of killing, dismembering, and in some cases eating sixteen young men.

On an average day, 135,000 children bring real guns to school. Not surprisingly, teenage violence and homicides are growing throughout the country — particularly in large cities.

Shortly after American troops were sent to Somalia, a graphic cartoon depicting handgun violence in America appeared in the *Cincinnati Enquirer*. The cartoon posed the following question: "Where is

---

15. John Gray, "Does Democracy Have a Future?" *New York Times Book Review*, January 22, 1995, p. 24.

the U.S. working the hardest to curb the use of guns?" Answer: "Somalia."

Many colleges and universities still offer credit for courses in ROTC. Paradoxically, while American medical schools are teaching physicians how to save lives, professors of military science at these same institutions are helping produce more efficient killers. When the University of Richmond needed a keynote speaker for the dedication of its new Jepson Leadership School, it turned to General H. Norman "Stormin' Norman" Schwarzkopf, the man who orchestrated the computer-controlled, high-tech deaths of two hundred thousand Iraqis during the Persian Gulf War.

Is it any wonder that President John F. Kennedy, Senator Robert F. Kennedy, and Dr. Martin Luther King Jr. were gunned down at the hands of assassins, or that Presidents Gerald Ford, Ronald Reagan, and Bill Clinton, as well as Governor George Wallace, were also the targets of assassination attempts?

Two weeks after Bill Clinton was elected president, the Secret Service forced the Central Florida Young Republicans Club to cancel its annual "turkey shoot" fund-raiser. The Young Republicans had planned to use enlarged photos of President-elect Clinton as bull's-eye targets.

Hardly a week goes by in which we don't read about a multiple homicide somewhere in the United States — usually in a big city. The story of Kitty Genovese, who was stabbed to death in New York City in 1964 while dozens of her neighbors watched without offering her any help, serves as a vivid reminder of urban indifference and insensitivity to violent crime. Not only is it unsafe to live in most big cities, no one seems to care.

Social scientists have identified at least five causes of urban crime: (1) an inadequate criminal justice system, (2) poverty and inequality, (3) the breakdown of the family and community, (4) violence in the mass media — particularly television, and (5) racism. To this list we would add another, *meaninglessness.*

To combat urban crime and drug abuse, our politicians call for tougher law enforcement, capital punishment, and more prisons — little of which seems to work in most places. No matter how tempting it may be to bomb the drug lords of Colombia and Peru, there is no military solution to America's drug problem. People take drugs because they are alienated and powerless and have no sense of meaning in their lives. All the aircraft carriers and battleships in the world will not make

---

Origin of Crime

The sheer physical size of a social aggregation seems responsible not only for the number of crimes committed by its component individuals or groups; more significantly and dangerously, the frequency of crime, growing with the increasing size of the group, seems to be responsible also for the development of a corresponding frame of mind, a condoning philosophy.[16]

Americans less dependent on drugs. Government cannot give people the meaning sufficient to keep them from destroying themselves. Drug abuse and violence are very human problems and cry out for bottom-up human solutions, not public relations gimmicks or top-down government enforcement programs.

To deter teenage crime, President Bill Clinton has urged more towns and cities to impose curfews on their youth. A jury in an upscale Detroit suburb recently convicted the parents of a wayward adolescent of a misdemeanor for failing to keep their son under control.

No matter which label we use — alcoholic, drug addict, child abuser, rapist, murderer, or polluter — all are examples of the consequences of separation and alienation for which our political leaders have little understanding or empathy. Tougher law enforcement, gun control laws, chain gangs, and capital punishment may help politicians get elected and remain in office, but they do little to get at the root cause of urban crime — size. Urban crime is out of control because our cities are too large, not because we are too easy on criminals.

Top-Down Urban Revitalization

Since the Truman administration launched urban renewal in 1949, the federal government has spent tens of billions of dollars pursuing the fantasy that it is somehow possible to fix inner-city ghettos by injecting large amounts of cash into them. Nothing could be further from the truth.

16. Leopold Kohr, *The Breakdown of Nations* (New York: E. P. Dutton, 1978), p. 29.

Urban Renewal

The rap on it, wholly justified, was that it bulldozed neighborhoods, especially black neighborhoods (hence its nickname, "Negro Removal"), and replaced them with highways, sterile housing developments and municipal office complexes that looked wonderful when planners presented them at Chamber of Commerce meetings but, when built, only hastened the city's decline.[17]

The level of federal spending for urban revitalization increased significantly in the 1960s with President Johnson's War on Poverty and Model Cities programs. These were followed by President Ford's community development block grants, President Carter's urban development action grants, Presidents Reagan and Bush's enterprise zones, and more recently President Clinton's empowerment zones. While pretending to be bottom-up, coordinated, neighborhood, community development programs, what they all had in common was that they were top down, extremely bureaucratic, very expensive, and almost unbelievably ineffective.

The Myth of Community Development

Politicians like it. Foundations like it. It sounds good to conservatives and liberals alike. But history shows that of all possible solutions to the crisis in ghettos, it's the one most likely to fail.[18]

As we said in the introductory chapter, inner-city problems of poverty, unemployment, homelessness, education, crime, and drug abuse don't lend themselves to solutions imposed by bureaucrats sitting in Washington, the statehouse, or city hall. They require the bottom-up participation of the victims, who ultimately must take full responsibility for their own destiny. Many urban minorities — particularly blacks, Jews, and Hispanics — have been treated badly in our country. But it

17. Nicholas Lemann, "The Myth of Community Development," *New York Times Magazine,* January 9, 1994, p. 29.
18. Lemann, p. 27.

is wishful thinking to think that big government can make right decades or centuries of wrongdoing.

Downsizing

Not unlike corporate America, we believe American cities are too big, too crowded, and too dehumanized to survive in their present form. The only way out is downsizing. If the people living in a city want it to become smaller, three options are available — entry restrictions, exit incentives, and secession.

Urban Decision Making

Our cities grow, factories are built and inventions proclaimed, all powered by forces few can understand and no one seems able to control. Decisions affecting the quality of life, and even the prospects for life itself, are made by remote officials in distant places. And, more terrifying, no decision seems even to be made at all.[19]

Entry Restrictions

When Deng Xiaoping came to power in China in 1978, there were over 800 million people living in the Chinese countryside. To avoid replicating the urban problems of countries like Brazil and Mexico caused by the immigration of poor farmers to Rio de Janeiro, São Paulo, and Mexico City, Deng did two things. First, he introduced his initial economic reforms in the countryside rather than in the cities. Second, he imposed a $1,000 head tax on anyone moving into a city like Beijing. In most cases, one would have to bribe several Chinese officials even to get in a position to pay the head tax.

Just as a country can choose to impose barriers to immigration along its borders, so too should a city or a state be allowed to restrict entry into its territory. Unfortunately, the U.S. Constitution prohibits such entry restrictions by states and cities. However, high taxes, overcrowding, traffic congestion, crime, pollution, and general urban decay

19. Goodwin, p. 15.

have served as increasingly effective limits to urban growth in recent years.

Drastic though it might be, the most effective way to discourage people from moving to cities and to encourage many to leave would be to eliminate all direct federal subsidies to cities. If a city cannot sustain itself, why should it continue to exist?

Exit Incentives

Several years ago the owner of Leunig's, a popular watering hole in downtown Burlington, Vermont, endeared himself to local liberals by offering to purchase one-way bus tickets to Boston for homeless people sleeping outside his bar. At first blush, such a scheme may seem harsh and inhumane, but it does raise an interesting point. Should large cities consider the possibility of paying people to relocate outside the city's boundaries?

With the high cost of education, law enforcement, incarceration, rehabilitation of drug and alcohol abusers, health care, and other public services, would it not be prudent to pay people to leave New York, Chicago, Los Angeles, or Philadelphia? It might well be financially viable for cities to develop relocation settlements in rural areas for those willing to take the risk of starting a new life outside the city. Relocation settlements would be self-contained planned communities with their own infrastructure and public services financed initially by the city offering relocation incentives. Incentives to small manufacturers to locate in the planned communities would also be part of the package. Of course, such relocation schemes must be completely voluntary. But over the long run they might prove to be a much more humane alternative than entrapment in the inner city.

Cities might also consider organizing and financing Israeli-style kibbutzim in the countryside. A kibbutz is an open-ended agricultural and industrial collective of several hundred members in which all property and productive assets are owned by the commune. Membership is open to anyone and no initiation fee is required. Members are free to leave at any time. Land is leased from the Israeli government on a long-term basis. Wages and profits are shared equally by the members, and there are no hired workers from outside the community. The kibbutz builds and furnishes homes for its members, pays for their medical care, provides their food and clothing, and even does their laundry. It also takes care of the elderly.

All of the resource allocation decisions are made by the community, including what is to be produced, when it is to be produced, how it is to be produced, and what is to be done with the proceeds. For the most part, kibbutzim, with their high degree of community involvement, are more efficient than other Israeli farms. Today most kibbutzim have diversified economies, which include manufacturing as well as farming.

In recent years kibbutzim have become more pragmatic, less democratic, and more profit-oriented. They can now form joint ventures with outside firms, have outsiders on their boards of directors, hire outside workers, and pay workers overtime.

Before summarily dismissing exit incentives, one should consider the possibility of a deal between large cities which have far too many people and small rural towns which are withering on the vine everywhere. As we shall see in the next chapter, many a small town can no longer afford to support its own school, fire department, and water-sewer system. The possibility of an injection of funds, buildings, new infrastructure, and people looking for a new start, all financed by a big city, may not be rejected by some small, struggling towns. Everyone gains by such an arrangement — the big cities, the small towns, and the relocated people. And the federal government need not be involved at all. Indeed, one way to guarantee its failure would be to create a new federal urban relocation program administered from Washington.

Secession

Frustrated by their relatively insignificant voice in a vast unsympathetic urban government, the people of Staten Island, New York, voted to secede from New York City in November 1993. However, the results of this election are not likely to bear fruit anytime soon, since secession in New York requires the approval of the governor and the state legislature, neither of which is enthusiastic about the breakup of New York City.

There is a certain irony to Staten Island's attempt to secede from New York City, since for years conservatives in upstate New York have fantasized about the possibility of seceding from New York City, which they perceive to be a bottomless pit draining off financial resources from the taxpayers of upstate New York. And back in 1969 Norman Mailer called for the creation of an independent state of New York City which would return power to the neighborhoods. Wrote Mailer:

You Can't Fight City Hall

In recent years the interests of the people of Staten Island have become lost among the interests of the four larger boroughs. Staten Island has become a dumping ground, literally and figuratively — first on the list for the most undesirable aspects of city government and last when it comes to desirable services rendered.

Guy V. Molinari
Staten Island Borough President

Power to the neighborhoods! In the new city-state, every opportunity would be offered to neighborhoods to vote to become townships, villages, hamlets, subboroughs, tracts, or small cities, at which legal point they would be funded directly by the fifty-first state. Many of these neighborhoods would manage their own municipal services, their police, sanitation, fire protection, education, parks, or like very small towns, they could, if they wished, combine services with other neighborhoods. Each neighborhood would thus begin to outline the style of its local government by the choice of its services.[20]

There is a serious move afoot in California to enable the 1.8 million people who live in the San Fernando Valley section of the city of Los Angeles to secede from Los Angeles. As B. Drummond Ayres Jr. expressed in the *New York Times*, "There has always been this nagging suspicion that Los Angeles is more a state of mind than a proper city, a place too scattered, literally and figuratively, to hang together as a metropolitan whole."[21] A Miami citizens' group has proposed dividing the city into smaller community governments.

If any city ever had a legitimate claim for independence, it would be Washington, D.C., with the stranglehold the U.S. Congress maintains over its internal affairs.

But at one level, secession is nothing new in urban America.

20. Norman Mailer, "An Instrument for the City," *New York Times Magazine*, May 18, 1969.
21. B. Drummond Ayres Jr., "Los Angeles, Long Fragmented, Faces Threat of Secession by the San Fernando Valley," *New York Times*, May 29, 1996.

Wealthy New Yorkers, for example, have always lived in exclusive, tightly secured, high-rise apartments completely separated from the rest of New York. They travel to and from their apartments in air-conditioned, chauffeur-driven limousines, eat in posh restaurants and clubs, and send their kids to elite private schools. These affluent New Yorkers live in an island unto themselves. They seceded from New York City years ago.

This modern form of secession includes the millions of urban Americans who have fled from cities to isolated, private, closed-off gated communities, condominiums, and cooperatives. We know one couple who spends five days a week in an exclusive gated community near Dallas. Each weekend they fly to San Antonio, where they live in a second gated community. The real issue is not whether or not one favors the right of a subdivision of a city to secede, but rather whether this right is reserved only for the wealthy and well-to-do who can buy their way out of the urban morass and into tightly secured communities.

There is but one solution to the problems of urban America — radical downsizing now.

Strategies for Empowering and Downsizing Cities

1. Abolish the U.S. Department of Housing and Urban Development.
2. Eliminate most federal subsidies to towns and cities.
3. Repeal most federal statutes regulating towns and cities.
4. Allow towns and cities to limit the number of people living within their borders.
5. Introduce voluntary exit incentives to encourage people to leave town.
6. Allow cities to secede from the state in which they are located and form independent city-states.
7. Permit sections of a city to secede from the city itself.

---

4 Rural America: Our Last Hope

> My feeling is that, if improvement is going to begin any-
> where, it will have to begin out in the country and in the
> country towns. . . . In rural communities there are still
> farms and small businesses that can be changed according
> to the will and desire of individual people.[1]

The American Countryside

The mass exodus of Americans from rural America to the city continued
throughout the 1980s, resulting in fewer than 25 percent of the population now living in the countryside. However, between 1990 and 1995,
1.6 million more people moved from cities and suburbs to rural areas
than went the other way. This new development reflects the effects of
the continued deterioration in the quality of urban life leading to the
out migration of people living in cities like Los Angeles and New York
to states like Washington and Oregon and Vermont, respectively.

Since the 1930s the message to rural Americans has been loud
and clear: "The path to fame and fortune lay not in the countryside but
in the city." If you were intelligent, hardworking, or highly motivated,
once you finished high school or college you moved to the city. Only

1. Wendell Berry, *The Work of Local Culture* (Great Barrington, Mass.: E. F.
Schumacher Society, 1988), p. 16.

Rural America

The news from everywhere in rural America has been almost unrelievedly bad: bankruptcy, foreclosure, depression, suicide, the departure of the young, the loneliness of the old, soil loss, soil degradation, chemical pollution, the loss of genetic and specific diversity, the extinction or threatened extinction of species, the depletion of aquifers, stream degradation, the loss of wilderness, strip mining, clear-cutting, population loss, the loss of supporting economics, the deaths of towns.[2]

the country bumpkins and the dregs remained behind in the countryside. All of the economic, political, social, and cultural action was in the city. And our government, in its wisdom, did little to stem the flow of people from the country to the city. Farm subsidies were aimed primarily at the large corporate farms, not the small family farms. Higher paying jobs, higher social welfare benefits, and government-subsidized urban infrastructure drew rural Americans to our cities like magnets. Karl Marx wrote, revealingly, of "the idiocy of village life."

Land was viewed as just another resource to be overused, abused, and abandoned.

Care of the Land

A nation will destroy its land and therefore itself if it does not foster in every possible way the sort of thrifty, prosperous, permanent rural households and communities that have the desire, the skills, and the means to care properly for the land they are using.[3]

No region was more enamored by the urban-industrial paradigm than the South. Traveling through the region in the 1920s, a journalist made this observation: "Down in Dixie they tell you and always with

2. Wendell Berry, *Sex, Economy, Freedom, and Community* (New York: Pantheon, 1992), p. 5.
3. Berry, *Sex, Economy, Freedom, and Community*, p. 4.

Foreign-Owned Automobile Plants in the South[4]

Location	Automobile	Jobs	Cost
Smyrna, Tenn.	Nissan	6,000	$1.2 billion
Spring Hill, Tenn.	Saturn	5,900	$3 billion
Georgetown, Ky.	Toyota	4,000	$2 billion
Greer, S.C.	BMW	2,000	$450 million
Vance, Ala.	Mercedes-Benz	1,500	$300 million

good cheer that the South is the new frontier. . . . There is a feel in the air: Big tomorrows are just around the corner." Unfortunately for the South, the "big tomorrow" turned out to be a very mixed bag — a combination of rapid urban-industrial growth along with racism, rural poverty, the demise of small towns, and increased dependency on the federal government. Enticed by the South's low-wage, nonunion environment; state subsidies; tax breaks; warm weather; low living costs; and relaxed lifestyle, dozens of multimillion-dollar plants — particularly automobile plants — have been drawn to the rural South.

The Dark Side of the Rural South

Small towns that were once economically stable and racially mixed are becoming pockets of poverty and overwhelmingly black — 75 to 100 percent so.

The pattern is so striking that some experts say a new kind of ghetto is evolving: rural instead of urban, but sharing many conditions of the inner city: white flight, black poverty, a disappearing job base, reliance on government welfare payments, rising crime and social isolation.[5]

4. Peter Applebone, "A Sweetness Tempers South's Bitter Past," *New York Times*, July 31, 1994, p. 1.

5. Peter Applebone, "Deep South and Down Home, but It's a Ghetto All the Same," *New York Times*, August 21, 1993, p. 1. However, the research of William Julius Wilson in his *When Work Disappears: The World of the New Urban Poor* (New York: Knopf, 1996) indicates that, compared with the urban poor, African Americans in rural areas of the south are safer, less likely to be imprisoned, and healthier, though their income is considerably less.

German chancellor Helmut Kohl, in chiding German factory workers, recently warned them that they could be losing their jobs to "third world countries — like South Carolina."

Of those left behind in rural America, African Americans, Native Americans, and Mexican Americans have fared the worst. Unemployment, poverty, disease, and despair remain at the nation's highest levels among these groups of rural Americans.

The Rural Great Plains

What remains of human settlement in the rural Great Plains is a Federal welfare project, sustained by Government farm programs and even more by Social Security and Medicare. This is the country of lonely old women, the widows who don't want to move South and whose children have gone elsewhere to find jobs. There are small towns in western Kansas, in the Dakotas and in the Oklahoma panhandle where nothing thrives except the drugstore and the clinic, if there is one.

Depopulation of the rural Great Plains has been going on for decades. Now begins its endgame — the disintegration of local institutions. Towns are withering, and rural counties are becoming too empty to continue as separate entities. If enough of them become that empty, at some point someone will ask this question: Is North Dakota necessary?[6]

In spite of all of these adversities, if there is hope for America, it lies in the countryside, because in the countryside farms, villages, towns, schools, churches, and governments are still small enough to fix.

Agriculture

The number of farms in America has dwindled to fewer than 2 million — down from a 1935 peak of 6.8 million. Furthermore, the number of

---

6. Jon Margolis, "The Reopening of the Frontier," *New York Times Magazine,* October 15, 1995, pp. 52-53.

The Virtues of Farming

Those who labor in the earth are the chosen people of God, if ever He had a chosen people, whose breasts He has made His peculiar deposit for substantial and genuine virtue. It is the focus in which He keeps alive that sacred fire, which otherwise might escape from the face of the earth. Corruption of morals in the mass of cultivators is a phenomenon of which no age or nation has furnished an example. It is the mark set on those, who, not looking up to heaven, to their own soil and industry, as does the husbandman, for their subsistence, depend for it on casualties and caprice of customers. Generally speaking, the proportion which the aggregate of the other classes of citizens bears in any State to that of its husbandmen, is the proportion of its unsound to its healthy parts, and is a good enough barometer whereby to measure its degree of corruption.

Thomas Jefferson
Notes on Virginia

---

people employed in farm occupations has dropped to 2.9 million from a peak of 11.6 million farm workers in 1910. Not only has the number of farms and farmers declined precipitously, but the average farm size has increased to 473 acres per farm. However, as the number of farms and the amount of total farm acreage have continued to decline, crop sales have actually been increasing.

High energy costs, the increased cost of mechanization, sagging farm prices, and a government farm subsidy program, which primarily benefits huge corporate farms, have taken their toll on small family farms. Today over a third of farm produce comes from only 1.4 percent of our nation's largest farms. Throughout the 1980s federal farm subsidies averaged nearly $15 billion annually. Seventy-three cents of every farm program dollar ends up in the pockets of 15 percent of the nation's megafarms.[7]

Among the many critics of American farm policy is Osha Gray Davidson:

7. Osha Gray Davidson, "Farming the System," *New York Times*, January 4, 1993, p. A15.

Despite a glutted market, farmers are paid a subsidy for every bushel of corn they produce. This encourages even the most conscientious growers to plow highly erodible land and to use enormous amounts of fertilizer and pesticides, polluting limited ground water.

Our new farm policy should encourage farmers not to grow more, but to grow more efficiently. And such a policy should take environmental and social costs into account. We pay to clean water polluted by farm chemicals. A more rational policy would hold farms responsible for environmental costs, perhaps by adding a tax to the price of toxic chemicals.[8]

Although Václav Havel's remarks were directed at the breakup of large state-owned farms in Czechoslovakia after the collapse of communism in 1991, he might very well have been talking about the American farm scene when he said,

Agriculture should once again be in the hands of the farmers — people who own the land, the meadows, the orchards, and the livestock, and take care of them. In part these will be small farmers who have been given back what was taken from them, in part larger family farms, and in part modest cooperatives of owners or commercial enterprises. The farmers themselves know best — and new farmers will quickly learn — how to renew the ecological balance, how to cultivate the soil and gradually bring it back to health. I also believe that a portion of the agricultural land should simply be left fallow, converted to pastureland, or reforested.

The Vermont Family Farm

In 1994, in a symbol of massive national transformation, the U.S. Census Bureau dropped its long-standing survey of farm residents — a painful reminder of the reduced importance of the family farm on the American landscape. Farm residents now constitute only 1.9 percent of the national population, compared with 40 percent at the turn of the century. The final farm report set the farm population at 4.6 million — down from 23 million in 1950, when farm residents constituted 15

8. Davidson, p. A15.

percent of the population, and 6 million in 1980, when farm residents made up 2.8 percent of the population. Today almost a third of farm managers and 86 percent of farm workers live away from the farm and commute to the fields.

One place where the family farm is still alive, although not so well, is in tiny Vermont. Even though farming now ranks only third behind manufacturing and tourism as a source of income in Vermont, the family farm is still arguably the heart and soul of the state. As Frank Bryan and John McClaughry have pointed out in their provocative book *The Vermont Papers,* it was not by chance that the statue atop the Vermont statehouse is that of Ceres, the patroness of agriculture, rather than either Vulcan, the patron of manufacturing, or Mercury, who might be loosely construed to be the patron of tourism.[9]

This Land Vermont

For centuries the Vermont landscape has evoked strong emotions, from the rhapsodies of the artist and poet to the exuberant joys of the vacationer and skier. But more important than these outbursts has been the quiet but deep-seated attachment of the Vermonter to his native soil. The Vermonter's attachment to his land has recognized its aesthetic and productive and sometimes its market values, but more commonly it has been an attachment of the soul. It sprang not only from the soul's affinity for a place, but also from its need to possess, protect, and pass on improved.[10]

According to a popular myth, not so many years ago there were more black-and-white Holsteins, Brown Swiss, and Guernseys in Vermont than there were people. Although the myth turns out to be just that — a myth — many Vermonters wish it were true. Today there are less than seven thousand farms in Vermont, of which fewer than two thousand are dairy farms. In 1950 there were over eleven thousand dairy farms alone, but reduced government milk subsidies, oversupply, and the rising cost of technology have driven thousands of Vermont

---

9. Frank Bryan and John McClaughry, *The Vermont Papers* (Post Mills, Vt.: Chelsea Green, 1989), p. 242.
10. Bryan and McClaughry, p. 22.

Sugaring

One joy of sugaring is that you take advantage of the inconstant weather. In fact, the more capricious the weather — the more spring seems to come and then dances away again — the better the sugaring. You can't do it at all without freezing nights and warm days. . . . A late wet April snow is simply frustrating for the motorist, or a suburbanite impatient to get to work on his lawn. For a syrup maker it is a cause for rejoicing, because maples run their fastest on such a day. . . . That night you boil until midnight, and there is a holiday atmosphere.[11]

The Vermont Farmer

For all Vermonters it is the farmer (along with logger and quarryman) who produces closest to the land. Historically, during the centuries when agricultural life gave form and substance to Vermont, the farmer was not a party to the manipulation of paper values and the realization of windfall gains, or to a life without hard physical work in such conditions as the changing seasons would provide. His was the world of the genuine, the natural, the God-given. He arose before dawn, conformable to the needs of his livestock. He savored the pungent aroma of the cow barn, the fragrance of the apple blossoms in May, the smell of the new-mown hay. He and his farm wife planned their life together to do what had to be done, cutting wood for the winter and the sugaring, fixing fence, seeing the milk safely to the dairy, guiding their son's hands for the first time he steered team or tractor, putting up food for the long winters. Affluent the farmer was not, but strong in mind and spirit, an essential working part of a beautiful though sometimes severe world which made sense — and was profoundly satisfying — to those who dwelt within it.[12]

11. Noel Perrin, *Third Person Rural* (Boston: David R. Godine, 1983), pp. 18-19.

12. Bryan and McClaughry, p. 242.

farmers off the land. Even though dairy products still account for three-fourths of agricultural income, cattle, vegetables, apples, hay, and maple syrup are also important cash crops. Average farm size in Vermont is only 219 acres, less than half the national average.

Although Vermont farm income is less than a half-billion dollars, total agribusiness income, including ice cream, cheese, chocolates, specialty meats, maple sugar houses, and farm tours, exceeds one billion dollars. Over 44,500 people are employed in agribusiness.

Farming — particularly the family farm — has left its mark on the character of Vermont. Vermont values such as individuality, resourcefulness, hard work, education, versatility, and inventiveness can be traced directly to the family farm.

Country Towns

Community still thrives in Vermont, with its town meetings, Congregational churches, county fairs, red barns, covered bridges, maple sugaring, and picturesque Green Mountains. Its bucolic population evinces independence, democracy, nonviolence, a strong work ethic, and a deep sense of community.

Eudora Welty on Towns

You could see a town lying ahead in its whole, as definitely formed as a plate on a table. And your road entered and ran straight through the heart of it; you could see it all, laid out for your passage through. Towns, like people, had clear identities and your imagination could go out to meet them.

Eudora Welty
One Writer's Beginnings

Although the backwoods of Vermont's hills and valleys fosters self-sufficiency, it also provides a hospitable climate for real community seldom found in America. From the outset, the combination of the harsh winters and the small farms, villages, and towns has engendered a variety of communal activities, including barn raisings, work bees, electric co-ops, and — more recently — cohousing and intentional communities.

Vermont Communities

The imperatives of Vermont's geography are important to its identity. For Vermont is a place of ups and downs. Its land seems to cluster people in little communities by nature. The winters are cold, the coldest in New England. The snow comes early and lasts and lasts and lasts. The soil is rocky, the living tough. Vermont's geography contains a dual imperative: it cradles settlements and it makes living difficult.

So Vermonters, harkening to humankind's basic need for cooperation, come to huddle like the Swiss in small communities, mountain towns and villages. They seek the safety of unity, of Congregationalism, of neighbor, church and town. Their spirits crave liberty, but the land compels union.[13]

Vermont is a cityless state. Its largest town, Burlington, has a population of only forty thousand. Among the better-known Vermont towns are Bennington, Brattleboro, Middlebury, and Rutland. Brattleboro and Middlebury have been ranked among the one hundred best towns in America in which to live.

Unfortunately, the automobile, interstate highways, shopping malls, fast-food restaurants, suburban sprawl, state government centralization, and the union (consolidated) high school movement have taken their toll on Vermont towns and villages. Once charming, quaint villages such as Essex Junction, Williston, Jericho, Richmond, Shelburne, and Hinesburg are now little more than Burlington bedroom communities filled with apartments and condominiums. Others such as Grafton, Stowe, and Woodstock have been overrun by tourists — particularly skiers.

Despite these setbacks, community is still very much alive in many of the towns and villages of Vermont — in places like Bristol, Chelsea, Ludlow, Newport, Peacham, and Quechee, to mention only a few. Although we have not been able to come up with a prescriptive formula for a successful Vermont community, there are some common elements shared by many Vermont villages — a town hall, a school, a

13. Bryan and McClaughry, pp. 30-31.

library, a Congregationalist church, a post office, a country inn or a couple of bed-and-breakfast establishments, and several stores including a general store. The traditional Vermont general store was a precursor to the shopping mall. In the not too distant past, it was not uncommon for a general store to include a grocery store, an apothecary, a post office, a pub, a barbershop, and a doctor's office. More often than not, it was some combination of the town meeting and the local church which provided the spiritual glue which held the community together.

Whether it be eating a plateful of turkey pie at the New Haven town meeting, fighting to preserve local control of the Charlotte middle school, or blocking a real estate development project in East Middlebury — evidence of community is everywhere. Dozens of Vermont towns have some sort of annual festival each summer. One can spend the entire summer attending festivals ranging from the sophisticated, world-class Vermont Mozart Festival held on the lawn of the Inn at Shelburne Farms overlooking the sunset on Lake Champlain to the hot-air balloon festival held near Quechee each year. A typical festival is the week-long Middlebury festival in which friends and neighbors are treated to a variety of different types of music each evening on the village green — classical, jazz, international, bluegrass, and Cajun.

Burlington's annual First Night festival is a community-based, alcohol-free New Year's Eve celebration of the performing arts. Participants can pick and choose among dozens of different musical events and performances scattered all over town in colleges, schools, theaters, churches, and auditoriums. Over fifteen thousand people participate in the festival.

Not big enough to attract the Ringling Brothers and Barnum & Bailey Circus, Vermont is fortunate enough to be included on the tour of the Big Apple Circus, a small not-for-profit performing arts community founded in 1977 to introduce American audiences to "the intimate and interactive environment of the classic, European one-ring circus." With its emphasis on theatricality, artistry, and audience participation, the Big Apple Circus incorporates aspects of traditional theater, including original music, lighting, choreography, sets and costumes, with classical circus acts. Set in an intimate one-ring tent where no one sits more than fifty feet from the action, the Big Apple Circus appears to have been custom-designed for Vermonters.

Perhaps the most unusual festival in Vermont — and one of the largest — is the annual Bread and Puppet performance of Our Domestic Resurrection Circus. Each summer over fifteen thousand pilgrims find their way to a remote, abandoned gravel pit now used as an amphitheater near the tiny village of Glover in the Northeast Kingdom of Vermont. There they are treated to a free outdoor puppet circus complete with sideshows, music, pageant, and delicious, free, homemade German sourdough rye bread made personally by Bread and Puppet founder Peter Schumann.

On a somewhat less esoteric level, there are dozens of country fairs scattered all over Vermont each summer, of which the Tunbridge World's Fair is probably the best known. This legendary fair has been around since 1861 and got its nickname from a politician's bombast back in its rowdier days.

Hear That Lonesome Whistle Blow

Nothing creates a more nostalgic longing for the countryside than the mournful sound of a distant train's whistle traveling through the night. Fifty years ago most of the towns and villages in the United States were connected by an extensive network of passenger trains.

In the 1940s when one of us used to visit his grandfather in a small Mississippi village, the most important event each day was the arrival of the Mobile-to-Saint Louis passenger train known as the Rebel. The Rebel brought the mail, merchandise for Granddaddy's general store, and a handful of passengers — sometimes from faraway places. Black and white farmers alike sat on benches in front of Granddaddy's store dipping snuff, drinking soda waters (soft drinks), and gossiping about who came and went on the Rebel.

Sparsely populated rural Mississippi was crisscrossed by four other crack, streamlined trains — the Panama Limited, the City of New Orleans, the Southerner, and the Crescent. Even tiny Vermont had a dozen or so passenger trains with wonderful names like the Green Mountain Flyer, the White Mountain Express, the Milk Train, the Montrealer, the Ambassador, the Ski Meister, the Red Wing, and the Alouette.

Of these trains, only two — the City of New Orleans and the Crescent — still run, neither of which operates daily. Other than along the Northeast Corridor between Washington, New York, and Boston, railroad passenger service, for all practical purposes, has ceased to exist in the United States.

History may show that the passage of the 1956 Interstate Highway Act contributed more to the demise of the railroad passenger trains in this country than any other event. In the name of "progress," we sold the soul of America to the Big Three automakers, multinational oil companies, coast-to-coast truckers, and mega–road builders. The combination of low-cost foreign oil and our vast, federally subsidized highway network made it virtually impossible for passenger trains to compete with the automobile.

With the automobile one has the feeling of freedom, power, independence, and control. It enables us to maintain our individualism and our separation from each other. Not only are automobiles and trucks less energy efficient and more environmentally hostile than trains, but they are antithetical to community building.

But on a train friends, neighbors, and complete strangers may converse and experience a sense of connectedness. Trains foster community between passengers and between towns. Automobiles perpetuate separation, alienation, pollution, traffic congestion, and urban sprawl.

All of this is in stark contrast to Europe, where even the smallest towns and villages are connected by an impressive network of passenger trains. Through efficient, high-quality railroads, village residents have easy access to neighboring villages as well as cities such as Paris, Rome, Geneva, Munich, and Zurich. Trains engender a sense of community within one's own country and with the rest of Europe.

Two hundred European cities are linked by modern, high-speed trains traveling at maximum speeds of between 90 and 125 miles per hour. Not only do these trains run on time, with minimal border crossing delays, but they are clean and comfortable. Most offer elegant dining car service as well. Train travel in Europe is a hassle-free, pleasurable experience affordable by most.

The efficiency of European trains was dramatically illustrated on a recent trip to Switzerland by Thomas and his family. Fifteen minutes after our Vienna-to-Zurich express left Innsbruck, we were informed that because of a collapsed bridge ahead, all passengers would disembark at the next village and board buses to the station just beyond the accident site. Within fifteen minutes all passengers and luggage had been loaded on six awaiting buses. Forty-five minutes later, west of the bridge, we boarded a Swiss train configured identically to our Austrian train. In typical Swiss fashion, we arrived in Zurich on schedule.

The combination of our love affair with the automobile and the death of passenger trains has done irreparable damage to small towns everywhere. We have paid dearly in terms of loss of community by turning our backs on passenger trains.

Amtrak

It is unlikely that Amtrak can overcome its problems in financing, capital investments, and service quality — and continue to operate with the present nationwide system — without significant increases in passenger revenues and/or subsidies from Federal, State, and local governments. Continuing the present course — maintaining the same funding level and route system, even with the proposed cuts in service — is neither feasible nor realistic because Amtrak will continue to deteriorate.

Government Accounting Office

North Carolina and Vermont have experienced some success in bringing trains back. North Carolina now has two state-subsidized commuter trains running between Raleigh and Charlotte each day. The governor of Vermont saved Amtrak from extinction in Vermont by subsidizing the St. Albans-to-Washington, D.C., Vermonter, which replaced the discontinued Montrealer. He has also supported a new ski train between New York City and Rutland called the Ethan Allen and a commuter train south of Burlington.

Nowhere is the case for passenger trains expressed more poignantly than in the classic American hobo song "The Wabash Cannon Ball."

The Wabash Cannon Ball

From the Great Atlantic Ocean,
To the wide Pacific shore.
From the Sweet Old Glory mountains,
To the Southland by the moor.
She's mighty tall and handsome,
She's known quite well by all.
She's the mighty combination,
Called the Wabash Cannon Ball.

She came down from Birmingham,
One cold December day.
As she rolled into the station,
You could hear the people say.
There's a girl from Tennessee,
She's long and she's tall.
She came down from Birmingham,
On the Wabash Cannon Ball.

Our Eastern states are dandy,
So the people always say.
From New York to St. Louis,
And Chicago by the way.
From the hills of Minnesota,
Where the rippling waters fall.
No chances can be taken,
On the Wabash Cannon Ball.

Here's to Daddy Claxton,
May his name forever stand.
He'll always be remembered,
Throughout our mighty land.
His earthly race is over,
And the curtains round him fall.
We'll carry him home to glory,
On the Wabash Cannon Ball.

Listen to the jingle,
The rumble and the roar.
As she glides along the woodland,
Over hills and by the shore.
Hear the mighty rush of engines,
And the lonesome hobo squall.
Riding through the jungles,
On the Wabash Cannon Ball.

Sustainable Rural Communities

The idyllic words of Wendell Berry remind us how far removed most of our rural towns and villages are from the sustainable ideal.

> The standard must be the health of the *whole* community: ourselves, the place where we live, and all the humans and other creatures who live there with us. It is better, even if the cost is greater, to buy near at hand than to buy at a distance. It is better to buy from a small, privately owned local store than from a chain store. It is better to buy a good product than a bad one. Do not buy anything you don't need. Do as much as you can for yourself. If you cannot do something for yourself, see if you have a neighbor who can do it for you. Do everything you can to see that your money stays as long as possible in the local community.[14]

Is it possible to reinvent rural America so that more people from our big cities will be attracted to the countryside and not just to the nearby suburbs? We believe the time has come for a paradigm shift away from the urban renewal model and toward rural redevelopment.

One country enjoying a resurgence of rural villages is tiny Finland, with a population of only 5 million people. During the 1980s and early 1990s, forty thousand more Finns moved to rural villages from cities than moved to cities from villages. This dramatic reversal of the rural-to-urban migration pattern which had persisted in Finland since the 1940s is attributable primarily to the Finnish Village Action Movement.

Today there are over thirty thousand Finns involved in three thousand self-governing Village Action committees which run the week-to-week activities of their villages. According to Hilka Pietilä, their work has an important impact on the lives of over half a million people in the Finnish countryside.[15]

The objectives of the Village Action Movement are twofold. First, to stop the migration from the villages by making them attractive, socially rewarding, and cozy places to live. Second, to tempt and persuade more people to move in and settle in the villages.

14. Berry, *Sex, Economy, Freedom, and Community*, pp. 16-17.
15. Hilka Pietilä, "The Villages in Finland Refuse to Die," in *Rebuilding Communities*, ed. Vithal Rajan (Devon: Resurgence, 1993), pp. 120-27.

Talkoot

A general problem in all villages is that whatever they want to do, they have practically no money to do it. But they have skillful and motivated people. They have reactivated their "secret weapon," an old Finnish tradition of voluntary teamwork, called *talkoot*. People have devoted millions of hours of work during these years in the villages for the common good without pay. Work substitutes for money and rewards more than money![16]

Among the many accomplishments of the Village Action committees are:

1. They have created new economic opportunities, increased political influence, and enhanced community-spirit and self-confidence.
2. They have improved community infrastructure, including roads, buildings, lighting, sports facilities, schools, shops, banks, and post offices.
3. "They have restored local traditions and heritage in the form of festivals and celebrations, village books and histories, collections of handicrafts, tools, suits, and dresses, the restoration and renovation of old buildings and houses, and preparing miniature replicas of their villages in their former state."[17]

If there is hope for America, it lies in the countryside. We are not advocating a massive infusion of federal aid to small towns and villages. If small towns are to stage a comeback, the initiative must be their own, not imposed by Washington or the statehouse. Rural America cannot be rebuilt by displaced urban planners. However, as federal subsidies are lowered for cities, highways, and expressways, the reduced federal tax burden on rural communities may free up local funds which can be spent for local development initiatives — schools, libraries, town halls, recreational facilities, etc.

In the previous chapter we proposed the possibility of cities

16. Pietilä, p. 121.
17. Pietilä, p. 125.

subsidizing the relocation of urban dwellers to the countryside. The flip side of that proposition is villages providing positive incentives to those disillusioned with urban life to move to rural villages. Village Action committees might be an excellent tool to attract people back to the villages. No doubt there are many other incentives as well.[18]

The history of the world tells us that big cities come and go. We can live without big cities, as we have before. But without small farms and rural towns and villages we cannot survive, for they are the wellspring of our nation. They are truly our last hope!

Strategies to Revitalize Rural America

1. Eliminate all federal subsidies to towns and cities.
2. Allow towns and cities to limit the number of people living within their borders.
3. Permit cities to introduce voluntary exit incentives to encourage people to leave town.
4. Abolish the U.S. Department of Agriculture.
5. Subsidize small family farms, not large corporate farms.
6. Revoke the state's authority to control, consolidate, and close local schools.
7. Introduce Village Action committees similar to those found in Finland.
8. Reduce federal subsidies to interstate highways and reallocate these funds to restore passenger train service connecting our towns and cities to our rural villages.
9. Patronize local merchants, farmers, banks, newspapers, sports events, and cultural activities.
10. Boycott the products and services of large national chains as well as mail-order houses.

---

18. For those considering a move to the countryside or to a small town, we recommend two books by Wanda Urbanska and Frank Levering — *Simple Living* (New York: Viking, 1992) and *Moving to a Small Town* (New York: Fireside, 1996).

5 *Digitizing America's Schoolkids*

Mass public education no longer works.

> Louis V. Gerstner Jr.
> Chairman and CEO of IBM

Only 75 percent of the students who enter American high schools actually graduate, and many of these are considered functionally illiterate. Twenty percent of all Americans cannot write a letter or read a newspaper. More than 80 percent of American eighth graders cannot calculate fractions, decimals, and percentages. Forty percent of fourth graders cannot differentiate between northeast and southwest on a map.

Although we spend over $300 billion annually on the 45 million children enrolled in our 84,500 public schools, only our ill-conceived social welfare system attracts more political flak than our failing public education system. While there is widespread criticism of our public schools, there is little agreement as to the causes of their decline or what will be required to fix them. Furthermore, it is not clear whether our schools are failing because our nation is in decline or our nation is failing because our schools are in decline.

94

The Meaning of Education

When people ask for education they normally mean something more than mere training, something more than mere knowledge of facts, and something more than a mere diversion. Maybe they cannot themselves formulate precisely what they are looking for; but I think what they are really looking for is ideas that would make the world, and their own lives, intelligible to them. When a thing is intelligible you have a sense of participation; when a thing is unintelligible you have a sense of estrangement. If the mind cannot bring to the world a set — or, shall we say, a tool-box — of powerful ideas, the world must appear to it as a chaos, a mass of unrelated phenomena, of meaningless events. Such a man is like a person in a strange land without any signs of civilization, without maps or signposts or indicators of any kind. Nothing has any meaning to him; nothing can hold his vital interest; he has no means of making anything intelligible to himself.[1]

The Symptoms

Business leaders like Louis V. Gerstner Jr., chairman and CEO of IBM, are concerned primarily with the implications of our failing education system on our competitive position abroad:

> American students are falling behind. They are doing worse today than students have done historically; our children are performing much worse than children from nations with whom they compete internationally.[2]

In a March 1996 speech to our nation's governors, Gerstner voiced the following concerns about America's declining competitive position in education, relative to other countries:

1. E. F. Schumacher, *Small Is Beautiful* (New York: Harper & Row, 1973), p. 89.
2. Louis V. Gerstner Jr., *Reinventing Education* (New York: Plume, 1995), pp. 4-5.

In Germany, 37 percent of high school students take advanced placement exams, and 95 percent of them pass. In the U.S. 7 percent of
high school students take advanced placement tests, and of those,
only 66 percent pass.

Japanese students start taking algebra two full years ahead of
U.S. students, and overall do five times as much homework per
week as American children.

Eighth graders in France spend more than half their math class
time studying geometry, while American eighth graders spend less
than one percent of their math class time on geometry.

Mr. Gerstner demonstrated a particularly strong interest in the
education of America's schoolkids when he was CEO of RJR Nabisco,
one of the largest manufacturers of cigarettes in the world. His work
at RJR Nabisco resulted in the publication of his book *Reinventing
Education,* which is a broadside attack on public school policymakers,
administrators, teachers, and students. Among his many concerns are
inadequate national standards, a lack of accountability, the shortness
of the school day and the school year, insufficient discipline and motivation, an increasing technological gap, and a need for more emphasis
on mathematics, science, and computers. Gerstner feels our public
schools are unchallenging, too easy, and that they fail to prepare high
school graduates for an increasingly competitive, market-oriented
world.

All fifty American states require that children attend school.
While state laws vary as to the ages and circumstances of compulsory
school attendance, generally they require that formal schooling begin
by age six and continue to age sixteen. On average, American kids go
to school 180 days each year in contrast to Japanese kids, who are in
school for 243 days a year. This is a major concern to Mr. Gerstner and
his followers, who fear American workers will fall further behind their
Japanese counterparts. Big Blue would lengthen the school day and
increase the length of the school year — all in the name of keeping
America free and great!

What happened to the view that all work and no play makes
Johnny (Jill) a dull boy (girl)? Would you like for your kids to be forced
by the state to go to school two hours longer each day for twelve months
a year so they can go to work for some big American company like
IBM? Some, including President Bill Clinton, advocate an additional
year of high school, saying we need at least thirteen years to do the job.

On the other hand, fundamentalist conservatives of the religious right feel that our schools are dominated by destructive liberal ideas that preclude the possibility of real learning. They reject the permissive philosophy of many public schools and advocate school prayers and Bible reading. Liberals respond that our schools are rigid, inflexible, and racist. They would give students more freedom, not less.

Character Education

Education worthy of the name is essentially education of character. For the genuine educator does not merely consider individual functions of his pupil, as one intending to teach him only to know or be capable of certain definite things; but his concern is always the person as a whole, both in the actuality in which he lives before you now and in his possibilities, what he can become.

Martin Buber
Between Man and Man

The problem of public education in America is that we live in a multiracial, multicultural, multireligious, multi-income, multipolitical, multi-interest society in which one's educational philosophy is shaped by one's race, religious faith, socioeconomic status, political philosophy, and special interests, not to mention a host of external factors associated with where one lives, works, and plays.

Competing with the Japanese, Mr. Gerstner's great concern, may be important to some parents, but by no means all. Some find the whole

---

A Libertarian View

Why is it that whenever CEOs turn their attention to education, their prescriptions are for top-down management, centralized control, and rigorous impersonality? When my daughter enters school in a couple of years, I'll be damned if she'll be taught to "compete with the Japanese."

Bill Kauffman

---

idea of basing an education system on competitive advantage to be morally and intellectually repugnant.

Another view of public education is that it is impossible to have stable schools in urban neighborhoods steeped in crime, violence, drug and alcohol abuse, poverty, teenage pregnancies, and broken families. A 1994 Carnegie Corporation report entitled "Starting Points: Meeting the Needs of Our Youngest Children" pointed out that the United States ranks near the bottom of the industrialized nations in providing universal health care, subsidized child care, and extensive leaves from work for families with children under age three, despite scientific evidence that these early years are critical in the development of the human brain. To expect our urban public schools to be able to solve all of the socioeconomic problems of urban America is utterly unrealistic. It's impossible to fix New York's schools without first fixing New York. But are New York, Washington, and Los Angeles fixable?

The academic requirements of entry-level jobs at many high-tech companies like IBM exceed those of some of our best colleges and universities. Many high school graduates are simply not qualified for high-tech blue-collar jobs.

Is what's best for an $80 billion multinational company like IBM good for America's public schools?

Schooling

Schooling (as opposed to education) has become our modern dogma, a sacred cow which all must worship, serve, and submit to, yet from which little true nourishment is derived. Schools have failed our individual human needs, supporting fallacious notions of "progress" and development that follow from the belief that ever-increasing production, consumption, and profit are proper yardsticks for measuring the quality of human life.[3]

Still others blame the demise of public education not on teachers, administrators, and politicians but rather on the "value-free" atmosphere which has evolved in our schools since the 1960s. So afraid are

3. Ivan Illich, *Deschooling Society* (New York: Harper & Row, 1970), book jacket.

academic bureaucrats of offending a particular racial, religious, or special interest group, and thus undermining public support for our schools, that they go to ridiculous extremes to avoid any discussion of morals, values, religion, or spirituality. While pretending to be value-neutral, our schools are in fact busily at work worshiping the gods of careerism, consumerism, technology, and multicultural separatism, says education philosopher Neil Postman in his provocative book *The End of Education.*[4]

In an address to the National Education Association, television producer Norman Lear challenged American teachers to develop a new concept of "progress" based less on materialism and technology and more on the needs of the human spirit:

> A civilization cannot progress when the majority of its youth devote their interests and energies to the materialistic pursuit of the sensory or outer world. When the young neglect to interest themselves in ethics, philosophy, the fine arts, religion and cosmology — or in the values of truth, beauty, goodness, love, loyalty and devotion — civility itself ceases.
>
> So wouldn't it be wonderful if, in the process of teaching — you uncover or discover a new, more spiritually satisfying notion of "progress" — one that relies less on a millennial faith in technology and rediscovers the center of our Being? One could imagine this search taking place through other institutions in our society. But none is as suited to this task, or as likely to have as great an influence as you.
>
> You could not aim higher, or better prepare the next generation for the world that we live in, than to teach it to look deeper into itself, to that place where humans from the very beginning of time have shared the same sense of awe and wonder as they groped for meaning.[5]

Curriculum is another area of concern where there is little agreement among critics of America's public schools. Some favor a common national curriculum carefully monitored by national standardized testing. Those subscribing to this view often advocate more mathematics,

4. Neil Postman, *The End of Education* (New York: Alfred A. Knopf, 1995).
5. Norman Lear, "Education for the Human Spirit" (speech before the National Education Association Convention in Kansas City, Mo., July 7, 1990).

science, and foreign language courses to enable Americans to be more "competitive." Still others feel that America's public schools — whether they be Northern or Southern; rural or urban; rich or poor; academic, general track, or vocational — are all too much alike.[6] According to this perspective, curriculum decisions should be decentralized to the local school level and custom-designed to meet the specific educational needs of the local community.

Although some feel that our schools are seriously underfinanced, this view is not a very popular one, since few Americans favor increased taxes as a way of improving our schools. However, there is widespread agreement that our federal, state, and local bureaucracies do not do a very efficient job of allocating our scarce educational resources. Lack of accountability is perceived as a serious problem among grassroots critics of the education establishment.

The Role of the Arts in Schools

The arts humanize the curriculum while affirming the interconnectedness of all forms of knowing. They are a powerful means to improve general education.

With a subject matter as broad as life itself, the arts easily relate to aspects of almost everything else that is taught.

Schools that do not teach the arts are, quite literally, creating a generation that is less civilized than it could be, more barbaric than it should be.

The arts provide a more comprehensive and insightful education because they invite students to explore the emotional, intuitive, and irrational aspects of life that science is hard pressed to explain.[7]

The Problems

We believe that underlying all of the symptoms of our failing public education system are three fundamental problems: (1) excessive centralization, (2) overregulation, and (3) absence of community.

6. Gerstner, p. 186.
7. Charles Fowler, "Strong Arts, Strong Schools," *Educational Leadership*, November 1994, pp. 4-9.

Excessive Centralization

Education research studies as far back as the 1960s began raising serious doubts about the efficacy of large consolidated public schools.[8] Yet throughout this century public school policymakers have argued that smaller schools were less efficient, provided students with fewer academic options, and should be closed, and students should be be bused — often far away from their homes — to larger, modern consolidated schools boasting their own cafeteria, auditorium, library, gymnasium, modern science equipment, computers, and student counseling service. One- and two-room schools were considered anathemas — candidates for extinction. Many a neighborhood, village, or small town was left isolated and disempowered when its school was closed — always in the name of "progress."

Big School, Small School

If there are a lot of people in any one setting — a meeting, for example, or a classroom — then each person has less influence on it, less chance to participate in it, less sense of responsibility for what goes on within it. If there are only a few, the chances are that each person involved will participate more, influence the events more, and have more intense reactions to what goes on.[9]

An assembly-line mentality pervaded education. Because of so-called economies of scale, large schools were said to be a more cost-effective way of training the future employees of corporate America. Those being prepared to work on Henry Ford's assembly lines needed to be obedient, uniform, consistent, and punctual. They needed to move by the bell. If you were going to spend most of your life working in a big factory, it made sense to be educated in a similar environment. Interestingly enough, our philosophy of mass public education differs little from that of our former archenemy, the Soviet Union.

8. Roger B. Barker and P. V. Gump, *Big School, Small School* (Stanford, Calif.: Stanford University Press, 1964).

9. Kirkpatrick Sale, *Human Scale* (New York: Coward, McCann & Geoghegan, 1980), p. 278.

Swiss One-Room Schools

The Swiss mountain village of Binn put an ad into lowland papers, calling for families with children to come and settle at 1,500 meters (4,950 feet). With small, school-age children, please, because Binn would have to close its one-room school next year: there would be only six kids left, and the canton of Wallis demands a legal minimum of seven children to keep supporting a village school and a teacher.

Binn, with 250 inhabitants forty-five years ago has only 162 left — most of them older people. The next larger village is Ernen, six miles down the road, and sometimes blocked off by snow in winter.

Those who left the village to find an easier life further down the valley don't help those who want to stay and keep the village alive.

Teacher Carmen Imhof grew up in Binn, and she'd like to stay. But unless families with children come to Binn, she will be out of a job at this time next year.

Swiss American Review
January 31, 1996

More recently the bigger-is-better philosophy has come under siege as an increasing number of educators now question the wisdom and cost-effectiveness of large consolidated schools — particularly big urban high schools. In an economy where creativity and individual initiative may be more valuable than uniformity and punctuality, our present megaschools seem oddly out of sync. Some Chicago, New York, and Philadelphia high schools with over five thousand students have actually been broken up into schools of five hundred students. As Susan Chira has pointed out in the *New York Times:*

> A generation ago, educators endorsed large high schools because they could offer a wide range of subjects and extracurricular activities at a relatively low administrative cost. But now many educators see big urban high schools — those with 2,000 to 5,000 students — as Dickensian workhouses breeding violence, dropouts, academic failure and alienation.
>
> By contrast, students in schools limited to about 400 usually have fewer behavioral problems, better attendance and graduation rates, and sometimes higher grades and test scores. At a time when

more children have less support from their families, students in small schools can form close relationships with teachers. Educators argue that small schools allow students, teachers and parents to know each other well, building bonds that are particularly vital during the troubled years of adolescence.[10]

Overregulation

Not only are our public schools too big and overcentralized, but they are literally drowning in a sea of federal, state, and local school district regulations. According to Kirkpatrick Sale, the fifteen thousand local school boards in our country, "though still empowered to *raise* money at the local level, are practically powerless to *spend* it as they see fit: from 90 to 99 percent of all expenditures now are mandated by state and Federal requirements and by contracts with government-sanctioned unions."[11] Federal directives play a major role in settling such local school issues as racial balance, pupil selection, curriculum content, textbook selection, teacher qualification, school architecture, and the treatment of special-needs students.

In the state of Vermont, for example,

the state controls teacher certification for all public-school teachers. The state maintains a list from which local school boards can choose superintendents, and woe unto the school board that desires some hard-headed practical citizen instead of a person who has all the right qualifications (and hasn't gotten crossways with the Department of Education in his previous job). The state controls teacher training. The state prescribes courses of study and number of days in school. The state establishes the school-leaving age. The state decrees the boundaries of superintendency districts and can change them without local approval. The state can, and does, forbid towns from seceding from union districts. The state demands local compliance with its Public School Approval Standards, or else an erring local district will apparently be consigned to some sort of educational receivership.[12]

10. Susan Chira, "Is Small Better? Educators Now Say Yes for High Schools," *New York Times*, July 14, 1993, p. 1.

11. Sale, p. 127.

12. Frank Bryan and John McClaughry, *The Vermont Papers* (Post Mills, Vt.: Chelsea Green, 1989), p. 185.

Professors in university schools of education write the regulations for teacher certification, ensuring that prospective teachers must take their courses in order to be certified, ensuring the professors' jobs for the future, ensuring that most prospective teachers will be forced to attend colleges and universities with schools of education — despite an increasing body of research that indicates that schools of education and their poorly educated majors are the source of our schools' problems, not their solution. The best training for a lifetime of teaching is a good liberal arts education, not indoctrination into the bogus science of "education."

One form of government control facing declining public support and possible extinction is the U.S. Department of Education. Created by President Jimmy Carter in 1980, the Department of Education is perceived by many Republicans — perhaps not unfairly — as a payoff to the National Education Association for its support of the Democratic Party. Public education mandates from the U.S. Department of Education are being met with increasing hostility at the grassroots level by parents, teachers, and school administrators alike.

Government Control of Education

Where the control of education is taken out of the hands of the family and the community, and schooling gets further and further away from the people who have a direct stake in it, the quality suffers. It is that which accounts in largest part, for the deplorable state of American education today. Yes, the government now controls education . . . but is it worth controlling?[13]

No form of government regulation has been less effective than court-ordered desegregation and busing. According to a 1993 Harvard University study on "School Desegregation" led by Professor Gary Orfield, four decades after *Brown v. Board of Education* our nation's schools are now more segregated than they have been in nearly twenty-five years. Whether caused by white backlash or white flight to the suburbs and segregation academies, many of our public schools — particularly our urban schools — are as segregated as ever.

13. Sale, p. 127.

Public Education

The fundamentalists are right: What Christians get in public schools is destructive of the Christian faith. It is not destructive of the Christian faith, however, because science in and of itself undermines the presuppositions of creation, though often the way science is taught as a mechanistic system does challenge some of the basic presuppositions of the Christian faith. Rather, the deep problem of Christians in public education is that it's not "public education." It is nationalistic education. Horace Greeley, the foundational theorist for public education, was quite clear that the purpose of compulsory, state administered education was to integrate the swarming masses of immigrants into America.

Recently, in a radio interview, a Native American activist was asked, "What would you like this country to do for you and your people?"

"Well," he answered in a quiet, unemotional voice, "one small thing the government could do for us is to return Mount Rushmore to the state in which they found it."

"What?" asked the astounded interviewer.

"It would be a start, a small thing, but a start. You can imagine how humiliating it is for us to have had one of our sacred mountains defaced with the images of some of the bloodiest leaders in history — Roosevelt, Washington, Jefferson, and a man like Lincoln. It's bad for our children to look up and see those images carved into stone. Some of them might take them as examples they ought to follow. What if some of our children grew up to be like Jefferson?"

We daresay that here was someone who had escaped the indoctrination of the public schools. Here was someone working out of a very different story about the way the world is.

Stanley Hauerwas and William H. Willimon
Where Resident Aliens Live

We both grew up in the South under state-enforced segregation — truly an evil system. We have until recently supported and worked for government-mandated school integration plans. But have we traded one evil system for another?

As the great black novelist and folklorist Zora Neale Hurston once noted, *Brown v. Board of Education* was not only an insult to black schoolteachers, but it led to the demise of black community schools with their own unique Afro-American curricula.[14]

Furthermore, in exalting race as the major criterion for educating children, other factors like economic opportunity are neglected. Increasing numbers of African American leaders are saying that racial equality without economic empowerment masks the ways in which African Americans are continually oppressed by this culture. Today, an army of government bureaucrats and teachers' union officials, having made careers on the basis of the politics of race, are a major hindrance to recognition of the host of factors which keeps ethnic minority children uneducated and locked into the cycle of poverty and despair.

Court-ordered integration and busing are classic examples of top-down attempts to impose community on unwilling subjects. A sense of community cannot be forced on anyone from above — perhaps the single most important lesson to be gleaned from the nearly seventy-five-year history of the Soviet Union.

The Resurrection of Separate but Equal

Back in 1954, the segregationist doctrine of separate but equal appeared to have been slain by a nine-headed St. George known as the United States Supreme Court. In its landmark ruling in *Brown v. Board of Education,* the justices overturned what had been for 60 years the legal underpinning of America's system of racial separation.

Four decades later, though, a mixture of white resistance to integration, population shifts, an increasingly conservative judiciary and black impatience and political empowerment seem to be converting separate but equal from a dead dragon into a rising Phoenix.

The once discredited doctrine is making a comeback, embraced in varying degrees by such divergent figures as Louis Farrakhan, the head of the Denver school board and Supreme Court Justice Clarence Thomas.[15]

14. We are indebted to Bill Kauffman for this observation.

15. Steven A. Holmes, "Look Who's Saying Separate Is Equal," *New York Times,* October 1, 1995, sec. 4, p. 1.

Absence of Community

That there is little sense of community in many of our overcentralized, oversized, overregulated public schools should come as a surprise to no one. Excessive centralization, bigness, overregulation, and forced integration and busing are all antithetical to a feeling of connectedness among parents, teachers, and administrators in local schools. How is it possible for the parents of inner-city African American kids bused to predominantly white, upper-middle-class suburban schools to avoid feelings of separation, alienation, and powerlessness over their children's education? The key to the education of African American children is not to place them in physical proximity to Caucasian children. It is rather to empower African American parents to ensure the same quality of educational opportunity enjoyed by those parents who have, through economic power, seceded to the suburbs.

A strong sense of community between parents and teachers is the glue which binds effective schools everywhere. Without this spir-

---

The Local Community

The child is not educated to return home and be of use to the place and community; he or she is educated to leave home and earn money in a provisional future that has nothing to do with place or community. The local schools no longer serve the local community; they serve the government's economy and the economy's government. Unlike the local community, the government and the economy cannot be served with affection, but only with professional zeal or professional boredom. Professionalism means more interest in salary and less interest in what used to be known as disciplines. . . . There must also be love of learning and of the cultural tradition and of excellence. And this love cannot exist, because it makes no sense, apart from the love of a place and community. Without this love, education is only the importation into a local community of centrally prescribed "career preparation" designed to facilitate the export of young careerists.[16]

---

16. Wendell Berry, *The Work of Local Culture* (Great Barrington, Mass.: E. F. Schumacher Society, 1988), pp. 11-12.

itual glue a public school becomes a dehumanized, mechanistic instrument of the state. Is it any wonder that so many of our public schools are failing?

Pseudosolutions

To resuscitate our moribund public schools, business, political, and education leaders have proposed a number of knee-jerk solutions to these problems, some of which include national performance standards, student portfolios, high technology, longer school days, and year-round schooling — big solutions to make our school problems even bigger.

Not surprisingly, IBM CEO Gerstner is a strong advocate of national performance standards and testing as a means of sorting out America's public schools:

> The business adage "what gets measured gets done" must be accepted by schools. Clear goals must be measured with unequivocal yardsticks. In particular, we must evaluate our schools with the same productivity focus that is used to measure efficiency in other areas. How much do students learn each month or year that they attend school? How great are these learning gains per dollar spent? How satisfied are the customers of education — parents and students — with the services they receive? We need national tests that allow us to determine whether students have achieved targeted goals. Beyond this measurement of school performance against absolute standards, school performance must be measured relative to other similarly situated schools. Firms constantly compare, or "benchmark," themselves against their competitors, both at home and abroad, as well as against noncompeting firms: Xerox, for example, compares itself to L. L. Bean for inventory control and to Florida Light and Power for customer-service response time. Schools should do no less. Wealthy suburban districts, for example, should not take satisfaction in comparing themselves to impoverished inner-city schools. Rather they should compare themselves to the best suburban districts, the best magnet schools, the best private schools, and then they should compare themselves to the competition: Berlin, Taipei, Seoul, Tokyo, Paris.[17]

17. Gerstner, pp. 69-70.

It is not by chance that IBM is referred to as "Big Blue." For decades the company imposed a strict code of conduct on its executives, including a rigid dress code consisting of a dark blue business suit, a white standard-collar dress shirt, and a conservative tie. Exceptions to the dress code were not tolerated. There was a certain consistency, a sameness about IBM employees, IBM offices, IBM factories, and IBM equipment. They were all blue!

Apparently Mr. Gerstner would like for all American children to be alike. But an eccentric Vermont farmer living in a small rural village probably couldn't care less whether he knows as much mathematics as a Japanese or German factory worker. By what logic does one arrive at the dogmatic conclusion that life is all about competing with foreigners? How much calculus, physics, and chemistry does a budding young artist or composer need to know?

As an alternative to standardized performance testing many educators now advocate the use of a systematic collection of a student's work selected largely by that student to provide information about the student's attitudes and motivation, level of development, and growth over time. Such a collection is called a *portfolio* and typically includes samples of a student's writing, math, art, science, social studies, and music. Although the pros and cons of the use of portfolios as student evaluation tools are still being debated by educators, on balance they appear to offer considerable merit.

In April 1995, Mr. Gerstner announced a $2 million grant to the Vermont Department of Education to "digitize" the portfolios of Vermont schoolchildren:

> Imagine students with a CD ROM disk with a complete student record; not just letter grades, but examples of work — essays, themes, research papers. Or examples of extracurricular activity: marching band or football in living color and sound. Or examples of editorials or articles in the student newspaper, video footage of lab work, or video footage of community service. The sky's the limit.[18]

Although there are only one hundred thousand public school children in Vermont whose portfolios might be digitized by IBM, the possibility of digitizing 45 million American schoolkids must resonate in

18. Gerstner, p. 104.

the hearts of all IBM stockholders. But why would anyone want to do this to our children and their schools? Who besides IBM and several other computer hardware and software vendors will benefit from digitizing our kids' portfolios? Comparing portfolios of math, science, art, and music is a little like comparing apples, oranges, peaches, and grapefruit. There are no known mathematical or social science formulas available for reducing student portfolio information down to a common denominator suitable for objective comparisons. This is a blatant form of computerization for the sake of computerization. Furthermore, digitizing student portfolios provides endless opportunities for the invasion of privacy and the commercialization of confidential information about our children. It represents high-tech paternalism carried to ridiculous extremes.

Low-Tech Schools

In no other part of the economy is the absence of technology so startling and so complete. Even our oldest, most enduring and traditional institutions — churches, mosques, and synagogues — use technology more inventively and more effectively than schools. In the economy as a whole, including private-sector "teaching and learning services," technology reigns supreme. Put most vividly and simply, the schools of the present are like a nineteenth-century farm: labor-intensive and low-tech. Like farms before tractors and fertilizer before milking machines and hybrid-seed corn, the school comprises a low-capital, low-productivity system. Despite the invention of a staggering array of new information tools that store and communicate knowledge, and that entertain, challenge, and extend the power of their users, schools transmit information as they have since Gutenberg.[19]

To gain support for Big Blue's national strategy to standardize America's schools and digitize our kids, Mr. Gerstner convened a National Education Summit in March 1996 at IBM's Executive Conference Center in Palisades, New York. Cosponsored by the National Governors' Association, the conference attracted President Bill Clinton,

19. Gerstner, p. 12.

forty-one state governors, forty-eight CEOs of some of America's largest corporations, and a number of education "experts."

As evidence of the success of the 1996 Education Summit in achieving IBM's self-serving objectives, the National Governors' Association issued the following policy statement to all conference participants:

> Technology can be a powerful ally in the quest to reform schools. Ambitious academic standards for students call for new ways of teaching and new ways of organizing schools to support higher performance. Higher standards mean that all students need to master basic skills as well as become adept at thinking analytically, solving problems, and communicating clearly. In addition, educators and business leaders agree that students must be able to use a variety of technologies if they are to succeed in the workforce of the twenty-first century.
>
> Computers, telecommunication, and interactive cable are among the many technologies that have immense potential to help schools reach higher standards. Yet, the sad truth is that schools are technologically impoverished. They have not even caught up with the computer revolution of the last decade, let alone become part of the telecommunications revolution of the 1990s.
>
> Equally disturbing is the fact that when technology is present in schools, it is all too often used with styles of teaching that fail to maximize its full potential. This is not surprising. Few teachers or administrators receive adequate preparation during their preservice or inservice training about how to integrate technology into classrooms and schools.
>
> To realize the potential of technology to support high performance, it is of paramount importance that policymakers and educators rethink teaching and learning together with technology purchases. Governors, working with educators, parents, business leaders, and communities can play a valuable role in this process by helping to ensure that all schools have access to technology and use it to support high quality instruction.

Just as Herbert Hoover once promised Americans "a chicken in every pot," to prepare our children for life in the high-tech fast lane, President Bill Clinton and Vice President Al Gore have proposed a computer in every classroom so that every child can be connected to the Internet.

The High-Tech God

Driven by our obsession to compete, we have embraced the electronic god with a frenzy. Soon, blessed with fax, voice- and E-mail, computer hookups and TV's with hundreds of channels, we won't have to leave our lonely rooms — not even to write a check, work, visit, shop, exercise or make love. We will have raced at incredible speeds to reach our final destination — nothing.[20]

But is all of this computer power really necessary? Neil Postman thinks not: "the problem of giving people greater access to more information, faster, more conveniently, and in more diverse forms was largely solved one hundred years ago."[21] Our problem today is not too little information, but information overload. We are bombarded with so much information at such high rates of speed from so many computers, radios, television sets, telephones, fax machines, newspapers, periodicals, books, billboards, and pieces of advertising junk mail that we haven't a clue as to what to do with it all. What we need from our

What Do Computers Teach?

What exactly is being taught using computers? On the surface, pupils learn to read, type and use programs. I'll bet that they're really learning something else. How to stare at a monitor for hours on end. To accept what a machine says without arguing. That the world is a passive, preprogrammed place, where you need only click the mouse to get the right answer. That relationships — developed over E-mail — are transitory and shallow. That discipline isn't necessary when you can zap frustrations with a keystroke. That legible handwriting, grammar, analytical thought and human dealings don't matter.[22]

20. Bill Henderson, "No E-Mail from Walden," *New York Times*, March 16, 1994, p. A21.
21. Postman, p. 42.
22. Clifford Stoll, "Invest in Humanware," *New York Times*, May 19, 1996, p. E15.

The Nine Assumptions of Modern Schooling

1. Government school is the essential force for social cohesion. It cannot happen any other way. A bureaucratized public order is our defense against chaos and anarchy.
2. The socialization of children in groups monitored by state agents is essential; without this, children cannot learn to get along with others in a pluralistic society.
3. Children from different backgrounds and from families with different beliefs must be mixed together. Robert Frost was wrong when he maintained "good fences make good neighbors."
4. The certifiable expertise of official schoolteachers is superior to that of lay people including parents. The protection of children from the uncertified is a compelling public concern.
5. Coercion in the name of liberty is a valid use of state power. Compelling children to assemble in mandated groups for mandated intervals with mandated texts and overseers does not interfere with academic learning.
6. Children will inevitably grow apart from their parents in beliefs as they grow older and this process must be supported and encouraged. The best way to do this is by diluting parental influence and discouraging the children's attitudes that their own parents are sovereign in either mind or morality.
7. The world is full of crazy parents who will ruin their children. An overriding concern of schooling is to protect children from bad parenting.
8. It is not appropriate for any family to unduly concern itself with the education of its own children, but it may expend unlimited effort on behalf of the general education of everyone.
9. The State has the predominant responsibility for training, morals, and beliefs. Children schooled outside government scrutiny frequently become anti-social and poverty stricken.[23]

23. John Taylor Gatto, *Notes on Education, Schooling, and Curriculum,* reprinted in the *Education Liberator,* November 1995, p. 4.

schools and our universities is not more or faster computers, but more effective tools to help us make sense of all of this information. What we're dying of, as a society, is not lack of information but rather a paucity of virtues like vision, creativity, and courage — *none* of which is fostered by technology.

Digitizing student portfolios and connecting every classroom to the Internet are public relations gimmicks aimed at conning the American people into believing that there are simplistic short-term solutions to enormously complex problems. The problems of low-tech public schools require bottom-up, low-tech solutions, not top-down, high-tech fads imposed by Washington, the statehouse, and corporate America. Big Brother, Big Blue, and big education want all of us to be the same — just like them. There are no high-tech, quick fixes to America's public education problems, which are deeply rooted in excessive centralization, overregulation, insufficient competition, and the absence of local community involvement.

Some Real Solutions

Neither increased computer power nor fine tuning or patching will turn our badly failing educational system around. Anything short of radical restructuring of the entire system will be insufficient to halt the public education free fall. What is required is nothing less than the dismantling of the federal and state educational bureaucracies and the complete transfer of power back to locally controlled neighborhood and village school boards.

While it's one thing for conservative politicians to rail against the federal government and denounce federal control of education, it's quite another for local communities to step forward and assume complete responsibility for their own schools. We can't have it both ways. We either bite the bullet and take charge of our schools, or we abdicate the responsibility to Big Brother or Big Blue. Local control of schools comes with a price, but a price we cannot afford not to pay.

Downsizing

For starters, we would abolish the U.S. Department of Education and close every office in Washington concerned with federal aid to education (i.e., federal *control* of education) for both public schools and higher education alike. The federal government should simply get out of education, and stay out.

State departments of education should be completely restructured as independent, nonprofit educational service bureaus providing a whole range of services to local schools on a fee basis. These bureaus must be free from the stranglehold of that state's university schools of education. Services might include architectural consulting, curriculum development, educational standards and testing, accounting and financial services, personnel recruiting, computer services, textbooks, educational supplies, teacher training, management development, and strategic planning. They may be purchased by local schools from state service bureaus or from other vendors who may offer similar services. The state will no longer have monopolistic control over the local school districts. Individual schools will be free to purchase support services from any vendor they choose.

Nietzsche on Public Education

In large states public education will always be mediocre, for the same reason that in large kitchens the cooking is usually bad.

Any individual school should have the right to secede from its city, town, county, or regional school district. The local community, whether it be a town, village, or neighborhood, should have absolute control of the school and total responsibility for its financial support. The buck no longer stops at the state department of education or the U.S. Department of Education, but rather at the local school board.

City, county, and district departments of education should either be shut down or become education service bureaus selling their services to local schools. A local school should not be required to purchase services from its city, county, or district service bureaus. Local schools should be operated as either public or private schools and financed by either local taxes, tuition and fees, or vouchers issued to the poor, or some combination thereof.

We recommend that no school have more than three hundred children, whether it be an elementary school (kindergarten through fifth grade), middle school (sixth through eighth grade), or high school (ninth through twelfth grade). However, decisions about the size of a school lie entirely with the local school board.

The Town's School

Each town is its own story, blessed with a uniqueness wrought by decades of natural and human action. When you kill a school, something in that town dies, and it can never be resurrected.[24]

One way to downsize large schools — particularly high schools and middle schools — or to prevent them from getting any larger is to decentralize some of the educational services they provide. Indeed, one of the real benefits — in contrast to some of the fantasized benefits — of modern technology is that it may greatly facilitate such decentralization.

It should not be necessary for a high school student to spend eight hours a day, five days a week in a particular building. Even if one attends a consolidated high school, some classes might take place in the child's neighborhood or village school building. In some cases these off-site classes might make use of television. In other cases they may be taught by a local expert living nearby.

Obviously E-mail and the Internet make on-line telecommunications between the student and his or her teachers a viable alternative to straight classroom lectures.

Advanced high school students may also take courses in local colleges and universities. Music students and artists may take private lessons for which they receive high school credit. Work-study programs are another possibility.

There is no reason why a high school or middle school student need be bused ten miles each way every day to a huge, impersonal, drug-infested degree factory where little attention is devoted to his or her individual needs.

Recently, helping a friend deposit his son at their local high school, it occurred to one of us: *This is the dumbest thing I've ever seen.*

---

24. Bill Kauffman, "The Miseducation of America, Part II," *Family in America,* April 1996, p. 6.

Nothing we know of human development, of educational methodology, of the nature of sixteen-year-olds and their needs, would lead us to believe in the educational wisdom of depositing a thousand of them in one place, for seven hours, with minimal adult interaction. Some years ago, Ivan Illich declared that if we did not already have schools and classrooms, no one would invent them.

By combining our imaginations with our sophisticated technology, we may be able significantly to decentralize the delivery of education services. This will make it much easier to downsize our public schools.[25]

Deregulation

Our public schools not only must be downsized significantly, but they must be deregulated as well. For starters, we would repeal all federal statutes aimed at regulating and controlling public schools. This would include all legislation dealing with racial integration, racial quotas, forced busing, school prayer, curriculum content, special-needs students, building construction, transportation, textbooks, and the like. We would also rescind all state government rules and regulations affecting our public schools. All coercive city, county, and regional school districts should be abolished. Only voluntary associations of schools should survive.

Rules and regulations affecting individual schools should originate only with the local school board. Neither the federal government nor state governments should be in the business of telling local schools what to do or how to behave.

Ultimately what we are talking about is replacing all large, government-controlled schools with much smaller, locally controlled schools accountable only to the local school board. Whether the school has only one room or twenty rooms is a decision for the local school board.

Competition

One of the reasons change has been so slow in coming to public education in America is because throughout this century the state has

25. If you would like to know more about the movement to downsize schools, contact: The Smaller Schools Project, P.O. Box 12888, Research Triangle Park, NC 27709.

maintained monopolistic control over our schools. Of the 50 million or so kids in grades K through twelve in America, only 11 percent attend private schools.

We think there should be a wide variety of different types of schools, including public, private, and parochial, as well as home schooling. State and local governments should be in the business of subsidizing students, not educational bureaucracies. We favor an educational voucher system where the child may use the voucher to purchase educational services at the school chosen by his or her parents. Above all we support increased competition for the public schools so as to encourage innovation at all levels of education.

Community of Learners

If our schools are fixable, they will be fixed at the local grassroots level by creating a community of learners in the town, the neighborhood, or the village. The school is the focal point of the learning community which empowers the community, parents, school administrators, teachers, and students. What is best for the students will be decided by the school board in collaboration with parents, teachers, and community leaders. Heavy parental involvement in the school is not only encouraged but is an absolute requirement for a successful, locally controlled learning community.

Empowering the Local School

- Empowering the community by empowering the school
- Empowering the school by empowering the principal
- Empowering the principal by empowering the teachers
- Empowering the teachers by empowering the students
- Empowering the students by empowering the parents
- Empowering the parents by empowering the community

Thomas H. Naylor

One such school that has very high academic standards and a truly remarkable track record of parental and community involvement is the Charlotte Central School located in the Champlain Valley of

> ## Characteristics That Foster Self-Initiated Learning
>
> - An environment rich in resources, where students can become highly focused and develop long-term attending skills.
> - An environment that allows children the freedom to explore their own interests and ideas, an environment that promotes a continuous exchange of ideas.
> - Teachers who are trained to act as coach, guide, model, thinker, prodder, therapist, moderator, raiser of questions, issues, and alternative perspectives.
> - A school that functions as a community of inquiry, a limited democracy where children practice good social skills, good human skills, on a minute-by-minute basis.
> - Teachers who are willing to accept the possibility that children can have ideas intellectually beyond their own.[26]

Vermont. With five hundred students in kindergarten through the eighth grade, Charlotte Central is a model of parent-teacher-student empowerment. The school makes extensive use of multigrade classes, team teaching, parent aids, and parent-teacher teams. For example, there is a Keystone team led by four teachers who teach two first/second–grade classes and two third-grade classes. By the time a Keystone child enters the fourth grade, he or she has experienced the positive benefits of being in a warm and friendly student-teacher-parent community. Community activities include joint social studies projects, field trips, holiday meals, sporting events, and fine arts performances. The Vermont family farm, the meadow, the local community, Lake Champlain, traditions, and endangered species have been among the joint projects studied by Keystone kids over the past two years. Some Keystone parents and students think the Keystone teachers walk on water.

Charlotte Central School works because it is small and its hard-working teachers and administors enjoy strong parental and community support. Unfortunately, it too suffers from the usual morass of rules and regulations imposed by Washington, Montpelier, and the five-

26. Raymond H. Hartjen, *Empowering the Child: Nurturing the Hungry Mind* (Port Tobacco, Md., 1994), p. 25.

school regional district of which it is a member. The school has managed to carve out a unique niche for itself even though the local school board possesses only limited power as a result of the regulatory environment.

For those interested in creating a learning community in their own local school, we recommend the excellent book by Raymond H. Hartjen entitled *Empowering the Child: Nurturing the Hungry Mind* (Port Tobacco, Md., 1994).

Implementation

The implementation of downsizing, deregulation, and learning communities may require a very tough sell. The biggest obstacles to the implementation of these strategies for restructuring public education include the public school establishment, the U.S. Supreme Court, the U.S. Congress, many state legislators, and schools of education.

But if we want to save our public schools from self-destruction, we must act now, and we must act decisively! It's later than we think, and the risk of having our kids digitized by IBM or someone else is far greater than most realize. For ethnic minorities, the stakes are particularly high since education is a primary path to empowerment. Even though the public schools have failed our ethnic minorities, they continue to act as if they have a monopoly on concern for America's racial educational problems. We celebrate those inner-city churches and community organizations, those advocates of educational vouchers, whose primary concern is to rescue ethnic minority children from a failing public school system, a system which has demonstrated in numerous cities that the key to making schools work for ethnic minority children is not having ethnic minority bureaucrats managing essentially unmanageable school systems, but rather in having smaller classrooms, smaller schools, and smaller school systems. For the sake of our children it is high time that we regain control of our schools at the local community level.

Public School Deregulation and Downsizing Strategies

1. Repeal all federal statutes regulating public education.
2. Abolish the U.S. Department of Education.
3. Eliminate the regulatory authority of state, county, city, and regional departments of education and transform them into nonprofit service bureaus which provide a broad range of services to local schools on a fee basis.
4. Replace state and local grants to schools with an educational voucher system which may be used by parents to purchase educational services for their children.
5. Begin downsizing schools with more than three hundred children.
6. Construct no new schools with a capacity greater than three hundred children.
7. Decentralize the delivery of educational services for schools for which there are significant political or financial obstacles to downsizing.
8. Encourage the development of a wide variety of different types of public and private institutions to deliver educational services.
9. Create a community of learners at the local school level that includes parents, students, teachers, administrators, and community members.

6 The Crisis in Higher Education: Metaphor for America

Academic Behemoths

Our colleges and universities ought to provide cutting-edge solutions — or at least some solutions — to our nation's many social, economic, political, and environmental problems, many of which are grounded in bigness. But as we pointed out in our book *The Abandoned Generation: Rethinking Higher Education*,[1] few solutions have been forthcoming from our institutions of higher education, which have themselves become mirror images of our country's problems — *a metaphor for America*.

Too many of today's college students are into consumerism, hedonism, anti-intellectualism, and unabashed individualism which give rise to alcohol abuse, indolence, and excessive careerism.

If one listens to college students talk in the dining hall, the library, or the student union, the expression heard most often from them on many campuses is, "I can't believe how drunk I was last night." College students spend over $5.5 billion annually on alcoholic beverages and consume over 4 billion cans of beer — the equivalent of thirty-four gallons of beer per student. A Harvard School of Public Health study released in 1995 found that 44 percent of the students surveyed at 140 colleges nationwide went on a heavy drinking binge at least once

---

1. This chapter draws heavily on our book *The Abandoned Generation: Rethinking Higher Education* (Grand Rapids: Eerdmans, 1995). A condensed version of this chapter appeared in a paper by the authors entitled "The Essential Mission: Teaching Undergraduates," *Academic Questions*, fall 1996.

during the two-week survey period. Nineteen percent of the respondents indicated they had binged three or more times during the two weeks.

Nothing better characterizes the self-image of college students than one of their favorite self-designations — "We work hard, we play hard." But how is it possible to work hard and maintain the kind of lifestyle which pervades college campuses today? How often do stu-

> You can lead me to college, but you can't make me think.
>
> University T-shirt slogan

dents think hard in an environment in which they receive higher grades for doing less work in fewer courses than was the case a few years ago? With no Saturday classes, few early morning classes, and the widespread use of work-saving personal computers, students have more free time on their hands than they can effectively use.

Students at Duke's School of Business were asked by Thomas to write a personal strategic plan for the ten-year period after graduation. "What do you want to be when you grow up?" With few exceptions, they wanted three things — money, power, and things (very big things, including automobiles, yachts, and even airplanes). Primarily concerned with their careers and the growth of their financial portfolios, their personal plans contained little room for family, intellectual development, spiritual growth, or social responsibility.

Their mandate to the faculty was, "Teach me how to be a money-making machine. Give me only the facts, tools, and techniques required to ensure my instantaneous financial success."

Most colleges — in response to market pressures — are so preoccupied with careerism that they do little to facilitate students' search for meaning. The absence of meaning leads to drunken, fraternity-house bashes, date rape, vandalism, and acts of violence. Students have no incentive to delay gratification, because they place so little faith in a future that has no meaning for them. Instead, they pursue the elusive dream that it is possible "to have it all and to have it now" — a dream that turns out to be a lie, a materialistic cover for lacking meaning.

While subscribing to an ideology that raises individualism to almost godlike status, most college students behave as world-class conformists. Some have tried — often in vain — to find meaning through the approval of parents, personal computers, excessive television viewing, rock music, spectator sports, physical fitness, and sexual promiscuity. Ironically, lacking any sense of direction, any inner conviction about what their lives ought to mean, they become the compliant victims of external pressures imposed by their parents, their passions, and corporate America.

During the "roaring eighties" American colleges and universities said no to almost no one. They tried unsuccessfully to be all things to all people. In so doing they now find themselves in too many unrelated, disconnected businesses. They have become unmanageable academic behemoths.

Overspecialization and functional isolation are two reasons why college costs consistently outpace inflation. Each department or professional school is an island unto itself, cooperating with no one. Promotions and faculty salaries are closely linked to publications within one's narrowly defined discipline. Departments compete for students and resources. Research and writing are rewarded; teaching is not.

At the University of Pennsylvania in 1995 there were twenty-nine more students registered than there were in 1980. There were also 1,820 more administrators and their staffs.

According to the U.S. Office of Education, one-third of all professors at research universities teach less than four hours per week. Over 40 percent of the professors at private research universities teach just one course per semester. Some highly paid professors teach no courses at all — the ultimate status symbol on some campuses.

Another factor contributing to the high cost of a college education is a tenure system which provides lifetime employment to a professor regardless of his or her level of incompetence. It's nice work, if you can get it!

In some universities the business school, divinity school, law school, engineering school, and medical school each has its own separate library. The Fuqua School of Business at Duke University has its own dining hall, computer center, audiovisual center, placement service, alumni office, and luxury hotel for executive education programs.

The cost of high-tech research equipment soared in the 1970s and 1980s — particularly in engineering, physical science, and medicine. The cost of research in such fields as particle physics and molecular biology is prohibitively expensive. But is all of this high technology and computer power really necessary to provide undergraduates with a well-rounded liberal arts education? Must every undergraduate have his or her own personal computer for typing papers, playing computer games, and surfing the Internet? We think not.

Undergraduate education and state-of-the-art research are two quite different businesses. Does it make sense to try to combine them under one umbrella called a university? Middlebury College is an excellent undergraduate educational institution. MIT, Cal Tech, and the Stanford Research Institute are world-class research institutes. Should not Amherst, Middlebury, Mount Holyoke, Vassar, and Williams specialize in undergraduate teaching, and MIT, Cal Tech, and Carnegie-Mellon in basic and applied research? The necessary skills for successful research grantsmanship are not the same skills required to be a good undergraduate teacher. Why do so many academics pretend otherwise?

In all too many state universities and some private universities such as Duke, Notre Dame, and Southern California, intercollegiate athletics — particularly football and basketball — have achieved singular economic importance for the university. Big-time college football and basketball are high-profile businesses characterized by illegal recruiting, elaborate player perquisites, minimal academic standards, notoriously low graduation ratios, and a generally anti-intellectual ambience. Even at private universities that presume to have higher academic standards for football and basketball players, athletes pursue an academic program of carefully monitored courses supported by an elaborate network of tutors and teaching assistants.

So important is college football at the University of Florida and Florida State University that their head coaches each earn nearly $1 million annually in salary and other benefits.

College football and basketball are to the National Football League (NFL) and National Basketball Association (NBA) what the minor leagues are to professional baseball — training grounds for future major-league athletes. The beauty of this corrupted system is that the member universities of the National Collegiate Athletic Association (NCAA) finance literally all of the preprofessional training for the pros who play in the NFL and the NBA, although only a tiny fraction of college players will ever become professional athletes.

Intercollegiate football and basketball are the academic equivalent of the Roman games. College sports heroes are treated like pagan Roman gladiators. They are strong, self-assertive, and narcissistic. We conveniently overlook the dirty mixture of money, greed, and publicity that surrounds big-time college football and basketball. Millions of

American men and some women vicariously live out their fantasies of becoming college sports heroes by spending hours each week watching football and basketball on television. Even more importantly, wealthy alumni and influential state legislators are entertained and made to feel good about their alma mater. But at what cost to the intellectual integrity of the institution?

Big-Time College Football

Big-time college football programs like Florida State's turn huge profits, and turn players into violent machines. The psychic bruises are harder to heal.

The football players at Florida State, like those at other major colleges, are bred for 60 violent minutes on Saturday afternoon. At least the hits they take on the field will heal.[2]

Although many small liberal arts colleges and some major private universities like Chicago, Duke, and Stanford have wisely kept a lid on growth, the prevailing attitude among most state universities, caught in the competition for tax dollars since World War II, has been "growth for growth's sake" and "bigger makes better." The trend toward growth has decidedly slowed as we move through the nineties. Now we find ourselves burdened with huge institutions in serious need of downsizing.

We believe there are far too many universities in the United States. Some are so tiny that it is difficult to take their self-proclaimed university status seriously. Others are so large that they are fundamentally unmanageable. The state of North Carolina, for example — a relatively poor state with a population of 6.8 million — has no fewer than fifteen state universities plus another seven private universities. Racial politics in Mississippi — a state with only 2.6 million people — has resulted in eight public universities in a state that can hardly afford to support one. On the other hand, tiny Vermont sensibly has only one state university.

The proliferation of universities with the inherent duplication of programs, research facilities, libraries, athletic programs, and academic

---

2. Pat Jordan, "Belittled Big Men," *New York Times Magazine*, December 10, 1995, p. 68.

infrastructure has contributed significantly to the skyrocketing cost of higher education. America needs not more universities but more small undergraduate colleges. Plato believed that the ideal republic would have no more than 5,000 citizens, in order adequately to foster communication and argument. But we have acted as if size makes no difference when it comes to achieving the mission of higher education.

Countering the trend toward giantism in universities is well-managed Oklahoma City University with only 4,660 students, of which 2,400 are undergraduates. Although OCU's strong international programs have attracted students from seventy-one different countries, 75 percent of OCU's undergraduates — including many Native Americans — are from Oklahoma. OCU produces a high-quality product, at a moderate cost, without the social chaos found on many university campuses. The administrators of OCU seem to know what business they are in and have created an environment with a strong sense of community between faculty and students.

Just as there are too many small universities whose quest for university status has distracted them from the task of undergraduate education, there are also too many universities that have become dehumanized, multibusiness bureaucracies. Undergraduate, professional, graduate, and adult education; housing; food service; dental and health care services; book publishing; agricultural extension service; management consulting; public service; and semiprofessional athletics are among the plethora of unrelated businesses in which large universities find themselves.

With 52,183 students, 38,958 of whom are undergraduates, the Columbus campus of Ohio State University is the largest university in the United States. Arizona State, Michigan State, Ohio State, Penn State, Texas A & M, and the Universities of Michigan, Minnesota, Texas, and Wisconsin are more like small cities than academic communities.

Some members of the governing board of the sixty-four-campus State University of New York have compared the $5 billion higher education system to an East German steel mill in the eighties, "a centralized, overregulated system whose lackluster campuses have little incentive to improve."[3]

Most of these universities are the legacy of World War II and postwar growth rather than serious academic planning. Is quality un-

3. Emily M. Bernstein, "SUNY: Grand Vision and Pragmatism Collide," *New York Times*, May 4, 1996, p. 1.

Mega-Universities[4]	
	Enrollment
Arizona State University	43,635
Indiana University	36,076
Michigan State University	40,047
Ohio State University	52,183
Pennsylvania State University	38,446
Texas A & M	41,710
University of Michigan	36,626
University of Minnesota	38,019
University of Texas	49,253
University of Wisconsin	43,196

dergraduate education compatible with so diverse a portfolio of unrelated activities? We believe that it is time for us to take a critical look at the businesses of these mega-universities. Do mega-universities represent a cost-effective way to train future generations of Americans? Since 1980, tuition at our public colleges and universities has increased 138 percent compared to 77 percent in the prestigeous Ivy League. Has the time come to begin seriously thinking about downsizing these academic giants?

Throughout the 1960s many universities grew haphazardly without any well-defined sense of direction. It is as though some of them have attempted to replicate urban sprawl in an academic setting. New programs are generated by a combination of the latest academic fads and new sources of government funding. Not unlike the programs of the federal government, obsolete academic programs are seldom allowed to die. Instead, they continue indefinitely long after the original program rationale has faded.

We believe there are striking parallels to the problems of our government, our corporations, and our cities in most American universities. Although tuition continues to spiral upwards, the quality and real economic value of undergraduate education are declining. For example, a 1996 study by the National Association of Scholars of fifty

4. From *Petersons' Guide to Four Year Colleges,* 24th ed. (Princeton, N.J.: Petersons' Guides, 1994).

leading colleges and universities found that they have dropped most of the core academic requirements once considered vital to a liberal arts education. Mandatory courses in math, science, history, literature, and English composition are disappearing. Only a handful of schools require undergraduate theses anymore. The average length of the school year decreased from 204 days in 1914 to 156 days in 1993.

As evidence of how bad things have gotten on some campuses, an increasing number of former students are filing lawsuits against universities charging them with false advertising, breach of contract, fraud, misrepresentation, and negligence.

Restructuring Higher Education

We believe that what is called for in higher education is nothing less than a complete restructuring of universities, including the way they are organized, the way undergraduates are taught, and the substance of the curriculum. The ultimate aim of restructuring is to improve the quality of undergraduate education, increase its value, and reduce its costs — to create a community of scholars and teachers who will enhance students' critical thinking skills and their search for meaning.

While we know that smallness alone is no guarantee of a school's educational effectiveness, we do believe that a large size is a mostly negative factor in achieving the goals of higher education. Universities are particularly vulnerable to the law of decreasing returns with regard to increased size. We estimate that the optimum-size undergraduate learning environment is an academic community consisting of no more than three thousand students subdivided into English-style residential colleges of around three hundred students each. Large state universities with their dehumanizing high-rise dormitories, legions of graduate teaching assistants, and tens of thousands of undergraduates are antithetical to the pursuit of knowledge, meaning, and community. There are those who respond, "But don't many students at larger schools do quite well on standardized tests like the GRE or the LSAT?" Such arguments fail to move us. The quantification and standardization of education, represented in such tests, is precisely what we are arguing against. Even relatively small universities like Duke with 6,130 undergraduates and the University of Vermont with 7,925 are difficult to manage. Viable undergraduate learning communities at mega-universities are often unachievable.

We propose downsizing colleges and universities to a more reasonable scale and eventually decoupling undergraduate education from the largest of them. Growth at universities with more than 5,000 undergraduates should be brought to a halt. Proposals for new undergraduate dormitories, classroom buildings, research laboratories, computer centers, or libraries should be rigorously examined. Over the next decade, the aim of large universities should be either completely to spin off their undergraduate programs or significantly decentralize them in a manner consistent with the residential college mode. Too many of our universities resemble General Motors of the fifties. While American business has radically transformed the corporation of the fifties — the World War II–induced behemoths churning out haphazardly built, assembly line–produced vehicles — American higher education is still saddled with huge institutional relics that produce assembly-line graduates. American higher education must show some of the same creativity and courage that we have seen recently in much of American business. Downsizing is the order of the day.

The three best-known American examples of the residential college system are Harvard, Princeton, and Yale. Yale's twelve residential colleges are self-sufficient communities within Yale College, each with its own dining hall, library, courtyard, seminar rooms, practice rooms, and numerous other facilities from darkrooms to printing presses, from game rooms to saunas. At the end of their first year, Harvard students are assigned to a house in which they will live for the remainder of their undergraduate career. Each house has a master, a senior tutor or dean, a tutorial staff, a library, and dining facilities. All houses are coeducational, and much of the social, athletic, extracurricular, and academic life at Harvard centers on the house. At Princeton all freshmen and sophomores live and dine in one of five residential colleges. A small number of juniors and seniors live and eat in the residential colleges; but most live in the upperclass dorms, and more than half dine in Princeton's well-known independent eating clubs.

In no sense are we suggesting that the residential college system as practiced by the aforementioned universities is a panacea. We know that the residential college experiments at the University of Virginia and at Princeton have had their critics. Yet we do defend the notion that size is an important issue. Even with the residential college system, size mitigates against the benefits of residential colleges when, as is the case at Harvard, there are 6,672 undergraduates dominated by 11,601 graduate students and professional students, or at Yale where there are

5,194 undergraduates out of a total enrollment of 11,129. Although Princeton, with just 4,525 undergraduates, is the smallest of the three, it struggles with a destructive social environment. Middlebury College, with just 1,960 students, has attempted to emulate some aspects of the residential college system, but with only mixed success.

In 1994, tiny Bennington College in Vermont, known for its non-traditional approach to education and its high tuition, sent shock waves through the American higher education establishment when it announced its plans to implement one of the most radical college restructuring schemes ever conceived. The reconfiguration called for faculty and staff reductions, the abolition of tenure, the elimination of traditional academic departments, a 10 percent cut in tuition and fees, the adoption of an alternative contractual system for faculty, and the establishment of a revolving venture-capital fund to support innovative new faculty ideas.

A Call to Action

The Bennington Trustees decided that business as usual was no longer tenable and that the only thing that made any real sense was to seek the most compelling response to the questions that matter in undergraduate education. They did so in the context of a college with a genuinely innovative vision of liberal education, driven by a passion for excellence and a penchant for irreverence, and they did so at a time in American history when the questions of the plight of liberal education were burning questions having a rare urgency — a sense of time running out and of very high stakes.

Elizabeth Coleman
President, Bennington College

All of this was in response to declining enrollments, a $1 million deficit, serious erosion of academic standards, poor faculty morale, and organizational chaos. Bennington was not only out of control; it was in a death spiral.

But to its credit, Bennington was small enough and flexible enough to reinvent itself. Most large colleges and universities are not! Unlike many college boards, Bennington's was not only paying attention to what was going on, but it was prepared to take risks to save a great college.

Over the long term, during the next decade, we are proposing that large universities basically withdraw from the undergraduate teaching business. The university of the future would consist of a collection of professional schools, graduate degree–granting programs, high-level research institutions, adult education, and professional outreach services. State universities would provide support services to a network of colleges not located on the central university campus, including administrative and financial services, library services, central computing facilities, as well as specialized courses for advanced undergraduates. Seniors in satellite colleges affiliated with the university might be allowed to take a limited number of graduate courses at the university.

Moreover, we encourage those who charge that these proposals would be extravagantly expensive to be honest about the extravagance, the waste, and the redundancy present in the large educational institutions. For decades, principally as a result of its participation in a wartime economy, American business thought that bigness, standardization, and assembly-line production techniques saved money. In the past ten years, American business has confronted the diminishing returns in regard to size. There are some tasks, particularly those that thrive on communication, interaction, and cooperation, in which cost and efficiency decline in exact proportion to size. Downsizing is not a call for withdrawal from commitment to educate the largest possible number of qualified students, but rather an attempt to give all of our students the best possible education by the most efficient means.

To finance the shift toward decentralized liberal arts colleges, we would close many redundant state-supported professional schools and graduate programs. For many states — not including California, New York, and Texas — there is little need for multiple, state-supported medical schools, law schools, and engineering schools. Many underfinanced, undersubscribed universities should be downsized back to colleges. Having experienced a couple of decades during which numerous colleges and two-year institutions frantically moved toward pinning the name "university" upon themselves, we must now help these schools recover the dignity, the focus, and the efficiency that comes from reclaiming their identity as colleges dedicated to undergraduate education.

It is not obvious that every state needs a dental school, a veterinary school, or state-of-the-art research institutions in nuclear physics and microbiology. The Cold War is over, and we do not need nearly so many nuclear physicists, mathematicians, chemists, and defense-related engineers. As taxpayers demand cutbacks in the so-called defense budget, research universities will discover painfully how much of their intellectual activity has been dictated by the Pentagon. A preoccupation with short-run profitability and stock prices has prompted American companies to reduce expenditures for basic research. Thus not only is there less demand for PhDs in basic science and engineering, but there is less private and government funding available to support expensive high-tech research in these fields. As the federal government returns previously federally funded programs back to the states, state governments will turn to their higher education budgets as sources for funds.

Perhaps the massive cutbacks in government- and business-funded research can be seen as an opportunity, rather than an impending disaster, an externally induced invitation for us to return to the basic purpose of education. Be well assured that if our faculties and administrators do not take this opportunity, they shall then be led through the humiliating process of having legislators and mere market pressures hack their schools to pieces, bit by bit.

Graduate education has always cost more than undergraduate

education because of small class sizes and laboratory equipment requirements. Universities should become much more selective in choosing departments and fields in which to offer PhD degrees. The manner in which some graduate departments continue to produce PhDs in fields already oversupplied borders on the immoral. Those who would defend the mega-universities on the basis of their altruistic desire to provide the largest possible number of students with access to higher education ought honestly to examine how much potential undergraduate funding is siphoned off at these institutions by expensive, glamorous, but relatively unproductive graduate and professional programs. For too long undergraduate colleges have seen their main value as feeding their students into the university for graduate and professional work. We want to reverse that process, inviting universities to see themselves as existing for and supportive of the task of undergraduate education.

Since professors in newly emerging liberal arts colleges will not be under the university publish-or-perish mandate, they can be expected to teach more — perhaps as many as four or five courses per semester.

As universities begin downsizing and cutting back on their undergraduate programs, former undergraduate dormitories can either be transformed to graduate and professional dormitories or converted to apartment buildings or much-needed housing for the elderly. We see educational value in colleges attempting to foster more interaction between the generations. Surplus undergraduate classrooms and office space may either be adapted to graduate and professional use or temporarily rented.

With modern telecommunications networks, universities may offer their satellite colleges televised courses on topics too specialized to be included in the curricula of most small colleges, such as Chinese, Japanese, advanced physics, and molecular biology. Universities might be seen as resource centers that offer support for strong undergraduate colleges, the strong undergraduate colleges being the basic units of American higher education, with the universities functioning for their support rather than as their norm to emulate.

Why should universities continue to support big-time football and basketball programs? University stadiums and basketball field houses could be sold or rented to nearby professional teams. In downsizing, intercollegiate athletics would return to the scale on which it existed before World War II. Small colleges would compete among themselves for the pleasure of it, not to train professional athletes and

Higher Education Downsizing Strategies

1. Downsize universities with more than ten thousand students by decoupling from them undergraduate education, and spinning off colleges consisting of no more than three thousand under- graduates subdivided into English-style residential colleges of around three hundred students each.
2. Reconstitute universities as collections of professional schools, graduate programs, high-level research institutions, and pro- fessional outreach services which support networks of off-site colleges.
3. Reduce federal aid to higher education and eliminate all federal regulations.
4. Replace tenure with long-term contracts and increase the number of courses taught by faculty members.

hype alumni and state legislators. If athletic scholarships were con- tinued, their educational usefulness, not simply their athletic value, would need to be demonstrated.

With an effective residential college system, fraternities and sororities would receive much-needed competition; they would possibly become obsolete. For decades, on many campuses, fraternities and sororities have provided a second-best alternative to the residential college system in America. In their fraternity or sorority, students found the sense of community they craved, but which the college or university failed to provide. Indeed, the very existence of the Greek system may at least partially explain why so few colleges and universities have adopted the English residential college plan.

Obviously, restructuring higher education will be a long and arduous task taking several decades to complete. But just as multimil- lion-dollar industrial conglomerates have outlived their usefulness and have given way to more creative adaptations, so too will large mega- university degree factories. It is not surprising that small colleges such as Amherst, Dartmouth, Middlebury, Mount Holyoke, Smith, Vassar, Wellesley, and Williams command premium prices in the marketplace. They charge high tuition because they provide a high value-added product.

By attempting to be all things to all people, large-scale universities have allowed their most important business — undergraduate education — seriously to be eroded. For too long university trustees and state legislators have been biased toward professional schools and graduate education. It's time to turn the situation around, to recover the centrality of undergraduate education.

Is it possible that what's good for AT&T, the former Soviet Union, Eastern Europe, and the USA may also be good for higher education? If higher education is to survive, it too must begin downsizing.

7 Give Me That Old-Time Religion

Not unlike our schools and our colleges and universities, many of our religious institutions have also grown too large — particularly mainline Protestant denominations.

Nothing better illustrates the problems of giantism in religion than the 1968 merger of the Evangelical United Bretheren and the Methodist Church to create the denomination with the largest number of churches in North America, The United Methodist Church. The economy was booming, corporate America was expanding, and the federal government was experiencing explosive growth. A bigger church would be a more effective, more efficient church. None of this was to be. A bigger church was a more bureaucratic church, a more authoritarian church, a less responsive, adaptive church, and a church in which too little power resided in the local congregations.

The year 1969 saw the beginning of a precipitous membership decline. United Methodists lost two million members in two decades, over a half million fewer people were attending Sunday worship. And an average of nearly four United Methodist churches closed every week.[1]

The unique feature of North American Protestantism is the invention, in the last century, of the Christian denomination. These large, voluntary religious organizations have contributed to the vitality and the character of American Christianity. Americans appear to like their

---

1. Andy Langford and William H. Willimon, *A New Connection: Reforming the United Methodist Church* (Nashville: Abingdon, 1996), pp. 21-22.

Christianity delivered in large doses, organizationally speaking. A few large denominations have dominated the North American religious scene for the past two hundred years. The churches of the United States report a total membership of 158 million members. Over half of this total is in three denominations: the Roman Catholic Church, the Southern Baptist Convention, and the United Methodist Church. A small number of denominations account for the great majority of members. The thirty-five denominations with membership greater than four hundred thousand account for more than 95 percent of the total membership.[2]

And yet, rather remarkable things have been happening in American churches. For several decades, the mainline Protestant denominations in the United States have been experiencing rapid membership decline, the first decline most of these denominations have ever experienced. Nineteen ninety-four was a rather typical year of decline for the following bodies:

Denomination	Membership Decline
The United Methodist Church	62,470
Evangelical Lutheran Church in America	13,737
Presbyterian Church (U.S.A.)	98,630
United Church of Christ	28,868
Christian Church (Disciples of Christ)	20,737

The membership decline in the mainline (perhaps now in honesty we ought to call these churches "old line" or even "sidelined") does not mean that Americans are less religious or more secular than we used to be. While the past couple of decades have been difficult for many large denominations, they have been years of spectacular growth for some churches. The decline of mainline Protestantism does not mean that people are turning away from organized religion in general. Nearly half a million persons joined denominations during 1994. The following churches continued to experience membership growth during that year.

2. These statistics, along with the other general church statistics used in this chapter, are from Kenneth B. Bedell, ed., *Yearbook of American and Canadian Churches: 1996* (Nashville: Abingdon, 1996).

Denomination	Membership Growth
The Roman Catholic Church	332,563
Southern Baptist Convention	215,418
The Church of Jesus Christ of Latter-Day Saints	93,000
Assemblies of God	52,897

Furthermore, the largest growth in Christian congregations occurs not in any of the historically top eight denominations but in the category "all others." That is, in 1820 Methodists accounted for 24 percent of all congregations in the United States, Roman Catholics for 11 percent. Today, Roman Catholic congregations constitute 7 percent of the total number of congregations, Methodists have precipitously fallen to 12 percent, while "all others" has risen to 33 percent of all congregations.[3] The latter part of this century has witnessed vast shifts in American religious life. The so-called mainline denominations are rapidly becoming sidelined by newer, younger denominations. Jehovah's Witnesses have surpassed the Christian Church (Disciples of Christ) in membership, for example. Denominations are becoming smaller and more numerous.

American-church historian Russell Richey characterizes various stages in the development of American denominationalism.[4] In the late nineteenth and early twentieth centuries, corporate or managerial organization typified the organization of denominations. Paralleling developments in American government and industry, the denominations looked like corporations. The churches went through a managerial revolution in the interest of efficiency and productivity. In a fascinating book, Rolf Lunden details the ways in which American churches attempted crassly to duplicate the techniques and the ethos of American business in their internal life.[5] Religious sociologist Gibson Winter called this increasingly bureaucratized organization of American religious life

---

3. Lyle E. Schaller, *Tattered Trust: Is There Hope for Your Denomination?* (Nashville: Abingdon, 1996), p. 16.

4. R. E. Richey, "Denominations and Denominationalism: An American Morphology," in *Reimaging Denominationalism*, ed. R. B. Mullin and R. E. Richey (New York: Oxford Press, 1994), p. 77.

5. Rolf Lunden, *Business and Religion in the American 1920's* (New York: Greenwood Press, 1988).

the most significant religious development in this century.[6] Further-more, it is a development which has remarkable parallels, said Winter, among Protestants, Catholics, and Jews, though with some variations.

Early Church Organization

After this the Lord appointed seventy others and sent them on ahead of him in pairs to every town and place where he himself intended to go. He said to them, "The harvest is plentiful, but the laborers are few; therefore ask the Lord of the harvest to send out laborers into his harvest. Go on your way. See, I am sending you out like lambs into the midst of wolves. Carry no purse, no bag, no sandals; and greet no one on the road."

Luke 10:1-4, NRSV

Larger, more interlocked and complex organizations were justified on the basis of the churches' desire for missionary expansion and benevolent transformation of American culture. They hoped, through these large organizations, at last to Christianize America. Alexis de Tocqueville's characterization of America as "a nation with the soul of a church" could be turned to say that many of the American churches have the soul of a nation. Denominations spoke of the need to build a "righteous empire," in which the church would dominate the nation for the betterment of all.

During this period, the organization of churches not only changed, but those who administered the denominations changed as well. Clergy became more professionalized, with more elaborate credentialing and accrediting processes, the requirement of a seminary degree, and in some denominations, the formation of the clergy into a veritable clerical guild. Historian Brooks Hollifield has chronicled the ways in which American Protestant clergy chameleon-like took on themselves the trappings of success as defined by the national culture.[7]

6. Gibson Winter, *Religious Identity: The Formal Organization and Informal Power Structure of the Major Faiths in the United States Today* (New York: Macmillan, 1968), p. 3.

7. E. Brooks Hollifield, *A History of Pastoral Care in America* (Nashville: Abingdon, 1983). See also William H. Willimon, "Clergy Ethics: Getting Our Story Straight," in *Against the Grain: New Approaches to Professional Ethics*, ed. Michael Goldberg (Valley Forge, Pa.: Trinity Press International, 1993), pp. 161-84.

In the nineteenth century, when entrepreneurial businessmen were transforming the country, clergy began to look like busy, efficient, macho business leaders. Later, in the mid–twentieth century, clergy looked like spiritual therapists, as the therapeutic mentality gripped the imaginations of Americans. Many clergy began to fancy themselves as efficient administrators, supervisors of a complex volunteer organization with a wide array of activities and services.

An interesting sidelight to this managerial revolution was the displeasure of some women who had led the relatively independent church mission agencies for women, now being brought under the control and accountability of male denominational leaders. In the first half of the nineteenth century, American women created some of the largest women's organizations in the world — the Women's Christian Temperance Union, for instance. These organizations gave women experience and power over their own lives and showed the energy and creativity they had to offer. As is typical of large organizations in the modern age, local initiative and lay leadership were sometimes considered a threat by the larger body. The need for coordination and approval outweighed the need for creativity and grassroots involvement.

Jesus on Participatory Management

You know that the rulers of the Gentiles lord it over them, and their great ones are tyrants over them. It will not be so among you; but whoever wishes to be great among you must be your servant, and whoever wishes to be first among you must be your slave; just as the Son of Man came not to be served but to serve, and to give his life a ransom for many.

Matthew 20:25-28, NRSV

Some of the churches' current mission funding crisis relates to this long process of professionalization and bureaucratization of the church's mission work.[8] Two critics of our current denominational mission funding procedures say mission funding has dropped precipi-

---

8. See Ronald E. Vallet and Charles E. Zech, *The Mainline Church's Mission Funding Crisis: Issues and Possibilities* (Grand Rapids: Eerdmans, 1995). If present church funding trends continue, by 2049, zero percent of congregational funds will be sent outside the congregation for mission and benevolence work, say John and

tously in the last two decades because those doing the mission lost touch with the local congregations who gave the funding. All church funding in America is voluntary. When the denominations forget the voluntary character of their churches, they are in trouble.

Organizational Development

Three basic trends characterize the Protestant denominations in their organizational growth: (1) elaboration of administrative staff; (2) centralized control of fund-raising and budgeting; (3) functional specialization through agencies and boards.[9]

Beginning in the late 1960s, says Richey, American mainline denominations became national religious regulatory bodies, devising complex guidelines and procedures for their respective bodies. In the era of government regulation, denominations looked less like a gathering of like-minded believers and more like a religious regulatory agency. Richey says these denominations now embody a complex of contemporary cultural forms, none of which is explicitly religious in origin: "The franchise, the regulatory agency, the caucus, the mall, the media."[10]

Up until the 1960s the largest Protestant denominations, along with the Roman Catholics, had a virtual monopoly in American religious life. If someone was going to be a Christian, that person had to practice Christianity when and where these churches demanded. Little wonder that in a denomination like the United Methodist Church — which has more congregations in more places than the U.S. Postal Service has post offices — the denomination began behaving like the U.S. Postal Service. A monopoly does not have to trouble itself with customer service.

Beginning in the sixties, America has seen a huge growth in independent, nondenominational, and younger denominational churches. These congregations have given the older denominations competition which was previously unknown. Americans are now religious consumers,

---

Sylvia Ronsvalle in their book *Behind the Stained Glass Windows* (Grand Rapids: Baker Books, 1996).

9. Winter, p. 30.
10. Richey, p. 77.

shopping around, demanding diverse services from their churches, and holding their congregations more accountable.

Large denominations have not been a pleasant place to be in recent years. The Episcopalians recently discovered that their national treasurer had embezzled millions, thus demonstrating to many in that church that their national body was unmanageable and unaccountable. The Southern Baptists went through a painful national division into fundamentalists and moderates with the concomitant dismantling of many of their cherished institutions, and a loss of energy in what had been a rapidly growing church. Some of the more liberal mainline denominations, like the Presbyterians and the United Methodists, find themselves a battleground for competing caucuses and special interest groups pushing feminist, gay and lesbian, and ethnic minority concerns; conservative theology; and other agendas. Might these groups be a symptom that many groups of members in these denominations feel they have little voice or impact upon the huge and unwieldy, directionless denomination? A caucus group provides its members a united voice, a public platform for their grievances, a budget, and status within the large, impersonal denomination.

Related to this fragmentation is the tendency of denominations to regulate and to legislate themselves more heavily. We have noted elsewhere that this is a characteristic of modern bureaucracy. Russell Richey says:

> Regulatory behavior . . . increasingly characterized all denominational agencies, which find themselves resorting to a variety of new mechanisms to achieve the results that used to come easier — to effect policy, to implement program, to disseminate resolutions. So agencies function at times like regulatory agencies, controlling through expectation or rule. In so behaving, denominations internalize one prevalent mechanism for continuing the rule from the top down . . . denominations here borrow from the repertoire of national and state regulatory agencies. Regulation — rule making, monitoring, on-site visiting, indicting, exposing, forcing adherence — reaches for the cooperation, unity, and coordination that used to link congregation to state, to region, to nation in denominational life. . . . Regulation, often adversarial in premise or tone, suggests a collapse of denominational cohesion and purpose.[11]

11. Richey, p. 89.

Professional Management

Protestant organization has brought professional, managerial personnel into the religious picture. Large-scale, highly rationalized organizations cannot operate on a familistic basis. They require skilled managerial personnel who can decide on objective criteria about program and advancement. This creates a conflict between the "organization men" and the constituency.[12]

One of us recently served as a delegate to his church's national convention. In the committee on which he served the Commission on the Role and Status of Women placed a monitor who kept track of the committee's discussion. At the beginning of every committee session, she reported how many women spoke and how many men spoke, whether or not the women's comments were responded to favorably by the men and whether or not the women seemed to be "taken seriously."

Internal regulation, legislative coercion, and adversarial monitoring are characteristics of an organization in deep trouble. Having lost its theological coherence or consensus, the denomination attempts to hold itself together through rules and structure in lieu of belief and practice. The trouble is surely deep when the organization is a Christian church which ought to operate on the basis of its theological principles, by persuasion, conversion, and education rather than by coercion and regulation. Church observer Lyle Schaller says most large denominations are organized on the basis of lack of trust. You can't trust the laity; furthermore, you can't trust the clergy either.

Aggravating the loss of members is a troubling demographic trend among the mainline denominations. There is a "graying" of mainline Protestantism. The average member of the mainline Protestant denomination is considerably older than the average member of newer denominations like the Assemblies of God. Among the reasons for this generational gap may be the size and the organizational structure of these older denominations.

Some church observers have noted generational differences in the ways in which Americans relate to their churches. The World War II generation, those Americans now over seventy, they call "Boosters."

12. Winter, p. 39.

These folk love to relate to, support, care for, and identify with institutions. Boosters have been incredibly generous, in gifts of time and money, to the institutions they love like their churches, colleges, and clubs.

The Boosters were followed by the "Boomers," those adults now between thirty and fifty who were members of the postwar baby boom. While Boomers have been ambivalent about their parents' institutions, after keeping their distance from organizations as young adults, many of them eventually returned to support institutions like the church. Yet the support of the Boomers tended to be halfhearted, and they did a poor job of integrating their children into institutions.

Which led, in some observers' view, to the "Busters," those who are now young adults and just older. This group takes a uniformly negative view of large organizations and is not much on institutional loyalty. They are cynical about politics and systems. While many of them have a decidedly altruistic bent, willing to give many hours to face-to-face, one-on-one charitable work like Habitat for Humanity, they tend to be uninterested in working in long-term, systemic solutions to social problems. They have given up hope in top-down, political, legislative solutions, preferring local, one-to-one action. Busters feel little long-term loyalty to schools, colleges, or churches. They stay on the move, value a diversity of experiences, and appear to be willing to roam from one institution to another over the course of their adult years.

These generational differences supply one reason why large mainline Protestant denominations are doing so poorly in attracting and retaining the young. These denominations are being run mostly by Boosters and an increasing number of Boomers. Boosters are older folk who love identification with large organizations and are great believers in the power of structures to bring about change, legislative coercion, rules, and mandates. Many of them feel they have benefited from the legislative quotas and affirmative action programs of the Great Society and its aftermath. They are elitists who believe that positive change occurs best when a few enlightened individuals at the top use their power to direct and to mandate change which trickles down to the less enlightened folk at the bottom. Although they like thinking of themselves as avant-garde liberals, they are organizational conservatives. If there is a good worth doing, it is worth legislating, mandating, and enshrining through a subsidy, a rule, or a committee. You can't trust the people at the bottom to know what's best for them. Those of us at the top, who have received enlightenment, must show the way to others.

To the Busters, this all looks rather dreary, even arrogant, a violation of the particularities of local differences and local needs. The Boomers and Boosters spend far too much time in committees, in meetings, in laborious process which attempts to ensure that every voice is heard, every point of view is considered, but which often means that the process takes too long to work, is too expensive to administer, and is manipulated by those bureaucrats who can understand the complicated procedures mandated by the organization.

Thus the Busters have deserted the mainline denominations, preferring instead the less heavily organized, less bureaucratized, more innovative younger churches. In fact, surveys indicate that since the late 1970s, no one is joining a denomination. People are joining congregations who happen to be affiliated with a denomination, but the denomination plays almost no role in why people select a church.[13]

We also believe that the large, bureaucratic, top-down organization limits these churches' ability to reach out to ethnic minority persons. During the past couple of decades, mainline churches have talked much about "diversity," "inclusiveness," and the need to attract more ethnic minority members. Many of them, such as the United Methodists, the Presbyterians, the Lutherans, and the Episcopalians, have spent millions in special funds to subsidize and to encourage ethnic ministries. Yet without exception, these efforts have failed. These denominations are as thoroughly Caucasian and middle class as when they began; most of them have even gone backward in regard to ethnic inclusiveness.

One reason is the organizational form of these churches. The corporate, bureaucratic model of organization is white-collar, corporate America through the sixties. Organizational form tends to be culturally specific. The imposition of this corporate management style of organization does not fit the needs and the peculiar ways in which different ethnic groups organize themselves. Therefore, if these churches are really serious about ministry with ethnic minorities, then they must encourage less uniformity and top-down control and more local leadership, organizational and structural diversity, and grassroots ownership of the church and its mission.

Will was visiting among leaders of the Church of God in Anderson, Indiana. He was told that one of that church's largest annual events

---

13. Milton A. Coalter, John M. Mulder, and Louis B. Weeks, *Vital Signs: The Promise of Mainstream Protestantism* (Grand Rapids: Eerdmans, 1996), pp. 16-17, 27-28.

was its Missions Conference where thousands of missionaries gather from all over the world for worship, singing, planning, and encouragement each summer. His own denomination, while much larger, has only a tiny fraction of that number of active missionaries around the world; in fact, there are more bureaucrats administering his church's mission program than actual missionaries in the field.

"Well, the Church of God's mission program is rather messy," said his host. "It's all very unorganized. Anybody, any member of our church who feels called by God to be a missionary, can stand up in his or her congregation and say so and start raising money to go be a missionary. Hundreds of them go every year."

Will, thinking of the paltry efforts by his own denomination in this area, said, "There is much to be said for being unorganized!"

Good-bye Ecclesiastical UN

The World Council of Churches is facing severe financial difficulties, and only "drastic action" on the part of the international ecumenical organization's 330 member churches can end the crisis. . . . the council had an income of about $64.3 million last year, down $7.4 million from 1994. Its expenditures in 1995 were about $81 million, compared with $91 million in 1994. . . . Approximately three-fourths of all contributions to the WCC come from four countries, . . . Germany gives 40 percent; Sweden, 15 percent; the Netherlands and the U.S. both give 11 percent.[14]

Part of the genius of American denominationalism has been its voluntarism, its ability to empower local, ordinary people, in thousands of places, to be faithful in their own time and place to the demands of Jesus Christ. This has led to an unprecedented diversity and vitality of religious expression. When that diversity and vitality were sacrificed for control — tight, interconnected, uniform, professionally managed organization — the churches forsook their birthright for a mess of big business pottage.

The denominations have only lately begun to sense that they are

14. "WCC Faces Financial Crisis," *Christian Century*, July 31–August 7, 1996, p. 743.

in real crisis. Huge membership losses are only a symptom of their problems. Though some national denominations like the Presbyterians and the Episcopalians have already experienced devastating financial crises, leading to the virtual dismantling of their national church structures, most mainline denominations have yet to experience the depth of the coming financial crisis. When the supportive and generous Boosters pass from the scene, leaving the churches and their mission to the less generous and more organizationally skeptical Boomers and Busters, there will be severe financial problems. Church historian Leonard Sweet says that, as a rule of thumb, Boosters give to institutions. Boomers give to causes, and Busters give to their friends.

The recent trend toward "megachurches," huge congregations of a couple of thousand members and higher, where Sunday worship draws a thousand worshipers or more, may seem to invalidate our "small is beautiful" thesis. These large congregations are a major factor in America's changing religious scene. Younger churchgoers are found in disproportionately large numbers in these large congregations. A majority of these megachurches were founded after 1970. Some mainline denominations (for example, the Evangelical Free Church of America and the Reformed Church in America) have designed programs to foster these large congregations. On the other hand, the United Methodists, during the same period, have sharply increased their proportion of smaller congregations (between 1980 and 1994, the United Methodists increased the number of congregations reporting an average worship attendance of fewer than twenty by 39 percent).[15] A major factor in United Methodist denominational decline appears to be the Methodists' support and subsidy of small congregations, coupled with a denominational prejudice against large congregations.

The typical growing congregation which is successful in attracting younger members has over two hundred persons in worship on Sunday morning.[16] Younger churchgoers tend to expect more of their churches. They want quality music and quality programming and preaching. They tend to value a wide array of program choices within the congregation. To many observers, the large regional church seems destined to replace the small neighborhood church. Lyle Schaller declares, "Large is replacing small as the descriptive term for where most people worship."[17]

15. Schaller, p. 58.
16. Schaller, p. 35.
17. Schaller, p. 15.

Yet two points ought to be considered before giving the future to the megacongregation:

1. What's disappearing in the American church is not the very small or the very large but the middle. Very small congregations are an amazingly tough, resilient part of American church life and will continue to be so. They have never depended upon denominational programs or top-down leadership for their lives. Denominations may pass away, but not the small membership church. The very large congregation is a new and, for the foreseeable future, vibrant part of American Christianity. But the small church will continue to characterize American Christianity.

The middle is shrinking. These congregations, whose average worship attendance is from twenty to two hundred, appear to be in trouble. Neither dynamically large nor intimately small, these congregations are dwindling. The United Methodists, for instance, have seen over seven hundred of their congregations of this size slip into the small congregation category between 1991 and 1994.

2. There are those who argue that there really is no such thing as the "large church." There are only clusters of small congregations meeting under the same roof who call themselves a large church. In fact, the organizational genius of these "megachurches" is that they have learned how to cultivate and cluster dozens of small "congregations." While their Sunday worship is huge, everything else in the church (other than their parking lots!) keeps small. They grow groups by the dozens. Alcoholics Anonymous, pottery classes, prayer groups, divorce recovery, yoga, assertiveness training, and Bible study were among the *twenty-eight* small groups who meet *every week* at one large church.[18]

So, far from being a uniformly strong assertion that "big is better," these megachurches may be proof that "small is everything." Their success in holding together a wide array of interests through small

18. The megachurches have thereby capitalized upon one of the most astounding "small is beautiful" phenomena in America — the small group movement. Millions of Americans are fleeing impersonal, large groupings in favor of small, face-to-face groups. Robert Wuthnow of Princeton claims that 40 percent of Americans belong to a small group, including 800,000 Sunday school classes, 900,000 Bible study groups, 500,000 self-help groups, 250,000 political action groups, and 250,000 sports/hobby groups. Note that the majority of these groups are somehow tied to religious practices, and many meet at churches. Robert Wuthnow, *Sharing the Journey* (New York: Free Press, 1994), also *I Came Away Stronger: How Small Groups Are Changing American Religion* (Grand Rapids: Eerdmans, 1994).

The Next Church?

[These] churches are remarkable chiefly for their size. Many of these (mostly Protestant) congregations count thousands of people in attendance on a weekend — in some cases more than 10,000. For their hugeness, they are often known, and often chagrined to be known, as megachurches. Among other labels one hears are full-service churches, seven-day-a-week churches, pastoral churches, apostolic churches, "new tribe" churches, new paradigm churches, seeker-sensitive churches, shopping-mall churches. . . . These very large and dynamic congregations may at the moment number no more than 400, but they are the fastest-growing ones in the country. Half of all churchgoing Americans, to cite a figure treasured in the Next Church community, are attending only 12 percent of the nation's 400,000 churches. To look at it another way, half of American Protestant churches have fewer than seventy-five congregants.

Big congregations endow a church with critical mass, which makes possible sizable budgets and economic efficiencies (such as very low staffing ratios) and formidable volunteer pools . . . these places have something in common, they whisper no word of denomination.[19]

groups may be their greatest attribute. The megachurches we have observed often have their problems — a charismatic but egocentric pastor, authoritarian leadership by the pastor, questionable theology, a troubling redefinition of Sunday worship into a professional performance rather than congregational participation, crass commercialism. Yet their curious blend of face-to-face small group commitment and Sunday morning major pageant is sure to be with us for the foreseeable future.

There is now a marked tendency, in all mainline Protestant denominations, for congregations increasingly to chart their own courses. Increasing numbers of congregations are coming to the renewed awareness that they, not the national denomination, are the basic form of the

19. Charles Trueheart, "Welcome to the Next Church," *Atlantic Monthly,* August 1996, pp. 37-57.

church. Congregations, tired of being treated by the denomination as no more than a franchise outlet for the denomination's programs, have begun to take responsibility for themselves. Not withdrawing from mission and outreach, these congregations are saying they have the ability to define mission and outreach at the local level, rather than waiting for the denomination to debate and to decide and then to inform the local church about what it ought to be doing to be faithful to Christian mission.

Some large congregations are forsaking traditional seminary training for their leaders, preferring to bypass the denomination's usual route for training clergy, choosing instead to train their own leaders in the skills they think necessary in their particular congregational situation. Independent publishing houses produce educational curriculum materials for congregations which previously would not think of using any "unofficial" literature.

As many as one hundred thousand Protestant churches are served today by a lay pastor who works at another job during the week. Lyle Schaller claims that this group of nonprofessional clergy is growing by 2 percent annually.[20] The dramatic shortage of priests among Roman Catholics is rapidly increasing the number of Catholic churches whose "priest" is a nun and whose laity are assuming more active parish leadership.

Schaller has also noted that there is less and less for a denomination to do these days, that every function once done exclusively by a denomination is now being done as well (many congregations think, better) on the local level. The last thing denominations do is to credential clergy. If local congregations, who pay the cost of the denomination, lose faith in the denomination's ability to train and to credential pastoral leaders, then those congregations will find alternative means of securing leadership.

Only six years ago, one congregation of our acquaintance was sending over a hundred thousand dollars a year to denominational headquarters to be used in denominational mission and benevolence work. Today that congregation does not send a dime to the denomination for this work, but instead sends three times that amount to non-denominational groups like Habitat for Humanity, Heifer Project International, Promise Keepers, World Vision, and other independent mission and benevolence agencies, having lost faith in the denomination's ability to administer these programs.

20. Schaller, p. 17.

In addition to the Episcopalians and Presbyterians, many other mainline Protestant denominations including the Lutherans and even the Southern Baptists are experiencing financial stress in the form of budgetary shortfalls. The Episcopal Church was forced to reduce its Manhattan headquarters staff by a third.

A number of contemporary observers say denominations may be breaking apart before our eyes in the latter part of the twentieth century.[21] Some denominations gave the illusion of growth and self-preservation with denominational mergers such as the creation of the United Church of Canada in 1925 or the more recent Presbyterian merger in 1983. These efforts to blend multiple ecclesiastical and regional traditions have been uniformly disastrous for the uniting churches, leaving them weaker and fractious. There is no more vivid argument against the "bigger is better" logic than the sad state of those denominations that merged. Throughout this period, most of these denominations also went through much restructuring and organizational tinkering. Most of this restructuring, until the last couple of years, resulted in larger, more complex ecclesiastical bureaucracy. Each denominational merger and restructuring added, rather than subtracted, levels of bureaucracy.

Fundamentalist Southern Baptists, in taking over their denomination's extensive agencies and institutions, may have come too late to the megadenomination game. Fundamentalists appear to be coming to embrace, at the end of the twentieth century, the project of mainline Protestantism at the turn of the century; namely, to produce a "Christian America" through their campaigns against abortion and for school prayer. This was the big church project of liberal Protestants during the past century, a project which is now in shambles.

Denominational structure gave the mainline big churches the illusion that they were still in control, that the Protestant hegemony over American life was still holding. Years ago, Gibson Winter noted that the Roman Catholic hierarchy had a false sense of contentment, assuming that just because it issued orders, its orders were being carried out at the local level. In a hierarchy, it is very difficult for those on the

---

21. See the work of Wade Clark Roof and William McKinney, *American Mainline Religion* (New Brunswick, N.J.: Rutgers University Press, 1987); and Robert Wuthnow, *The Restructuring of American Religion* (Princeton, N.J.: Princeton University Press, 1988). The Ronsvalles' research indicates that, if present trends continue, the mainline denominations, which in 1968 comprised 13 percent of the U.S. population, will by 2028 be zero percent *(Behind the Stained Glass Windows).*

top to know what is going on at the bottom because functionaries at the bottom have a stake in suppressing information which may be detrimental to the self-image of those administering the organization at the top.[22] Now, as the twentieth century ends, there is little way for big churches to deny that they are in big trouble. The time has come for the churches to recover the power of their essentially voluntaristic, local character.

We find ourselves in agreement with Russell Richey who, in concluding his survey of recent trends among mainline Protestants, says, "Denominationalism is a relatively recent phenomenon and may have outlived its usefulness."[23] The Disciples of Christ, the United Church of Christ, the United Methodists, and the Southern Baptists are among the denominations which are now either implementing or devising plans for downsizing their denominational structures.

We have expended an entire chapter pondering the demise of the mainline denominations, not only because they represent another area where big did not lead to better and not only because we are both active church members, but also because in a downsized, more diverse, more politically open America, mediating nongovernmental institutions like our churches, synagogues, and mosques play a crucial role. Religious institutions tend not to want to be legitimized on the basis of their social utility; they see their primary purpose as the worship and service of God, and only secondarily as being helpful to the wider society. Yet while religious institutions are praising God and indoctrinating their young into their faith, they also have a powerful effect upon the lives of others, even others who may not hold their faith.

We believe that religious institutions always and everywhere do a better job of social aid and support than the federal government.[24] We know that some of this country's more creative educational solutions have arisen from the educational initiatives of the religious community. Throughout history, religious institutions — such as women's missionary societies and the African American church — have given the powerless their first experience of political empowerment, their first skills in organization, and a forum to address issues which were ignored by the wider society. A reformed United States, in which power is

---

22. Winter, p. 107.
23. Richey, p. 92.
24. Our assumption of the primacy of religious-based care is confirmed by Marvin Loasky, *Renewing American Compassion: How Compassion for the Needy Can Turn Ordinary Citizens into Heroes* (New York: Free Press, 1996).

returned to the local community, is a people in great need of locally managed, empowered, mediating institutions like our churches. Besides this, we believe that the current American situation is not just a political or economic crisis; it is at heart a moral, spiritual crisis, a crisis of meaning which results in a political crisis. Strong, vibrant, confident religious institutions are therefore essential to the future of this society.

Strategies for Decentralizing and Downsizing Religious Denominations

1. Decentralize decision-making power to the lowest level possible — the local congregation.
2. Reduce the size of the denominational central office staff.
3. Broaden the base of participation of laypeople.
4. Decentralize the delivery of services.
5. Make the process of electing corporate denominational officers more democratic.
6. Empower local congregations and individual members through the cultivation of small groups.

---

8 Our Moribund Welfare State

The American welfare state is politically vulnerable because it does not rest on a sense of national community adequate to its purpose. The nationalizing project that unfolded from the Progressive era to the New Deal to the Great Society succeeded only in part. It managed to create a strong national government but failed to cultivate a shared national identity. As the welfare state developed, it drew less on an ethic of social solidarity and mutual obligation and more on an ethic of fair procedures and individual rights. But the liberalism of the procedural republic proved an inadequate substitute for the strong sense of citizenship the welfare state requires.[1]

Social Welfare

No American institution has been more maligned by conservative politicians and more recently by liberals alike than our all-encompassing, highly ineffective, self-defeating social welfare system. Long before Barry Goldwater, George C. Wallace, Ronald Reagan, Newt Gingrich, and Pat Buchanan discovered the political benefits of running against

1. Michael J. Sandel, *Democracy's Discontent* (Cambridge: Harvard University Press, 1996), p. 346.

155

our ill-conceived, often corrupt system of public welfare, one conservative politician after another had railed against this multiheaded monster. Previously, critics claimed that most of our public assistance programs were little more than coercive forms of taxation and socialism. However, more recently they have been attacked by political liberals who argue that many well-intended programs breed dependence among recipients and reward immoral and irresponsible behavior.

Low-income housing, rent subsidies, federal aid to education, college scholarships, Medicare, Medicaid, food stamps, job training, Social Security, unemployment insurance, and public assistance are but a few of the plethora of federal social welfare programs in place today. Nearly 60 percent of the $1.6 trillion federal budget is spent on income security, Social Security, health care, Medicare, veterans' benefits, and education and training.

The Welfare State Bill of Rights

The right to a useful and remunerative job . . . the right to earn enough to provide adequate food and clothing and recreation . . . the right of every family to a decent home, the right to adequate medical care . . . the right to adequate protection from the economic fears of old age, sickness, accident, and unemployment . . . the right to a good education.

Franklin D. Roosevelt
State of the Union Address
January 11, 1944

Franklin D. Roosevelt's New Deal, Harry Truman's Fair Deal, John F. Kennedy's New Frontier, and Lyndon B. Johnson's Great Society were all variations on the same theme — giant social welfare projects. And the fundamental assumption underlying each of these programs was always the same: "big government" knows best how to solve the problems of our states, cities, towns, and villages. Unfortunately, our state and local governments were all too willing to abdicate their responsibilities to the U.S. government.

Some politicians were euphoric in their claims for what was possible for big government to accomplish. In his 1961 inaugural address, President John F. Kennedy said, "Man holds in his mortal hands the power to abolish all forms of human poverty." And a few years later in his Great Society speech, President Lyndon B. Johnson proclaimed,

> The Great Society rests on abundance and liberty for all. It demands an end to poverty and racial injustice, to which we are totally committed in our time. But that is just the beginning.
>
> The Great Society is a place where every child can find knowledge to enrich his mind and to enlarge his talents. It is a place where leisure is a welcome chance to build and reflect, not a feared cause of boredom and restlessness. It is a place where the city of man serves not only the needs of the body and the demands of commerce but the desire for beauty and the hunger for community.

Regrettably, the optimistic promises of the big welfare state have not been realized. Neither hunger, poverty, nor homelessness has been eliminated, and in many inner cities and abandoned rural areas they may even be worse than they were thirty years ago. Instead of solving our social welfare problems, we have created an expensive, complex system of multigenerational dependency.

Centralized Social Welfare

The major difficulty . . . is that it tends to destroy a sense of local responsibility for the well being of the local townspeople; when the state pays relief costs there is a feeling that there is no need to worry about the matter.

Andrew Nuquist

In his short-lived presidential campaign in 1968, Senator Robert F. Kennedy, one of the architects of the New Frontier, must have realized that few Americans had taken seriously his brother John's 1961 advice, "Ask not what your country can do for you — ask what you can do for your country." Senator Kennedy was one of the first liberal politicians to acknowledge that our social welfare system was perhaps "our greatest domestic failure." He noted that

> Millions of our people are slaves to dependency and poverty, waiting on the favor of their fellow citizens to write them checks. Fel-

lowship, community, shared patriotism — these essential values of our civilization do not come from just buying and consuming goods together. They come from a shared sense of individual independence and personal effort.[2]

All of this is in sharp contrast to Japan, where only 0.7 percent of the population receives benefits from the government compared with the 4.8 percent of Americans who receive grants from Aid to Families with Dependent Children or the 9.7 percent who receive food stamps.

Robert F. Kennedy on the Welfare State

The inheritance of the New Deal is fulfilled. There is not a problem for which there is not a program. There is not a problem for which money is not being spent. There is not a problem or program on which dozens or hundreds or thousands of bureaucrats are not earnestly at work.[3]

Even though we spend hundreds of billions of dollars annually on social welfare, our nation's social health appears to be deteriorating rather than improving. According to Fordham University's Index of Social Health, our nation's social well-being has fallen to its lowest level in 25 years, with children and young people suffering the most. This is hardly surprising when you consider that the federal government spends five times more on Americans over 65 than on those under 18.

The index measures the sixteen social indicators listed on page 159.[4]

The Congressional Budget Office projects that the Medicare trust fund will be insolvent by the year 2001 unless Medicare benefits are reduced or Medicare tax rates are boosted. Only a few years later the Social Security system is expected to be bankrupt as well. For this reason

2. Robert F. Kennedy, press release, Los Angeles, May 19, 1968, in Edwin O. Guthman and C. Richard Allen, eds., *RFK: Collected Speeches* (New York: Viking, 1993), pp. 385-86. Cited by Sandel, pp. 302-3.

3. Robert F. Kennedy, Utica, N.Y., February 7, 1966, in Guthman and Allen, pp. 208-9. Cited by Sandel, p. 300.

4. Marc Miringoff and Marque-Luisa Miringoff, "America's Social Health: The Nation's Need to Know," *Challenge,* September-October 1995, pp. 19-24.

Children:	Infant Mortality
	Child Abuse
	Children in Poverty
Youth:	Teen Suicide
	Drug Abuse
	High School Dropouts
Adults:	Unemployment
	Average Weekly Earnings
	Health-Insurance Coverage
Aging:	Poverty among Those Over 65
	Out-of-Pocket Health Costs for Those Over 65
All Ages:	Homicides
	Alcohol-Related Highway Deaths
	Food Stamp Coverage
	Access to Affordable Housing
	Gap between the Rich and Poor

we favor decentralizing the ownership and control of Social Security to the states and allowing private alternatives as well.

In summary, our gargantuan system of public welfare is too big, too bureaucratic, too expensive, and too inhumane, and it leads to excessive dependency, a loss of community, and a sense of powerlessness among its clients and victims. In addition, it has had too little impact on the social problems it was designed to solve. However, in August 1996, the Congress did take an initial step toward the decentralization of social welfare benefits by passing a radical welfare reform bill. The long-term effects of this legislation are not yet known.

Lest we be misunderstood and mistakenly equated with traditional welfare bashers, who blame all of our social problems on the victims — "welfare moms" and their children — we hasten to add that we are in no way against compassion. We favor more educational and jobs programs to enable people to obtain and keep employment. We are particularly disturbed by the plight of poor children in our society. We favor decentralized compassion administered locally rather than nationally — compassion that is active, participatory, and effective.

The Birth of a Revolutionary Class

For the first time in human history, Western societies will have a large group of affluent, economically inactive, elderly voters who require expensive social services like health care and who depend upon government for much of their income. It is a revolutionary class, one that is bringing down the social welfare state, destroying government finances, altering the distribution of purchasing power and threatening the investments that all societies need to make to have a successful future.

No public interest is served by making parents rich at the cost of making children poor.

Quite simply, we have to generate values that allow us to go beyond the normal welfare calculus of capitalism to a mentality in which the satisfaction of building a better tomorrow outweighs the immediate appeal of greater and greater consumption.[5]

Conservatives are often critical of "entitlements of the poor" but say little about "entitlements of the aged" — Social Security and Medicare — or "entitlements of large corporate farms" — agricultural price supports. A major thrust of this book is substituting empowerment for entitlements as a means of problem solving.

As a positive alternative to our moribund social welfare system, consider the Swiss approach. In Switzerland, the primary responsibility for social welfare rests with its twenty-six cantons (tiny states) and 3,020 communes. Unlike the United States, 95 percent of all Swiss citizens are insured against illness by one of the four hundred *private* health insurance funds.

Swiss children are taught in public schools the virtues of self-sufficiency, hard work, cooperation, and loyalty to family and community. Since public assistance is funded from local sources, it behooves the local community to discourage public dependency and to work with social welfare clients so that they may become self-sufficient as soon as possible. Public welfare is viewed as temporary — lasting only so long as the victim is impoverished.

5. Lester C. Thurow, "The Birth of a Revolutionary Class," *New York Times Magazine*, May 19, 1996, pp. 46-47.

The Swiss Way of Welfare

The lessons of Switzerland for other Western nations are clear. Social problems cannot be resolved without provision of appropriate employment, without control of immigration, without well-planned and earned social insurances, without promotion of family responsibility, without appropriate child socialization, without effective schooling aimed at academic excellence, without vocational preparation, and without cooperative support of such efforts by the domestic relations courts.

Only in the local community or neighborhood is it possible for agencies of social service and social control to keep close touch with one another in the individualized treatment of clients. Even then, the agencies must necessarily be autonomous and not constrained by national regulations, which preclude the design and administration of unified case planning. Switzerland has demonstrated that such coordination at the local level can be achieved and effectively carried out. Swiss welfare is local, cooperative and nonpoliticized. Finally, as the Swiss have amply demonstrated, the control and prevention of welfarization and its related social ills requires involvement of the citizenry in the local community.[6]

Aid plans are custom-designed on an individual basis with strict time limits imposed. The contract between the client and the local welfare agency is approached from a win-win perspective in which the objective is to help the client get back on his or her feet. For a nominal fee, it is possible to obtain any individual's tax return without having to state a reason. This helps keep welfare clients, as well as others, honest.

The Swiss practice what many politically conservative Americans preach but rarely practice themselves — complete decentralization of the responsibility for social welfare. The inescapable conclusion engendered by a visit to Switzerland is that Switzerland works. What can a global superpower like the United States learn from a small country with only 7 million people? A lot.

6. Ralph Segalman, *The Swiss Way of Welfare* (New York: Praeger, 1986), p. 195.

Strategies for Downsizing and Decentralizing Social Welfare

1. Abolish *all* federal government social welfare programs.
2. Transfer *all* responsibility for social welfare to the states and local communities.
3. Decentralize the ownership and control of the Social Security system to the states.
4. Initiate local bottom-up community social welfare programs as alternatives to top-down federal government programs.

The Health Care Labyrinth

Americans pay more for health care per capita, and more as a percent of the overall economy (14.4 percent of GNP), than any other country in the world. Collectively, we spend nearly a trillion dollars annually on health care services — $410 billion for hospitals, $200 billion for doctors, $110 billion for nursing homes and home health care, $100 billion for medicine, $65 billion for insurance, and $100 billion for dentists, optometrists, physical therapists, pharmacists, etc., of which administrative costs have been estimated to be as high as 30 percent.[7] By comparison, Canada, England, Germany, Japan, and Sweden all spend less than 10 percent of GNP on health care. But 42 million Americans have no health insurance whatsoever and another 50 million are significantly underinsured.

Ironically, America's huge investment in health care has had little impact on life expectancy or the incidence of sickness, when compared with other developed countries. The United States ranks only eighteenth in life expectancy among the developed countries of the world. Overall, Americans die younger, lose more babies, and are at least as likely to suffer from chronic disease as those living in other industrial nations which spend much less for health care.

Ultimately, the high price we pay for health care is determined by two immutable forces — our inordinate fear of death and the greed of health care providers and insurers.

7. Robert Sherrill, "The Madness of the Market," *Nation,* January 9, 1995, p. 48.

The Meaning of Good Health

We have come to ever more desire what we cannot any longer have in unlimited measure — a healthier, extended life — and cannot even afford to pursue much longer without harm to our personal lives and our other social institutions. If we are to have any hope of finding a long-lasting solution to our health care crisis, we must start by taking a hard look at that desire, one I share along with everyone else. Perhaps the health care problem is not quite what appears on the surface, just as a matter of improved financing, equity, and efficiency. Perhaps it is a crisis about the meaning and nature of health, and about the place that the pursuit of health should have in our lives. Any serious consideration of health care must, in any case, begin with that basic issue.[8]

Our fear of dying stems from our dread of the complete loss of control over our lives and the possibility that death may lead to nothingness. Few of us know how to die happy. One reason so few die happy is that we refuse to plan for the one event in our life which is absolutely certain — our own death. In the words of Albert Camus, "There is but one freedom, to put oneself right with death. After that, everything is possible." To cope with our fear of death, we spend our entire lives denying that we are going to die. Rather than helping us prepare for a happy death, many health care providers exploit our tendency to deny death by providing us with one death-defying technology after another.

For those who can afford health insurance, the sky is the limit when it comes to the use of magnetic resonance imaging, ultrasound, CAT scans, nuclear diagnostics, complex multiorgan transplants, coronary bypass surgery, artificial kidney machines, death-defying prenatal procedures, and emergency helicopter service. Our favorite high-tech medical procedure is the pig liver transplant, which enables the swine's organ to live on long after the death of its original owner.

Intensive-care medicine is by far the most expensive form of

---

8. Daniel Callahan, *What Kind of Life* (New York: Simon and Schuster, 1990), p. 11.

> ## Enhanced Quality of Life
>
> Among the very real benefits of American medicine, in addition to prevention of disease, lies the enhanced quality of life provided patients treated with state-of-the-art surgical techniques, life-improving medications, and high-tech medical procedures.
>
> Burton E. Sobel, M.D.
> University of Vermont Medical Center

medical care money can buy. We have over eighty-seven thousand intensive-care beds in the United States — more than any other country. Over 80 percent of our lifetime expenditure for health care occurs in

> ## Is Death a Curable Disease?
>
> Half the energy of the medical industry one suspects, may now be devoted to "examinations" or "tests" — to see if, though apparently well, we may not be latently or insidiously diseased.
>   It is not clear, why death should increasingly be looked upon as a curable disease, an abnormality, by a society that increasingly looks upon life as insupportably painful and/or meaningless.[9]

the last six months of our lives, during which "health care" serves as a euphemism for futile death denial.

Neither our physicians, our psychotherapists, nor our priests and rabbis do a very good job of teaching us how to die happy. Instead our health care providers charge too much, perform too many unnecessary operations and high-tech diagnostic tests, and prescribe too much expensive medication for which our employers, our insurance companies, and our government are increasingly unwilling to pay.

Although England has a higher life-expectancy rate than the United States, Neil Postman has noted in his book *Technopoly* that

9. Wendell Berry, *Another Turn of the Crank* (Washington, D.C.: Counterpoint, 1995), p. 88.

American doctors perform six times as many cardiac bypass operations per capita as English doctors do. American doctors perform more diagnostic tests than doctors do in France, Germany, or England. An American woman has two to three times the chance of having a hysterectomy as her counterpart in Europe; 60 percent of the hysterectomies performed in America are done on women under the age of forty-four. American doctors do more prostate surgery per capita than do doctors anywhere in Europe, and the United States leads the industrialized world in the rate of cesarean-section operations — 50 to 200 percent higher than in most other countries. When American doctors decide to forgo surgery in favor of treatment by drugs, they give higher dosages than doctors elsewhere. They prescribe about twice as many antibiotics as do doctors in the United Kingdom and commonly prescribe antibiotics when bacteria are likely to be present, whereas European doctors tend to prescribe antibiotics only if they know that the infection is caused by bacteria *and* is also serious. American doctors use far more x-rays per patient than do doctors in other countries.[10]

Fifty years ago a physician was a devoted public servant who called on his patients in their homes, would accept payment in kind (a chicken, a sack of tomatoes, or a fifth of Jack Daniels), and frequently was not paid at all. Today physicians, private profit-making hospitals, drug companies, and health insurance companies are engaged in a never-ending struggle to extract as much money as possible from patients, employees, and the government. How can a physician work for a for-profit hospital and still be bound by loyalty to the patient? Large health care conglomerates now provide their customers with a complete range of integrated health services, including insurance, pharmaceuticals, other health care products, outpatient medical service, hospitalization, surgery, medical testing, psychiatric care, nursing home and convalescence care, hospice care, and funeral services.

Although physicians' salaries have declined in recent years to an average of $150,000 annually, in the 1980s salaries of $250,000 to $300,000 were not at all uncommon, and some surgeons were making over $1 million. A 1995 study by the Pen Health Professions Commission has questioned whether we need 125 high-tech medical schools and their expensive, often underutilized teaching hospitals. Does North

10. Neil Postman, *Technopoly* (New York: Vintage, 1993), p. 94.

The Story of Martha

When 86-year-old Martha was admitted to the hospital with internal bleeding, she was virtually unable to walk. The bleeding turned out to have been caused by an anti-inflamatory medicine and subsided within forty-eight hours after she arrived in the hospital and the medication was discontinued. In spite of the fact that the bleeding had stopped, she was then subjected to two very traumatic and highly intrusive tests — a colonoscopy and an endoscopy. In addition, she was given an MRI and a spinal injection.

On the fifth day of Martha's stay in the hospital, she suffered the first of two heart attacks, spent two days in the cardiac intensive care unit, and was finally released at the end of her second week there. The total tab for the two weeks was over $25,000.

When Martha left the hospital, she had little to show for the $25,000 outlay paid for by Medicare and Blue Cross & Blue Shield. She was much weaker than when she entered the hospital, less self-sufficient, and still could not walk.[11]

Carolina, a relatively poor state with a population of 6.8 million, need four medical schools? Does Ohio need six? New York fourteen? Some physicians have argued that the problem lies not with too many medical schools but rather with the wrong mix. Perhaps some medical schools should specialize in medical research, others in acute care, and still others in preventive medicine.

There are twelve hundred private health insurance companies in America. The government pays for the health care of some through Medicare, Medicaid, the military, and the Veterans Administration, and also for the health care of Native Americans living on reservations. This complex labyrinth of private and public payment plans adds significantly to the administrative cost of health care, since all of these plans follow different eligibility, underwriting, benefit, and reimbursement policies.[12] To collect fees from all of these agencies, a physician needs

11. Thomas H. Naylor, Magdalena R. Naylor, and William H. Willimon, *The Search for Meaning Workbook* (Nashville: Abingdon, 1994), p. 36.

12. Ed Cooper and Liz Taylor, "Comparing Health Care Systems," *In Context*, no. 39, p. 35.

an army of clerical assistants. Is it any wonder that solo family practitioners may soon cease to exist? The cost of dealing with all of these payers is staggering.

> ### Holistic Health Care
>
> The medical approach, which treats people as the sum of a series of body parts, often fails to incorporate the many inter-related facets of illness — emotional, spiritual, existential, and interpersonal. As a result, modern medicine has shown only limited capacity to reduce some of the most common diseases of the developed world, many of which are caused by unhealthy life-styles — smoking, drinking, over-eating, etc. — and unhealthy social and natural environments — exposure to toxins, excessive stress, violence.
>
> We need to revive the historic mission of health care — the healing of the whole self. Healing that treats people as a sum of body parts, isn't.[13]

Ironically, while millions are being forced out of corporate America because of restructuring and downsizing, the rapidly deteriorating situation in the American health care industry has forced droves of private physicians either out of business or into the arms of corporate America. Because of previous abuses among private physicians, hospitals, and insurance companies, the health care system is becoming more centralized, forcing private physicians into HMOs (health maintenance organizations) and other large managed-care networks. At least in the short run, the entire health care field seems to be headed toward even bigger clinics, hospitals, insurance companies, and drug companies. The personal touch of the friendly, family, neighborhood physician has been replaced by the large, bureaucratic HMO and megahospital. Medicine is no longer a healing art, but rather a very big impersonal business. How long will it take the public to discover that big medicine is not necessarily better medicine?

As further evidence of the trend toward even bigger medicine, in June 1996 two of Manhattan's giant medical centers — New York

13. Sarah van Gelder, "Making Sense of Health Care," *In Context*, no. 39, p. 11.

University and Mount Sinai — announced they would merge. Two weeks later two of the city's largest teaching hospitals, Beth Israel Medical Center and Long Island Jewish Medical Center, followed suit.

As a trillion-dollar business, the American health care industry is dominated by big medicine (the American Medical Association), big hospitals and big hospital chains (Columbia/HCA Healthcare), big government (Medicare and Medicaid), big insurance, big pharmaceuticals, big university health centers, and big technology. Even with all of the computer power and high technology in the world, it is not humanly possible to design and implement either a national health care system or a national health insurance system — private or public — to meet the needs of 260 million people in fifty diverse states.

Canada's single payer system, Japan's universal health insurance system, Germany's sickness funds, Sweden's decentralized delivery system, Hawaii's employer-mandated universal health insurance, and America's managed care plans all have their pros and cons. But any lasting solution to our health care problems must confront head-on widespread patient death fear, health care provider greed, the sheer size of our country and our government, our existing health care institutions, and the lack of community connecting patients, physicians, hospitals, and payers.

As a result of our obsession with providing individuals with the maximum freedom of choice in selecting health care options and our complete aversion to national health insurance and socialized medicine, we may have unwittingly created an unwieldy monster that combines the worst features of free enterprise medicine and socialized medicine. Our health care system is not only very expensive, unbelievably high-tech, increasingly bureaucratic, and dehumanizing, but we often leave the hospital in worse condition than when we entered. This is called progress!

We have the mistaken view that it is possible to make the individual well even though he or she lives in a community infested with poverty, pollution, traffic congestion, work-related stress, crime, and substance abuse. But unhealthy communities breed unhealthy individuals and increase the cost of health care.

The abuse of alcohol, drugs, and tobacco kills 520,000 Americans each year. According to a 1995 study by the National Public Services Research Institute, a nonprofit policy research organization, alcohol abuse costs society $128 billion annually, drug abuse $122 billion, and tobacco $94 billion.

Health Is Membership

When the choice is between the health of a community and technological innovation, I choose the health of the community. I would unhesitantly destroy a machine before I would allow the machine to destroy my community.

I believe that the community — in the fullest sense: a place and all its creatures — is the smallest unit of health and that to speak of the health of an isolated individual is a contradiction in terms.[14]

The only way to bring down the cost of health care while providing high-quality medical services is to downsize hospitals, clinics, nursing homes, and insurance to a more human scale, to stress prevention more than treatment, and create an environment in which patients, doctors, nurses, hospitals, insurers, and employers are all in community with one another.

So long as an individual feels he or she has the freedom to spend, say, $500,000 of the community's health care resources for his or her open-heart surgery without any financial consequences whatsoever or any feeling of guilt about sucking up that amount from the community's health insurance reserves, health care costs will continue to spiral upward. In the past, doctors and hospitals were paid their fees by the insurance companies, who simply passed them on to employers, who usually paid the health insurance premiums for their employees. There was no need for the patient to feel guilty about the increased premiums, since they would be absorbed by the employer rather than other community members. It was all a very impersonal series of financial transactions. No one was financially accountable to anyone. It was as though no one seemed to care.

Under this ill-conceived scheme, some older patients relished that they were getting their money's worth from their insurance by soaking the system for $50,000 hospital stays and $100,000 operations. "I've got mine, Jack, and the rest of you be damned" was an all too prevalent attitude. Or, "I'm entitled to every high-tech procedure available — regardless of the cost and the impact it might have on future

14. Berry, p. 90.

insurance rates." What is truly amazing is that this irresponsible system survived as long as it did without major modifications.

Big-ticket health care decisions which absorb large amounts of the community's health care resources should be community decisions, not individual decisions alone. Whether a patient is entitled to a heart-lung transplant is a community decision involving the patient, physician, hospital, and other community members. Not every person in the community who wants a heart-lung transplant or some other exotic medical procedure is entitled to one. How old is the patient? What is the overall condition of the patient's health? Does the patient contribute to the well-being of the community? Does the patient plan to remain in the community? These are among the tough questions community councils must answer before committing the community's health care resources to a particular individual.

Some may argue that community involvement in major health care resource allocation decisions is tantamount to politicizing health care. So what else is new? Our present inequitable system excludes many poor African Americans, Native Americans, Hispanics, and children from participation in the exclusive, high-tech medicine club whose membership is restricted to those who can afford the very best health insurance.

We must acknowledge up front that we don't have the resources to provide every patient who needs an MRI, a CAT scan, kidney dialysis, open-heart surgery, or emergency helicopter service with these very expensive services. Who is entitled to receive these services? Just the super-rich? The community providing the resources should have a say in who is entitled to service — the village, the town, or the neighborhood, but not the state.

We would significantly downsize all large hospitals to no more than a couple of hundred beds. Not every hospital must offer state-of-the-art diagnostic tests and other medical procedures. The community would decide whether or not to invest in MRI or CAT scan equipment, how to finance this expensive equipment, and who has access to it. Large urban and university medical center hospitals heavily subsidized by the state and federal governments would be scaled back. A group of towns or neighborhoods might opt to pool their limited resources and build a regional, high-tech, acute care hospital serving the communities which support it. But eligibility to use the regional hospital would again be controlled by the respective local communities that own it.

Strategies for Downsizing and Decentralizing Health Care

1. Abolish Medicare and Medicaid.
2. Close the U.S. Department of Health and Human Services.
3. Repeal all federal health care regulations.
4. Eliminate all federal health care subsidies.
5. Encourage states and local communities to come up with decentralized public and private alternatives for financing and delivering health care services.
6. Practice holistic medicine which treats the physiological, spiritual, emotional, and intellectual needs of individual patients as well as the community as a whole.
7. Promote local community responsibility for health care.
8. Spend less of the local community's limited resources on sophisticated, high-tech medical devices.
9. Spend more of the community's health care resources on teaching people how to live healthy, meaningful lives and how to die happy.

Medicare and Medicaid are failing. As a nation, we need a national debate on whether or not to continue costly, ineffective programs like Medicare, Medicaid, and the Veterans Administration hospitals.

If medical students require subsidies, they should be subsidized by the local communities to which they will return to practice medicine, not by the monolithic federal government. Just as we have argued that the federal government should get out of public education, higher education, and social welfare, so too should it get out of health care. The primary responsibility for the physical, mental, spiritual, and emotional health of a village, town, or neighborhood rests with the local community.

Most research and development in the health care industry would be privately financed by health care–related firms such as pharmaceutical companies. But there would be nothing to prevent a group of communities, a town, or a city from organizing and financing its own research and development center and collaborating with others concerning a health problem of particular concern to people in the area, such as AIDS, lung cancer, or some other malady. Medical research and development priorities should be driven by local needs, not by national public relations campaigns.

There is no national fix to America's health care problems. Local communities must become involved in the solution of their own health care problems. If conservative politicians are serious about improving the quality and containing the cost of health care, they must do more than rail against the federal government; they must start preaching serious local health care responsibility and preventive health maintenance as each citizen's responsibility.

Big Charities: Accountable to No One

As an alternative to government-supported social welfare programs, nonprofit charitable foundations, private colleges and universities, private hospitals, human service organizations, and religious institutions have considerable appeal. Annual revenues of nonprofits are nearly $1.5 trillion. Among the better-known nonprofit charitable organizations are United Way, the Red Cross, the Boy Scouts of America, Save the Children, and the National Association for the Advancement of Colored People (NAACP). Charitable giving amounts to nearly $150 billion each year in the United States.

However, the image of nonprofit charities was severely shattered in 1994 and 1995 by a series of scandals. William Aramony, the former CEO of United Way, the nation's premier nonprofit organization, was convicted of defrauding the organization of $1.2 million and sent to prison for seven years. The NAACP sustained a similar blow when its executive director was dismissed for giving $332,000 of the association's funds to a former employee who had alleged sexual harassment. The organization was also found to be $3.8 million in debt.

On a much larger scale, the Foundation for New Era Philanthropy, a tax-exempt charitable organization that solicited funds from colleges and universities, museums, and other nonprofit organizations with promises that it would double their money, filed for bankruptcy with liabilities in excess of $500 million. The United Nations Children's Fund acknowledged losing $10 million through serious fraud and mismanagement in its Kenya office. Finally, two child-sponsorship organizations, Save the Children and the Christian Children's Fund, were accused of overstating the percentage of sponsorship contributions which actually reaches poor children.

Although Americans are donating more to charity than ever before, the percentage of people who contribute declined from 73 per-

Big Foundations[15]

	Assets
1. Ford Foundation	$6.6 billion
2. Packard Foundation	6.3
3. W. K. Kellogg Foundation	6.0
4. J. Paul Getty Trust	6.0
5. Robert Wood Johnson Foundation	3.8
6. Pew Charitable Trusts	3.3
7. Lilly Endowment, Inc.	3.1
8. MacArthur Foundation	2.9
9. Rockefeller Foundation	2.4
10. Andrew W. Mellon Foundation	2.2

cent in 1993 to 69 percent in 1995 according to a Gallup poll. The survey also showed a growing distrust among Americans about how charities handle donations.

As an example of what can go wrong in huge nonprofit charitable organizations, consider the case of child sponsorship organizations. One of us, Thomas, had the opportunity to observe one such organization, the Christian Children's Fund (CCF), at very close range between January 1992 and April 1994 as a member of its board of directors. Shortly after I was removed from the board for "whistle-blowing," both the president and the chairman of the board resigned.

Hundreds of thousands of Americans are seduced by emotionally charged TV advertisements into sending monthly checks to private child-sponsorship organizations such as CCF, Childreach, Save the Children, and World Vision. Long before I joined the board of CCF, I had been a sponsor of a child in Bangladesh through Save the Children. The possibility of sponsoring one's own child in an impoverished Third World country has enormous appeal. It's neat, clean, tax-deductible, and hassle-free. You don't have to travel anywhere; you need not see or touch any smelly, filthy children; and you avoid the risk of disease and sickness. Even though you are completely detached from your child, writing a check makes you feel good.

15. Source: The Foundation Center, as reported in the *New York Times*, May 6, 1996, p. B9.

Can Public Trust in Nonprofits Be Restored?

Scandals have undermined society's most important institutions.

The performance of nonprofits is shrouded behind a veil of secrecy that is lifted when disasters occur.

Without information, the public can't know if an organization is fulfilling its mission.[16]

But are these nongovernmental charitable organizations all they are cracked up to be? How confident can you be that your contribution will actually benefit poor children? To whom are these organizations accountable?[17]

While poring over a troubling internal audit report alleging improprieties in a CCF office in Brazil, a fellow board member proclaimed, "This is scary stuff." Even though I had been on the board for eighteen months, it had not sunk in that being a board member of a $112 million charitable organization is an awesome responsibility.

At least in theory, board members have a fiduciary responsibility to the hundreds of thousands of sponsors and sponsored children. In practice they are accountable to no one. There are no stockholders or government regulations to protect the interests of sponsors or children. Neither sponsors, sponsored children, nor employees have any voice in the election of members to these self-perpetuating boards. Free of public regulatory pressures, charitable boards operate as islands unto themselves.

Unfortunately, when one joins the board of a large international charity, it is all too easy to be seduced by the don't-rock-the-boat culture in which strategic planning, performance results, accountability, and financial control are clearly secondary to organizational growth, public relations gimmicks, and international razzmatazz. A press release announcing a $10,000 grant for Indian earthquake victims is far more important than evaluating the grant's impact in a place where the charity has no on-site infrastructure or comparative advantage.

---

16. Regina E. Herzlinger, "Can Public Trust in Nonprofits and Governments Be Restored?" *Harvard Business Review,* March-April 1996, pp. 97-107.

17. Thomas H. Naylor, "The Trouble with Child-Sponsorship Organizations," *Chronicle of Philanthropy,* January 12, 1995.

If individual board members are not attentive, management is free to do what it chooses. It's easy to distract the board with issues such as choosing the right celebrity for the charity's TV spots rather than trying to determine whether sponsors' expectations are being realized in the delivery of services to poor children. Frequently the relationship between the board and senior management is based on the aphorism "Ask me no questions, and I will tell you no lies."

Child-sponsorship promotional literature trades heavily on the claim, for example, that eighty cents of every dollar contributed benefits children and their families. This is a very strong statement, but is it true? In reality neither the management, the board, nor the external auditors of these charities have a clue as to what percentage of each sponsor's contribution actually reaches children. The financial and management control systems required to make such bold statements do not exist.

The audited financial reports of these organizations are misleading, since they report only on highly aggregated macrofinancial data provided by management. The typical audit report contains no information about what is happening in particular countries or specific child development projects. How much is actually being spent on overhead and fund-raising in a given country is completely unknown to the outside auditors — not to mention funds which may have been misappropriated through incompetence, fraud, or corruption.

When told about a project leader in a rural village using sponsorship funds to start her own beauty salon, video rental shop, and school supply business, the chairman of CCF quipped, "You know how it is in these Third World countries." Monitoring child development projects in developing nations is a difficult business. But child sponsorship organizations shouldn't make unsubstantiated claims about how much money reaches children.

Another way charities play fast and loose with creative accounting is through the use of millions of dollars worth of unaudited gifts-in-kind. By acting as transfer agents distributing large gifts of food, medicine, and medical supplies for needy nations, child sponsorship agencies artificially inflate their income to counteract the effects of declining sponsorship revenues. The adverse effects of gifts-in-kind on cash available to children can be quite significant.

Suppose, for example, that a charity embraces the so called 80-20 rule, claiming that 80 percent of *all* contributions go to support children with the remaining 20 percent used for management and fund-raising.

For every $1 million received in gifts-in-kind, the organization can literally reduce cash outlays to children by $200,000 and still maintain the 80-20 rule. This is how CCF could afford to send twenty board members and fifteen senior officers to Poland in 1993 for a week in the most posh hotel in Warsaw. All of this is perfectly legal and consistent with "accepted accounting practices." That it is unethical and misleading doesn't seem to matter.

With no government agencies looking over their shoulders, the task of policing the financial affairs of child sponsorship agencies and other charities has been assumed by three private watchdog groups — the National Charities Information Bureau, the Philanthropic Advisory Service of the Council of Better Business Bureaus, and the recently formed American Institute of Philanthropy.

What these watchdogs have in common is that they publish evaluations of charities based almost entirely on information provided by the charities themselves. These toothless tigers possess neither the staff nor the resources to dig below the surface and investigate individual foreign country offices or child development projects. They too have no way of knowing what percentage of the sponsor's dollar reaches the children or their families.

Money magazine and *Forbes*, in turn, process the information provided by the charities and the watchdogs and publish their own periodic "independent" evaluation of charitable organizations. Individual contributors incorrectly conclude that if a charity has been endorsed by *Money* and *Forbes*, everything must be okay.

The rationale underlying child sponsorship as a form of charitable giving is that many Americans who will not contribute to the poor will pay twenty dollars per month to support "my own child." Throughout the 1970s and 1980s soul-wrenching TV spots depicting the plight of poor children generated hundreds of millions of dollars of child sponsorship income. As one CCF board member expressed it, "We always led the way in finding the right promotional gimmick." But as Americans have become better educated and more affluent, the appeal of tear-jerking TV spots has tapered off in the 1990s.

This decline in sponsorship income has prompted some child sponsorship agencies to seek help from the U.S. Agency for International Development (USAID) to bolster their income. But USAID is one of the most highly criticized agencies of the U.S. government. Not only did it have difficulty sorting out the differences between humanitarian aid and Cold War military assistance, but many of its Third World projects have been mired in inefficiency and corruption. Why would any self-respecting private child-development organization want to emulate USAID?

The sheer amount of record keeping required to support child sponsorship is enormous and quite expensive — notwithstanding modern computer technology. For example, there was some accounting mix-up with every contribution I made to CCF. A $500 gift to the agency's work in Guatemala resulted in three mutually contradictory thank you notes, thus making me wonder what actually happened to the funds I contributed. There are even occasional reports of dead children being sponsored. Proving a sponsor's contribution goes to a particular child is not easy under the best of circumstances. Sponsorship also creates a class system at the project level. Sponsored children are often viewed as superior to others. Loss of sponsorship can be psychologically damaging.

Child sponsorship is an inefficient way to raise money based on questionable ethical practices. Although hundreds of thousands of children have benefited from sponsorship, other alternatives should be considered such as family, village, or project sponsorship. For example, a Sunday school class might sponsor a family for $100 per month or a Rotary Club might support a school or village for a year for $5,000. Not only would this type of sponsorship be more cost-effective, but it overcomes some of the ethical questions underlying child sponsorship.

Is it really possible for a highly centralized bureaucratic organization to funnel over $100 million annually to four hundred thousand sponsored children in fifteen hundred child development projects in forty countries, and do so efficiently? We think not.

Big Little League Baseball

Little League Baseball is the largest organized youth sports program in the world with 3 million participants on 196,000 teams in ninety-one countries.

The downsizing of corporate America provides dramatic evidence that growth for growth's sake is a mixed blessing — that bigger no longer means better. Just as many a corporate giant has become too big to manage effectively, so too is the case with some global child sponsorship organizations and other large charities as well. The gap between sponsors (contributors) and children (clients) is simply too great for there to be any reasonable chance of effective project management and control. At CCF, for example, the development group attracts sponsors through advertising. Sponsor relationships are managed by sponsor services, which passes checks on to accounting and finance for transmittal to the agency's offices abroad. These offices may be responsible for over one hundred projects in countries like Brazil and India. Specific projects are managed by family councils at the village level. At least five levels of management are involved in every child development project.

These problems are generic to large-scale, multinational child sponsorship organizations and have little to do with the personalities of individual managers. The horror stories reported in the field are the logical consequences of too much money passing through too many organizational levels for the good of the children or their sponsors who live too far away.[18]

The problems of the poor, the underprivileged, and the disenfranchised are not amenable to solutions imposed by large hierarchical organizations — private or public — located thousands of miles away. Solutions require the bottom-up participation of those affected, as well as a sense of community connecting those who have been victimized (poor children and their families) with those in a position to influence the results. Maybe such organizations have to be located in the country or even the village where the children live to be truly effective. The number of management levels separating donors and children has to be reduced. Ultimately, there may be no substitute for two-way, donor-family engagement, and that is a higher price than most of us are prepared to pay.

One of us had extensive experience with Christian Community Development, an indigenous, grass-roots organization in Honduras that places North American church groups in the villages of Honduras for hands-on experience with Honduran hosts. These experiences empower the Hondurans and educate the North Americans.

While claiming to be a positive alternative to the highly central-

18. For a riveting analysis of the endless abuses of governmental and nongovernmental aid organizations operating in the Third World countries, see the book by Michael Maren, *The Road to Hell* (New York: Free Press, 1997).

ized, top-down approach to foreign aid practiced by the U.S. Agency for International Development, many large American international charitable organizations such as the Christian Children's Fund and Save the Children actually emulate the management style of the USAID. There is little difference between large-scale public and private foreign assistance organizations. Not surprisingly, public and congressional support for U.S. government foreign aid to developed countries continues to trail off. The United States now ranks twenty-first among the world's twenty-one leading industrial countries in the amount of foreign aid it gives in relation to its GNP. We spend only $7.3 billion annually on foreign aid, which represents 0.1 percent of GNP.

Four Maxims for Charitable Giving

1. Ask the right questions about the finances and delivery of services by large domestic and international charitable organizations.
2. Avoid contributing to large-scale multinational charitable organizations with inadequate financial and management controls.
3. Support smaller charitable organizations based in the region or country where the services are to be delivered.
4. Whenever possible become personally involved in the delivery of services yourself.

Empowering the Poor

The explosion of federal government intrusion into the world of the poor and dispossessed began in the New Deal. In his first inaugural address, Franklin Roosevelt called for a re-creation of America whereby our citizens would "move as a trained and loyal army willing to sacrifice for the good of common discipline." Citizens ought to be "ready and willing to submit our lives and property to such discipline," all for the "larger purpose." Translated this meant bigger government, solutions imposed from the top, and a vast array of governmental functionaries to enforce the solutions.

Later, John Kennedy would also call for the subordination of local interests in urging us to "Ask not what your country can do for you — ask what you can do for your country." It was not surprising when Lyndon Johnson took his cue from Roosevelt and reached for military metaphors to describe what he wanted to do to and for the poor: "War," said Johnson, "evokes cooperation . . . [and a] sense of brotherhood and unity."

The depiction of the nation in this presidential rhetoric was a mighty, all-powerful, completely able instrument to work good. The good that needed doing can only be worked if we are all unified, sacrificial, and moving to the beat of one drummer. The depiction of the poor is that of hapless, helpless, passive victims who are in need of a cadre of professionals who dispense programs through a vast bureaucracy.[19]

This arrangement was criticized years ago by Stokely Carmichael and Charles Hamilton in their book *Black Power,* where they urged blacks to "recognize the need to assert their own definitions, to reclaim their history, their culture; to create their own sense of community and togetherness." Carmichael and Hamilton thus saw the downside of federal government beneficence, the restrictive, oppressive nature of the calls for national unity and initiative. "We must begin to think of the black community as a base of organization to control institutions in that community," they said. Their thought, considered revolutionary at the time, makes more sense than ever today.[20]

At the beginning of the United States, Alexis de Tocqueville's *Democracy in America* celebrated the ability of Americans, at the local level, to form voluntary associations to right the wrongs within their society. These bottom-up solutions were a uniquely American invention, said Tocqueville: "Americans of all ages, all stations in life, and all types of dispositions are forever forming associations." A comparatively weak central state, Tocqueville noted, was a conscious invention of the Founders to insure that there was maximum political room for small, intimate, decentralized political action. The Founders "thought it also right to give each part of the land its own political life so that there should be an infinite number of occasions for the citizens to act

19. See the account of the relationship between a powerful federal government and poverty in Michael S. Joyce and William Schambra, "A New Civic Life," in *To Empower the People: From State to Civil Society,* ed. Peter L. Berger and Richard John Neuhaus (Washington, D.C.: AEI Press, 1996), pp. 11-29.

20. Stokely Carmichael and Charles V. Hamilton, *Black Power: The Politics of Liberation in America* (New York: Random House, 1967). William Julius Wilson, *When Work Disappears: The World of the New Urban Poor* (New York: Knopf, 1996), depicts the devastation wrought among the urban (predominantly black) poor. But his prescription is more top-down, big government paternalism and programs.

together and so that every day they should feel that they depend on one another."[21]

We believe that the most humane, empowering solutions for the plight of the poor lie in these local, bottom-up, voluntary associations, preferably those in which the poor participate. The best ideas will arise there, where the poor themselves have a hand in their empowerment. "Progressive" must not mean, as it has meant too often in our political past, more government, a more militaristic, bureaucratic approach to human action, but rather the local action of people joining together to better their lives.[22] In 1994, 89 million citizens over the age of eighteen gave an average of 4.5 hours per week in volunteer service to make their communities more compassionate and caring. We believe this sort of compassionate, grassroots action is the way to the future.

Considering the history of American politics since the New Deal and the Great Society, it is interesting how quickly Americans became disenchanted with top-down, heavy-handed federal governmental solutions to what ails us. As Michael S. Joyce and William Schambra have said in their piece "A New Civic Life,"

> After 1964, *no one* would again win the presidency by boasting about building a Great Society, a great national community in America. *No one* would again call proudly and forthrightly for a shift of power to Washington and away from the local organic networks. Indeed, every president from 1968 to the present has placed at the center of his agenda the *denunciation* of centralized, bureaucratic government, along with promises to slash its size and power and to reinvigorate states, small communities, and civil society's intermediate associations.[23]

21. Alexis de Tocqueville, *Democracy in America* (Garden City, N.Y.: Doubleday, 1969), p. 513.

22. For a detailed exposition of the ways in which local communities are mobilized to do a better job with charity than the federal or state government does with welfare, see the essays in Peter L. Berger and Richard J. Neuhaus, eds., *To Empower the People: From State to Civil Society* (Washington, D.C.: AEI Press, 1996).

23. Joyce and Schambra, p. 23.

9 Mighty Morphin Superpowers

> . . . the United States now runs the risk, so familiar to historians of the rise and fall of previous Great Powers, of what might be called "imperial overstretch": that is to say, decision makers in Washington must face the awkward and enduring fact that the sum of the total United States' global interests and obligations is nowadays far greater than the country's power to defend them all simultaneously.[1]

The Green Mountain Boys

On any given day one can see up to twenty gas-guzzling F-16 fighter jets flying in and out of Burlington International Airport. (The airport is called international even though there is no foreign country to which one can fly from Burlington.) Not only do these screaming Cold War relics endanger the lives of hundreds of commercial airline passengers each day, but they also fly at dangerously low altitudes over Burlington and the University of Vermont campus. At $20 million a pop, the F-16s are the pride of "the Green Mountain Boys," the Vermont Air National Guard unit named after legendary folk hero Ethan Allen's pre-Revolu-

---

1. Paul Kennedy, *The Rise and Fall of the Great Powers* (New York: Random House, 1987), p. 515.

Vermont Joke

A man pulls up to a Vermont woodcutter and says, "I want to place an order for a cord of firewood." The Vermonter recoils saying, "Look, I don't take orders from nobody!"

---

tionary minutemen volunteers. (The Green Mountain Boys now have one female F-16 pilot.) The original Green Mountain Boys helped carve out the independent state of Vermont from territory previously claimed by New York and New Hampshire and managed to avoid ever killing anyone — so the story goes.

But now that the Cold War is over, from whom are the F-16s protecting Vermont? With the closing of the Plattsburgh, New York, Air Force base, upstate New York hardly seems a threat. That leaves New Hampshire or possibly Massachusetts? Or is the real villain independence-minded Quebec to the north?

No major battle between European invaders and Native Americans ever took place on Vermont soil. Only one minor skirmish occurred in Vermont during the American Revolution. The lone Civil War engagement fought in Vermont, in Saint Albans, was more like a Jesse James — style bank robbery carried out by a handful of Confederate soldiers.

Why would anyone invade Vermont? Only Wyoming has a smaller population. Vermont has virtually no mineral resources of value, is one of the least-violent states in the nation, and has no military bases. What if a country such as Canada, China, Japan, or Russia were to invade the Green Mountain State? What would it do with Vermont? Would all of the black-and-white Holsteins be confiscated or perhaps the entire sugar maple crop be cut over? Imagine trying to force freedom-loving Vermonters into slave labor.

Vermont is too small, too rural, and too independent to be invaded by anyone. Furthermore, Vermonters, not unlike the Swiss, tend to stick to their own knitting rather than intrude into the affairs of their neighbors. Vermont has always been that way and probably always will.

No Duty to Retreat

As a nation our attraction to war and military solutions to problems is nothing new, since as we pointed out in our discussion of urban America, the United States is one of the most violent nations in the world. Our penchant for intergroup violence — ethnic, racial, agrarian, frontier, religious, and industrial — is without equal. Americans have always turned to violence when provoked by either domestic or foreign enemies.

Bombs Bursting in Air

Our history is filled with acts of public terror and mayhem in all parts of the country, from the first settlements onward. Hardly a decade has passed without deadly rioting, bombing or vigilante brutality. Vigilante attacks, among the most common forms of political violence, have almost always been meted out in the name of patriotism, moral decency, and law and order against perceived threats, be they from abolitionists, uppity blacks, undesired immigrants — or abortion doctors.[2]

Historian Richard Maxwell Brown provides convincing evidence in his book *No Duty to Retreat: Violence and Values in American History and Society* that America's history of violence has been strongly influenced by the common law of self-defense, of which the American version differs significantly from the original English doctrine:

> At the core of the English common law of self-defense was the concept of retreat. Thus, in the English common law going back to the middle ages the first obligation of a threatened individual in a personal dispute — even an individual without fault in the quarrel — was to flee from the scene. With one of two antagonistic individuals gone a homicide could not possibly occur. Should it be impossible, however, to get away, the English common law required the individual to retreat as far as possible — retreat "to the wall"

2. Sean Wilentz, "Bombs Bursting in Air, Still," *New York Times,* June 25, 1995, p. 40.

was the legal phrase — before resisting and perhaps killing in an act of lawful self-defense.

In essence, the legal duty to retreat was a command to individuals to forsake physical combat. To lawyers and judges, this doctrine became known as the DUTY TO RETREAT, and according to it you had to prove in open court that you had obeyed the duty to retreat before you could be found not guilty of committing murder in self-defense.

The colonists brought the English common law with them, but in the nineteenth century, American courts and judges made mincemeat of the duty to retreat and replaced it with the American doctrine of NO DUTY TO RETREAT — of the right to stand one's ground and, if need be, kill in self-defense.[3]

If one combines the no-duty-to-retreat doctrine with the American frontier spirit, then assassinations, riots, bombings, shootouts, gunfights, lynchings, and massacres become the rule — not the exceptions.

The American Frontier

The most important effect of the frontier has been in the promotion of democracy. The frontier is productive of individualism. Complex society is precipitated by the wilderness into a kind of primitive organization based on the family. The tendency is anti-social. It produces antipathy to control, and particularly to any direct control. The tax-gatherer is viewed as a representative of oppression.

To the frontier the American intellect owes its striking characteristics. That coarseness and strength combined with acuteness and inquisitiveness; that practical, inventive turn of mind, quick to find expedients; that masterful grasp of material things, lacking in the artistic but powerful to effect great ends; that restless, nervous energy; that dominant individualism, working for good and evil, and withal that buoyancy and exuberance which comes with freedom — these are traits of the frontier.[4]

---

3. Richard Maxwell Brown, "American Violence and Values in Historical Perspective" (paper presented at the Oklahoma City University Mid-Year Institute, January 3, 1996).

4. Frederick Jackson Turner, "The Significance of the Frontier in American History," *The Annual Report of the American Historical Association for 1893.*

> ### We're No. 1
>
> We proudly declare ourselves to be No. 1, the world's only remaining superpower. Naturally, the discontented of the world hold us responsible for their plight: their poverty, their ignorance, their weakness, their irrelevance. . . . We extol such principles as democracy, individualism, consumerism and the marketplace of ideas as though they were uncontested virtues. . . .
>
> We lead an economic system that has effectively buried every other form of production and distribution — leaving great wealth and sometimes great ruin in its wake. We purvey a culture based on mass entertainment and mass gratification: one that extols hedonism and accumulation even as it describes them as individualism and abundance. . . .
>
> Unlike more traditional conquerors, we are not content merely to subdue others: We insist that they be like us. And of course for their own good. We are the world's most relentless proselytizers. The world must be democratic. It must be capitalistic.[5]

These combined ideas also help explain how militarization has become the defining element in American history. We began assembling one of the greatest war machines of all time in 1940 and never got around to disassembling it. In his book *In the Shadow of War*, Michael S. Sherry discusses how for over fifty years military issues have shaped our politics, the expansion of our government, our economy, and our culture. The "war on poverty," the "war on drugs," and the "culture wars" are not just descriptive metaphors but evidence of a distinctively militarized national psychology. We simply know of no other means of national mobilization (see? another military metaphor!) than the model of the military.

Great Powers

Just as the Vermont Air National Guard maintains twenty F-16s, so too does the U.S. government continue to spend over $250 billion annually

5. Ronald Steel, "When Worlds Collide," *New York Times*, July 21, 1996, p. E15.

on military defense, even though the Cold War ended with the collapse of the Soviet Union in 1991.

In over two hundred years, the North American continent has not been attacked — nor even seriously threatened with invasion by Japan, Germany, the Soviet Union, or anyone else. But over a million Americans have been killed in wars and trillions of dollars have been spent by the military — nearly $13 *trillion* on the Cold War alone.

Far from defending our population, our government has drafted Americans and sent them to die in the battlefields of Europe (twice), on tropical Pacific islands, and in the jungles of Southeast Asia. On dozens of occasions over the past two centuries our political leaders have used minor incidents as provocation to justify sending troops to such far-flung places as China, Russia, Egypt, Greenland, Uruguay, the Samoa Islands, Cuba, Mexico, Haiti, Nicaragua, Panama, Grenada, Lebanon, and Iraq.

Global Superpowers

The great powers are the ones which are artificial structures and which, because they are artificial, need such consuming efforts to maintain themselves. As they did not come into existence by natural development but by conquest, so they cannot maintain themselves except by conquest — the constant reconquest of their own citizens through a flow of patriotic propaganda setting in at the cradle and ending only at the grave.[6]

During the 1980s, while accusing the Soviet Union of excessive military aggression, the Reagan administration was participating in nine known wars — in Afghanistan, Angola, Cambodia, Chad, El Salvador, Ethiopia, Lebanon, Morocco, and Nicaragua — not to mention our bombing of Libya, invasion of Grenada, and repeated attempts to bring down Panamanian dictator Manuel Antonio Noriega. Without any sense of irony whatsoever, President George Bush condemned Saddam Hussein for replicating in Kuwait precisely what Bush had done in Panama a few months earlier; namely, invading a tiny country

6. Leopold Kohr, *The Breakdown of Nations* (New York: E. P. Dutton, 1978), p. 58.

with a huge military force and setting up a puppet government. Bush then deployed five hundred thousand American troops, fifty warships, and one thousand warplanes to the Persian Gulf at the "invitation" of King Fahd of Saudi Arabia "to teach Saddam Hussein a lesson."

Global Supercop

The Cold War may have ended, but Washington policymakers don't seem to have noticed. America, facing no serious security threats, accounts for roughly 40 percent of the globe's military spending. Our expenditures outpace those of Russia by three or more to one; America spends twice as much as Britain, France, Germany, and Japan combined. What for? During the Cold War the doctrine of containment provided a coherent rationale for a large military in advanced outposts around the globe. That justification has obviously vanished, so today policymakers are busy concocting new "vital" missions to replace that of resisting communism. . . .

Today, anyway, not all international problems are our problems. Rather than dreaming up new purposes for Cold War institutions and forces, policymakers should stop encouraging Washington to act as an international cop out to police the rest of the globe.[7]

So common is war to Americans that it has become trivialized. When General Norman Schwarzkopf, commander of the allied forces in the Persian Gulf War, returned from the 1991 war, he led a victory parade down Disney World's Main Street, with Donald Duck and Mickey Mouse at his side.

But lest all of this sound like the United States is unique in its passion for war, nearly 40 million people have been killed by this century's international and civil wars. Even more disturbing is R. J. Rummel's book *Death by Government,* in which he concludes that during this same period "170 million men, women, and children have been shot, beaten, tortured, knifed, burned, starved, frozen, crushed, or worked to death; buried alive, drowned, hung, bombed, or killed in any other of the myriad ways governments have inflicted death on

7. Doug Bandow, "Uncle Sam, International Nanny," *Chronicles*, May 1996, pp. 16-18.

unarmed, helpless citizens and foreigners."[8] The explanation given by Rummel for all of this mass killing by government, *democide*, is that

> The more power a government has the more it can act arbitrarily according to the whims and desires of the elite, and the more it will make war on others and murder its foreign and domestic subjects. The more constrained the power of governments, the more power is diffused, checked, and balanced, the less it will aggress on others and commit democide.[9]

Democratic governments have proved to be as warlike and violent as nondemocratic governments with the single exception that democratic states do not make war on other democracies. Since more people have been killed in this century *by their own governments* than have died in war, one might be tempted to conclude that the most evil invention of humanity is the modern nation.

Twentieth-Century Megamurderers[10]			
Dictator	*Country*	*Period*	*Murders (thousands)*
Stalin	USSR	1929-53	42,672
Mao	China	1923-76	37,828
Hitler	Germany	1933-45	20,946
Chiang Kai-shek	China	1921-48	10,214
Lenin	USSR	1917-24	4,017
Tojo	Japan	1941-45	3,990
Pol Pot	Cambodia	1968-87	2,397

The Temple of Doom

Although right-wing politicians, religious fundamentalists, and American Sovietologists had been telling us since the late 1940s that "You can't trust the Russians," former President Ronald Reagan was

8. R. J. Rummel, *Death by Government* (New Brunswick, N.J.: Transaction Publishers, 1994), p. 9.

9. Rummel, pp. 1-2.

10. Rummel, p. 8.

without equal in terms of his ability to stir up anti-Soviet feelings among Americans.

Reagan was driven to show that literally everything the Soviets did was suspect and that no part of the Soviet arms buildup in the 1970s and 1980s was in response to American arms building or to the Soviets' perceptions of U.S. motives. Everything that was true and good was on our side, and the Soviets were to blame for everything that went wrong in the world. Simplistic though it may have been, the American people were mesmerized by this view of the Soviet Union.

The Readiness Gap

The U.S. has the finest and best financed military in the world. It is also the most ready, prepared to go thousands of miles on short notice. But it is inadequately controlled by civilian superiors. As a result, the "nonpolitical" admirals and generals running the military are taking all of us to the cleaners, using the readiness gap to snatch up precious dollars to defend against a threat that no longer exists.[11]

Psychologists use the term *character disorder* to describe the neurotic behavior of people who blame all of their problems on someone else. According to Ralph K. White, global superpowers such as the United States and the former Soviet Union suffer from three common neuroses — an exaggerated fear of their "enemies," "macho pride," and a complete inability ever to admit error.[12]

Most Americans had a paranoid fear of Soviet-style communism — particularly the repressive form that it took under Stalin. Although the Soviet Union changed a great deal after Stalin's death in 1953, many Americans still firmly believed that it was incapable of significant change. Since the Bolshevik Revolution in 1917, our politicians, our press, and our academic experts had viewed the Soviet Union as anathema. Not only was the Soviet Union constantly denigrated by the United States, but it was most often portrayed as evil, inhuman, and imperialistic. However, while the Soviets were our allies in World War II, we were conveniently able to overlook Stalin's atrocities of the 1930s.

11. Lawrence J. Korb, "The Readiness Gap," *New York Times Magazine*, February 26, 1995, p. 41.

12. Ralph K. White, *Fearful Warriors* (New York: Free Press, 1984).

The Soviets' paranoia toward the United States stemmed from a fear of foreign invasion. For over a thousand years the Russian territory had been the object of countless foreign invasions, the most disastrous of which was by the Germans in World War II, which resulted in 7½ million Soviet battle deaths and nearly 20 million Soviet civilian casualties — in contrast to the U.S. war losses of only 300,000. Although the Germans occupied the Soviet Union, our homeland remained untouched during World War II. Few Americans were aware that between 1918 and 1920 we actually sent troops to the Soviet Union to fight against the Revolution. Thus, when President Reagan spoke of "containing" Soviet aggression, the Kremlin was contemplating the risks of "encirclement."

Rogue States

Washington is obsessed with a handful of "rogue states," which are portrayed as major threats to U.S. and Western security. These countries, particularly Iraq, Iran, Libya, Syria and North Korea, have become the dominant enemy image in Washington. . . .

The rogue-state concept is a product of a determined Pentagon effort to create a new foreign threat to justify military spending in the wake of the cold war.[13]

The other form of paranoia shared by former U.S. and Soviet leaders was macho pride. Both sides had an excessively high moral self-image. Each side had a long list of deeply resented grievances against the other, which took the form of political, economic, and social injustices. Every time there was an alleged abuse by one side, the other side responded with a compensatory charge of its own. Both nations were full of self-righteous indignation and wounded pride. Each country could cite the most minor malefactions of the other in excruciating detail, but never accepted responsibility for or acknowledged the pain and suffering inflicted by its own policies.

According to the Center for Defense Information, three years after the Cold War ended, the United States was still selling annually a staggering $63 billion worth of weapons, military construction, and

---

13. Michael T. Klare, "The New 'Rogue State' Doctrine," *Nation*, May 8, 1995, p. 625.

Cold War without End

The United States had contingency plans for every conceivable twist of the cold war, except one: triumph.[14]

---

training to 142 nations, including 59 authoritarian governments such as Saudi Arabia, Indonesia, Morocco, Thailand, and Guatemala.

The Technocrats

Many of the Sovietologists who shaped American foreign policy throughout the Cold War were Soviet and East European émigrés who had suffered personally at the hands of the Soviet government. However, for the most part, the scientists, engineers, and technocrats who designed, developed, and implemented the sophisticated, high-tech, Cold War weapons systems had no firsthand contact with the Soviets. Their anticommunism was derived more from a psychological need to justify their decision to spend their lives producing instruments of death.

The Pentagon was the only institution in the world that could provide the high-tech enthusiasts with endless resources to do state-of-the-art research on the cutting edge of science. For many technocrats, the thrill of overcoming scientific and technological hurdles was the driving force motivating them to pursue ever more sophisticated weapons systems. To rationalize developing weapons capable of producing so much destruction, one must have a bigger-than-life enemy — a role the Soviet Union was willing to play for over forty-five years.

Beginning with the World War II Manhattan Project, and continuing with the Apollo moonwalks, the space shuttle, the B-1 bomber, the stealth bomber, the Trident II missile system, and the Strategic Defense Initiative (SDI), our government spent trillions of dollars on military and space-related high technology. After spending nearly $45 billion to build twenty B-2 stealth bombers — the most expensive warplane in history — the Pentagon hopes to build another twenty at a cost

---

14. Thomas L. Friedman, "Cold War without End," *New York Times Magazine,* August 22, 1993, p. 30.

of $30 billion. This Cold War relic has experienced a plethora of unresolved technical problems. Even though President Reagan's fantasy of developing "a security shield which can one day render nuclear weapons obsolete and free mankind from the prison of nuclear terror" has been thoroughly discredited by many of the scientists who worked on SDI in the 1980s, military enthusiasts have proposed that we spend an additional $40 billion on top of the original $36 billion for a smaller version of "Star Wars."

Star Wars II

One day, mathematically, something bad can happen and you ought to have a minimum screen on a continentwide basis, and that's doable.

Newt Gingrich, Speaker of the House

A 1996 General Accounting Office study concluded that the Pentagon and its principal military contractors significantly overstated the effectiveness of so-called smart weapon systems in the 1991 Persian Gulf War. Specifically, the study concluded that the Pentagon's claims for the F-117A stealth fighter ($106 million per plane), the Tomahawk land-attack missile, and laser-guided "smart" bombs "were overstated, misleading, inconsistent with the best available data, or unverifiable."

As evidence of business as usual in the Pentagon, the Army has proposed a new antipersonnel weapon, the Laser Countermeasure, which fires a beam powerful enough to burn out human retinas from up to three thousand feet away — all in the name of progress. And there is talk of resurrecting the supersonic transport (SST) which Congress killed back in 1971. A leading manufacturer of Russian warplanes has teamed up with the American aerospace industry to design a supersonic passenger plane for the twenty-first century.

The merger of McDonnell Douglas and Boeing aerospace companies, with a combined revenue of $50 billion annually and a workforce of over 200,000, will create even more opportunities and political pressure for new, large-scale, high-tech defense projects. The only thing new is that Lockheed Martin and Boeing-McDonnell Douglas will control most of the American aerospace pie.

The common and distinguishing characteristic of these high-tech

---

High-Tech Freedom

With the doubled-edge sword of technology, Americans have carved a world of gleaming aircraft and guided missiles. The airplanes that transport them, the cell phones and television cables and computers that link them, define how they live, how they work, how they take their pleasure. They are right up there with freedom of speech and religion, freedom from want and fear. They make America rich, powerful, and free.

But Americans cannot control technology; increasingly, it controls them. And when the people Americans fear get their hands on it, the fear is accelerated and amplified by 500 channels of interwoven media hype.

The airlines and telephones and E-mail that connect Americans connect those other people too. High technology may make a fine sword, but it is a flawed shield. It cannot stop every nut with a grudge. . . .

We — the United States — have the smart bombs, built with the billions that bankrupted Moscow and made America Number One. They — the furious and the powerless — have the dumb bombs, made from fertilizer and fuel oil, ignited by rage and religion. But the United States can't stop them all, not with its ever-tightening laws, not with its trillion-dollar military, not with its weapons and warheads.[15]

---

military adventures is managerial indifference to costs backed by the political will to foot the huge bill. Whenever a congressional policymaker has to make a decision based on technology that he or she does not fully understand, then that policymaker becomes vulnerable to being run over by a high-tech steamroller. The high priests of military technology come on so strong with their forecasts of gloom and doom that the Congress is easily intimidated into believing everything the Pentagon has to sell — all in the name of national security. Our Congress neither knows how to ask the right questions, nor how to evaluate the answers. This is one reason we are still spending $250 billion each

15. Tim Weiner, "The Devil's Bargain of a Better World," *New York Times*, July 21, 1996, p. E5.

> **Mighty Morphin Power**
>
> For whenever a nation becomes large enough to accumulate the critical mass of power, it will in the end accumulate it. And when it has acquired it, it will become an aggressor, its previous record and intentions to the contrary notwithstanding.[16]

year on defense. Since the Soviet Union is no longer around, military planners hype the alleged threat of nuclear, chemical, or biological attack by a dozen or so "rogue nations" such as Iran, Iraq, Libya, North Korea, and several former Soviet republics.

What Price Freedom?

When Baltic republic Lithuania demanded freedom from the Soviet Union in 1990, former Soviet leader Mikhail S. Gorbachev offered the Lithuanians the Soviet equivalent of a leveraged buyout. His conciliatory message to the defiant republic was, "If you don't like it here, you are free to go, but at a price." His initial asking price was $33 billion — probably more hard currency than could be found in all of Lithuania.

While providing Soviet republics with a legal secession mechanism, Gorbachev offered them economic incentives and political concessions to stay. Departing republics would have been obliged to pay relocation costs for their citizens who wanted to remain in the Soviet Union. They would have also been expected to compensate the Soviets for state-owned property, mines, oil fields, factories, public utilities, highways, schools, hospitals, etc.

In January 1991, President George Bush angrily demanded that any Soviet republic which wanted its freedom should be allowed to leave the Soviet Union. When the USSR collapsed later that year, secession became a moot point.

Fifteen minutes after the Black Sea cruise ship *Ayvazovskiy* landed in Yalta, in October 1991, our tour guide began calling for Crimean independence — independence from the Ukraine, to which it had been a part since the 1950s, and independence from the Soviet Union. Already

16. Kohr, p. 35.

secessionist fever was spreading within Soviet republics. But Crimean secessionists were soon thwarted by the threat of military action by the heavy-handed Ukrainian government. Russian president Boris Yeltsin consistently opposed the use of force against Crimea and once said that "Crimea has the right to make its own decisions."

But what is good for the goose is apparently not so good for the gander. When the tiny Muslim republic of Chechnya sought independence from Moscow in 1994, Yeltsin followed quite a different script. Fearing that Chechen independence might stir up secessionist feelings among other Russian republics and lead to the breakup of Russia, Yeltsin sent forty thousand Russian troops to the Chechen capital of Grozny to crush the revolt, resulting in over thirty thousand civilian deaths.

Concerned about the possible disintegration of Russia into a handful of small, heavily armed republics accountable to no one, Washington remained silent in the face of fierce, unrepentant Russian aggression against Chechnya. Yet only a few years earlier, the White House expressed outrage when Gorbachev deployed a handful of Soviet troops to Georgia and Lithuania to put down social unrest. President Bush once went on national television to condemn Gorbachev for the deaths of a dozen Lithuanians killed by Soviet troops. President Clinton's comparative silence in the matter of Chechnya perhaps betrayed his administration's policy that a big Russia, centrally administered by a quixotic Yeltsin, is better than a group of small republics. Is this one reason why the Clinton administration so fiercely opposed a second term for U.N. Secretary General Boutros Boutros-Ghali? He believes that,

> The time of absolute and exclusive sovereignty, however, has passed; its theory was never matched by reality. It is the task of leaders of states today to understand this and to find a balance between the need of good internal governance and the requirements of an ever more interdependent world.

The same principle of self-determination that led former Soviet republics to independence is the driving force underlying the secessionist demands of nearly a dozen Russian republics. But what if the principle of self-determination were to find its way across the Atlantic to the United States, where some claim it originated in the first place? How would the White House and Congress react if Vermont were to announce its intention to secede? Would Washington's response be any different from Moscow's overreaction to Chechnya? Only time will tell.

Little States — Little Wars

With the exception of a handful of megastates such as California, Texas, and New York, most American states would never be perceived by other states or other nations as a serious military threat. The average amount spent for defense by each American state is over $5 billion per year, which is comparable to the defense budgets of Sweden and Switzerland, which are not thought to be a threat to anyone. Yet collectively the United States of America is viewed by the other nations as an ominous military power second to none.

Military Might

A small-state world would not only solve the problems of social brutality and war; it would solve the problems of oppression and tyranny. It would solve all problems arising from power.[17]

Since 1791 when Vermont joined the original thirteen English colonies to become the fourteenth state, the United States has pursued an aggressive expansion path of annexation of previously independent states — Alaska and Hawaii being the most recent acquisitions. Although Puerto Rico is likely to become the next American state, some nationalistic American politicians have actually called for the annexation of the three Canadian Maritime Provinces of Nova Scotia, New Brunswick, and Prince Edward Island.

While the United States has continued to expand its power through annexation, the rest of the world has followed a quite different path since the end of World War II. At that time there were only 45 nations. With the breakup of the European colonial empire in Africa and the more recent disintegration of the Soviet Union, Czechoslovakia, and Yugoslavia, today there are 191 nations — 52 of which are in Africa.

Even though the Cold War is over, in 1995 there were nearly 150 wars or skirmishes taking place throughout the world — 100 of which were occurring within countries rather than between them. Some argue that as the world's only surviving superpower, the United States has a moral obligation to intervene and attempt to stop the fighting in war-

17. Kohr, p. 79.

Nation-States

I was brought up on an interpretation of history which suggested that in the beginning was the family; then families got together and formed tribes; then a number of tribes formed a nation; then a number of nations formed a "Union" or "United States" of this or that; and that, finally we could look forward to a single World Government. Ever since I heard this plausible story I have taken a special interest in the process, but could not help noticing that the opposite seemed to be happening: a proliferation of nation-states.[18]

torn areas such as Bosnia and Herzegovina. Others question whether we have the resources to stop the bloodletting in such far-flung places or whether these little civil wars have anything to do with us. Left to

Isolationism

How horrible, fantastic, incredible, it is that we should be digging trenches and trying on gas-masks here because of a quarrel in a faraway country between people of whom we know nothing.

Neville Chamberlain

their own means these conflicts will gradually dissipate. Be that as it may, the United States sent twenty thousand "peacekeeping" troops to Bosnia and Herzegovina — one of eight places where we intervened militarily since 1990. The others include Iraq (three times), Somalia, Haiti, Macedonia, the Taiwan strait, Rwanda, and Zaire.

Entangling Alliances

When President George Bush persuaded all of the global heavy hitters of the UN to join forces with the United States in 1991 and invade Iraq,

18. E. F. Schumacher, *Small Is Beautiful* (New York: Harper & Row, 1973), p. 67.

> ### Little-State Wars
>
> Its wars mean little, and are as little as the states between which they are fought. Its hatreds whittle down to rivalries, and it never suffers the double heartbreak of the great-power world which is constantly out to achieve the unachievable, and then invariably succumbs to the unpreventable.[19]

it was one of the very few times in history that they ever agreed on anything. One of us remembers hearing a Near Eastern businessman say, "Woe be unto us smaller nations, if the United States and the Soviet Union ever agree on anything." This man was from Iraq. His fears were prophetic. The UN proved itself to be every bit as violent and warlike as the nations it was supposed to keep at peace.

In 1994 when the UN was supporting peacekeeping operations in seventeen countries including Bosnia, Haiti, Iraq, and Somalia, UN Secretary-General Boutros Boutros-Ghali had this to say about the UN's inability to curb the genocide in Rwanda: "It is a failure for the United Nations; it is a failure for the international community. And all of us are responsible for this failure. Not only the great powers but the African powers, the nongovernmental organizations, all the international community."

> ### Shaw on the League of Nations
>
> The organization of nations is the organization of world war. If two men want to fight how do you prevent them: by keeping them apart, not by bringing them together. When the nations kept apart, war was an occasional and exceptional thing: now the League hangs over Europe like a perpetual war cloud.[20]

The track record of large multinational organizations in preventing war or restoring peace is singularly unimpressive. Just as the

19. Kohr, p. 61.
20. George Bernard Shaw, *Geneva* (New York: Dodd, Mead, 1947), p. 61.

The Global Village

In our villages, there may be an upsetting murder once in a decade. The rest of the time we live in unruffled peace. In a large community, on the other hand, there is murder, rape, and robbery every hour in some distant corner. But since we are linked with every distant corner, every local incident turns into an issue, a cause, a national calamity clouding our skies not once in a decade but all the time. From our local newspapers we learn that none of the massive misfortunes depressing the world ever happens in our town. Yet we must suffer because our unifiers have forced us to participate in millions of destinies that are not ours. This is the price of modern vast-scale living. Having drawn the entire human race to our anxious bosom, we have to share in all its miseries.[21]

League of Nations was unsuccessful in preventing World War II, so too did the United Nations have little to celebrate on its fiftieth anniversary in 1995. Not only was the UN unable to prevent a plethora of wars in China, Korea, Southeast Asia, Afghanistan, Africa, Central America, the Middle East, and Yugoslavia, it was impotent to bring them to an early conclusion. The 185-member megaorganization faced a monumental financial crisis in 1996 with over half of its member nations in arrears for payment of their membership dues and assessments amounting to a total of $3.1 billion. The leading deadbeat nation was the United States, which owed $1.5 billion. In response to the pending financial liquidity crunch, the UN secretariat began reducing the size of its staff.

But why should the UN be expected to bring peace to warring Balkan nations or African tribes? These conflicts are not new and in some cases can be traced back for decades, if not centuries in the case of Bosnia. Why do we keep pretending that the UN has the power to bring peace to such complex conflicts? These are local civil wars which have to be sorted out by the local people involved. With over seventy thousand civilian and military personnel, the UN is but one of many international organizations to which the United States belongs which is too large and

---

21. Kohr, p. 171.

Woodrow Wilson on Neutrality

Every man who really loves America will act and speak in the true spirit of neutrality, which is the spirit of impartiality and fairness and friendliness to all concerned.

The United States must be neutral in fact as well as in name during these days that are to try men's souls. We must be impartial in thought as well as in action, must put a curb upon our sentiments as well as upon every transaction that might be construed as a preference of one party to the struggle before another.

Speech, August 19, 1914

---

spread too thin in too many countries to be effective in any. Others include the World Bank and the International Monetary Fund.

Some say that NATO prevented another major war in Europe after World War II. But the hot wars between the United States and the Soviet Union took place not in Europe but in Vietnam, Afghanistan, Ethiopia, Angola, Nicaragua, and El Salvador. Furthermore, NATO has proven to be powerless to resolve the conflicts among the former states of Yugoslavia. Even so, during the 1996 presidential campaign President Bill Clinton and Senator Bob Dole agreed that the only way to make NATO more effective was to make it bigger. Both supported the expansion of NATO to include Poland, Hungary, and the Czech Republic.

The painful message of history is clear — military alliances among nations do not prevent war but may actually enhance the likelihood of war. The "Big Brother" approach is no more effective as a peacekeeping strategy than as a social welfare tool. The solution of local problems including local wars lies with those involved, not with politicians and bureaucrats located thousands of miles away in Washington, New York, or Geneva.

We are learning, in the later part of the twentieth century, the high cost of our schemes for unifying and centralizing humanity. Such totalitarian projects always required the violent imposition of some privileged grand narrative upon lesser privileged local narratives. Meaning and value which did not fit under the totalizing umbrella of the grand narrative were suppressed or ignored in favor of artificial homogeneity.

Now, we're rediscovering the power of local narratives, meaning

---

Military Defense Downsizing Strategies

1. Substitute constructive engagement, tension reduction, and power sharing for military confrontation as strategies of choice for resolving international disputes.
2. Reduce our commitment of troops and war-waging devices in Europe, the Middle East, and the Far East to reflect today's realities, not yesterday's fears.
3. Discontinue our role as self-appointed global policeman with the right to intervene in any minor skirmish anywhere in the world.
4. Disengage from the United Nations, the World Bank, and the International Monetary Fund.
5. Replace our compulsory military alliance among states with a voluntary alliance similar to NATO.

---

which seeps out beyond the scope of the organizing grand narratives. We're becoming more tolerant of things that cannot be fit within a single, massive whole. Out of conflict, dissension, and a variety of social voices arise creativity, imagination, and invention; they do not flow from imposed consensus and false claims of universality. Postmodernism theorist (and interestingly, French Canadian) Jean-Francois Lyotard, speaks of the postmodern "war on totality."[22]

---

22. Jean-Francois Lyotard, *The Postmodern Condition: A Report on Knowledge,* trans. Geoff Bennington and Brian Massumi (Minneapolis: University of Minnesota Press, 1984), p. 82.

10 Our States: Toothless Paper Tigers

> The trick is to reestablish and reempower governments of human scale — governments that serve the parts, which are indeed the heartland of the nation.
>
> Frank Bryan
> *Real Democracy*

Manifest Destiny

Throughout the Cold War American politicians and Sovietologists frequently condemned the Soviets for the heavy-handed manner in which they acquired their fifteen republics — particularly the forced annexation of Latvia, Lithuania, and Estonia, and parts of Finland, Poland, and Romania. But before we are so quick to judge the Soviets, we need to take a long, hard look at the process by which our fifty states were acquired and developed. Although our nation was founded on the principles of life, liberty, and the pursuit of happiness, the story of how Native Americans were relentlessly forced to abandon their homes and lands and move into Indian territories to make room for American states is a story of arrogance, greed, and raw military power. Our barbaric conquest of the Native Americans continued for several hundred years and involved many of our most cherished national heroes, including George Washington, Thomas Jefferson, James

Monroe, and Andrew Jackson, to mention a few. To add insult to injury, we have violated over three hundred treaties which we signed protecting the rights of American Indians.

Veni, Vidi, Vici

By what right or warrant can we enter into the land of these Savages, take away their rightful inheritance from them, and plant ourselves in their places, being unwronged or unprovoked by them?[1]

It was as though our conquest of the Indians was driven by a belief that our country had been chosen by God to rule all of North America, if not the entire world. But the Indians were by no means the only victims of American imperialism. In the words of Gary B. Nash in his provocative book *Red, White, and Black,* "The promise of American colonial society was intimately and unforgettably intertwined with the exploitation of African labor and Indian land."[2]

Christian Entitlement

Like other Europeans, Puritans claimed the land they were invading by right of discovery. This theory derived from the ancient claim that Christians were everywhere entitled to dispossess non-Christians of their land. A second European legal theory, called *vacuum domicilium,* bolstered Puritan claims that land not "occupied" or "settled" went by forfeit to those who attached themselves to it in a "civilized" manner.

Thus, in Puritan eyes, entitlement to the land of New England required nothing more than the assertion that because their way of life did not conform to European norms, the Indians had forfeited all the land which they "roamed" rather than "settled."[3]

---

1. Robert Gray, *A Good Speed to Virginia* (1609), quoted in Wesley Frank Craven, "Indian Policy in Early Virginia," *William and Mary Quarterly,* 3d ser., 1 (1944): 65.

2. Gary B. Nash, *Red, White, and Black* (Englewood Cliffs, N.J.: Prentice-Hall, 1982), p. xiv.

3. Nash, pp. 79-80.

The United States was the last major country to abolish slavery. Many of our founding fathers who fought against the Indians, including Washington and Jefferson, also owned slaves. One hundred years after the American slaves were freed, there were still laws on the books in the South and other parts of the nation condoning racial discrimination. Even though legal segregation has been outlawed, de facto segregation is still widespread in the United States.

Ethnic Cleansing Didn't Start in Bosnia

When it comes to the sorts of horrors now defining the Balkan conflict, the United States may not have written the book on ethnic cleansing, but it certainly provided several of its most stunning chapters — particularly in its treatment of the American Indian in the transcontinental drive for territory justified under the quasi-religious notion of "manifest destiny."[4]

With the exception of Hawaii, all of our states were pieced together from territory originally occupied by Native Americans. Some, like Louisiana and Alaska, were acquired through direct purchase from France and Russia, respectively. The military defeat of England, Mexico, and Spain paved the way for the annexation of others. The annexation of Texas, Oregon, New Mexico, and California was rationalized by the American equivalent of "Manifest Destiny" or "God's will," according to William W. Rankin, as was our intervention in Cuba, Puerto Rico, Hawaii, and the Philippines.[5]

President James K. Polk had this to say about the annexation of Texas in 1845:

> Our nation is a confederation of independent states whose policy is peace with each other and all the world. To enlarge its limits is to extend the dominion of peace over additional territories and increasing millions. . . . Foreign powers should look on the annexation of

---

4. Kenneth C. Davis, "Ethnic Cleansing Didn't Start in Bosnia," *New York Times*, September 3, 1995, sec. 4, p. 1.
5. William W. Rankin, *Cracking the Monolith* (New York: Crossroad, 1994), pp. 104-39.

America: Through a Different Looking Glass[6]

Where today are the Pequot? Where are the Narragansett, the Mohican, the Pokanoket, and many other once powerful tribes of our people? They have vanished before the avarice and the oppression of the White Man, as snow before a summer sun.

Tecumseh (Shawnee)

Their numbers were small, they found friends, and not enemies; they told us they had fled their own country for fear of wicked men and came here to enjoy their religion. The white people had now found our country, and more came among us . . . at length their numbers had greatly increased; . . . and many of our people were destroyed.

Red Jacket (Seneca)

They promised how we are going to live peacefully on the land we still own and how they are going to show us the new ways of living . . . , but all that was realized out of the agreements with the Great Father was, we are dying off.

Sitting Bull (Sioux)

Texas to the United States as diminishing the chances of war and opening to them new, ever increasing markets for their products.

While we may appreciate Polk's candor in linking the formation of our nation with "ever increasing markets," is this much to build a nation upon?

But when all is said and done, the history of the United States of America differs little from that of any other large empire, whether it be Greek, Roman, Turkish, Napoleonic, English, or Soviet. It is firmly grounded on imperialism — imperialism toward Native Americans, African Americans, and any other nation which happened to get in its way.

6. Cited by Russell Thornton, *American Indian Holocaust and Survival* (Norman: University of Oklahoma Press, 1987).

States' Rights

For nearly fifty years, "states' rights" was justly viewed by political liberals in this country as a not-so-subtle euphemism for racial segregation and the denial of basic rights to African Americans. Such thinking stems from the 1948 presidential campaign of Governor Strom Thurmond of South Carolina and his Mississippi running mate, Governor Fielding Wright, as candidates of the segregationist States Rights Party. Fiery racist Governors George Wallace of Alabama, Ross Barnett of Mississippi, and Lester Maddox of Georgia, as well as most other white politicians in the South in the 1950s and 1960s, ran under the states' rights banner.

Plessy v. Ferguson

If the two races are to meet upon terms of social equality, it must be the result of natural affinities, a mutual appreciation of each other's merits, and a voluntary consent of individuals. . . . Legislation is powerless to eradicate racial instincts or to abolish distinctions based upon physical differences and the attempt to do so can only result in accentuating the difficulties of the present situation.

1896

Even though I (Thomas) grew up in Jackson, Mississippi, in the 1950s, I am neither a racist nor a political conservative. I do not own a gun and have no plans ever to own one. By the time I was twelve years old, I had figured out that white supremacy was a lie, delighted in sitting in the section of city buses reserved for blacks, and refused to stand whenever "Dixie" was played at high school and college sports events. Although I voted for Richard Nixon in 1960, John F. Kennedy soon won me over, and I supported virtually every left-wing Democratic cause for the next thirty years, including the Civil Rights Acts and most of the Great Society programs.

Yet, I have learned the downside of imperious federal government to which the seedy history of states' rights once blinded me. Throughout my lifetime I have witnessed the steady erosion of the integrity of the states, beginning with the New Deal in the 1930s, ac-

> ### The Democratic Party Model
>
> The model of modern governance rests on one overarching idea. The idea is that, for the sake of America's social, economic, and moral well-being, the country must be led by a wise, powerful central authority, an activist federal government that will serve as a combination national social engineer and policeman. The government does for citizens, towns, cities, and states what they are too weak, poor, benighted, or corrupt to do for themselves.[7]

celerated by the Civil Rights Acts and Great Society programs of the 1960s, and reaching culmination in the 1980s with Ronald Reagan's multitrillion-dollar military buildup, resulting in one of the largest government bureaucracies in history. While pretending to be a decentralist, Reagan may have contributed to the massive concentration of power in Washington more than any other president. Yet in a speech in Chicago in 1975 he said:

> I am calling for an end to giantism, for a return to the human scale — the scale that human beings can understand and cope with; the scale of the local fraternal lodge, the church congregation, the block club, the farm bureau. It is the locally owned factory, the small businessman who personally deals with his customers and stands behind his product, the farm and consumer cooperative, the town or neighborhood bank that invests in the community, the union local. In government, the human scale is the town council, the board of selectmen, and the precinct captain.
>
> It is this activity on a small human scale that creates the fabric of community, a framework for the creation of abundance and liberty. The human scale nurtures standards of right behavior, a prevailing ethic of what is right and wrong, acceptable and unacceptable.

Since the onset of the Great Society, conservative politicians have been calling for a return to the U.S. Constitution — particularly the Tenth Amendment, which provides that "The powers not delegated to

7. Michael Kelly, "Rip It Up," *New Yorker*, January 23, 1995, p. 32.

> The states are the laboratories of democracy.
>
> Christine Whitman,
> Governor of New Jersey

the states by the Constitution, nor prohibited by it, are reserved to the states respectively, or to the people." Instead of a transfer of power from the federal government to the states, what the American people got from conservative politicians over the past thirty years was a menu of political rhetoric and Band-Aid policy changes packaged in TV sound bites as revenue sharing, new federalism, competitive federalism, and the short-lived Contract with America. The current buzzword for states' rights is *devolution*. Unfortunately, the sad reality is that American states are little more than *toothless paper tigers*. The myth of states' rights is just that — a myth.

The Devolution Model

Devolution argues that the central authority has improperly arrogated too much power to itself, and has become at once abusive of the rights of citizens and irresponsive to their needs. The solution is to strip away from the government many of its functions and to assign those functions to small units of polity — to the states, cities, and towns, ultimately the citizens themselves.[8]

Seeds of Dissent

So deep was the economic despair of the Great Depression that, if the New Deal and World War II had not come along when they did, one could imagine the possibility of states being pitted against each other in the competition for jobs and other scarce resources. But that was not to be. World War II, the postwar economic boom, and the Cold War not only provided much-needed jobs, but gave our nation a sense of direction and diverted our attention away from such nagging prob-

8. Kelly, p. 32.

lems as rural poverty, urban decay, aging infrastructure, increased crime and violence, and a complete breakdown of our sense of community.

With an increasingly sluggish economy and the absence of a viable external military threat, the attention of Americans has turned inward to such issues as abortion, crime, health care, and the cost of social welfare. Public opinion polls reflect a lack of confidence in our nation and its government. Ninety-one percent of the respondents in a *Time Magazine*–CNN poll said they had little or no confidence in our government in Washington for solving the nation's problems. A Harris poll found that 68 percent of Americans rate the state of the nation negatively. And three-fourths of the respondents of a Gallup poll said Americans are less patriotic than in previous decades.

Political Cynicism

In the United States the end of the cold war has intensified a mood of political cynicism. American public opinion expects little from its democratic institutions, and if the experience of the last decade or so is any guide, even its most modest expectations are likely to be disappointed.[9]

Although the American states may have once shared a number of common characteristics, this is much less true today than ever before. What do heavily industrialized states such as New York, New Jersey, Ohio, and Pennsylvania have in common with predominantly rural states such as Maine, Vermont, Mississippi, and West Virginia? The South is the fastest growing region in the nation demographically and economically.

Although African Americans represent only 12.6 percent of the American population, fourteen cities with populations over one hundred thousand have black majorities. Detroit and Washington, D.C., are 75.7 percent and 65.8 percent black, respectively. Vermont, on the other hand, with fewer than two thousand blacks in the entire state, has the lowest percent African American population among the fifty

9. John Gray, "Does Democracy Have a Future?" *New York Times Book Review,* January 22, 1995, p. 1.

Texas

Texas has the most farms, the most churches per capita, the biggest state fair, the most airports, the most insurance companies, the most species of birds, the most banks, the most football teams, the most holidays, among other things.[10]

---

states. The Mississippi Delta and the so-called Black Belt of the South have virtually nothing in common with the San Francisco Bay area.

A dozen American cities with populations over one hundred thousand have Hispanic majorities, even though only 10.2 percent of the national population is Hispanic. Miami leads the way with a 62.5 percent Hispanic population. Over 25 percent of the population of Texas is Hispanic. Not surprisingly, many Texans now identify more closely with Mexico than was previously the case. California is expected to have a Hispanic majority during the first quarter of the twenty-first century. And Los Angeles County will have one by the end of this century.

Despite all of the hype about the merits of multicultural pluralism, our cities are different and our states are different — very different. This is not a statement of racial or ethnic superiority of one state or city in comparison to others, but rather an acknowledgment that the problems of Houston and Miami bear little resemblance to those of Burlington, Vermont, or Laramie, Wyoming.

As further evidence of the differences among states, we shall consider the costs and benefits of the distribution of various federal government programs and subsidies. One example of the gross inequity of many federal subsidies is the savings-and-loan debacle we noted previously. The $500 billion bailout cost every man, woman, and child in America an average of nearly $2,000 to compensate depositors living mostly in Texas and a few other Sun Belt states for the greed inflicted on them by a few hundred of their own citizens. By what logic should Delaware's, Hawaii's, and Vermont's proportionate share of the bailout tab be $1.4 billion, $2.3 billion, and $1.1 billion, respectively, when none of these states had any savings-and-loan failures?

Even though its largest town, Burlington, has a population of

10. John Bainbridge, *The Super-Americans* (New York: Doubleday, 1961), p. 9.

only forty thousand and the state has no military bases whatsoever, Vermont's share of the cost of Star Wars I (SDI) amounted to $80.4 million. Star Wars II will cost Vermonters another $89.3 million. Vermont's share of the cost of the first twenty B-2 stealth bombers was $99.1 million. The next twenty will cost Vermont another $67.0 million. But as we said before, "Who would ever bomb Vermont — or New Hampshire, Maine, Montana, North Dakota, or Wyoming, for that matter?" Why all this military madness?

Because too many people choose to live in places like Chicago, New York, Houston, and Los Angeles, and because these cities may be perceived as a threat by other bully nations, why should tiny states like Maine, New Hampshire, and Vermont be coerced into footing the bill for the protection of the megacities?

Maybe Vermont needs The Green Mountain Boys more than ever — not to fight New Yorkers or the British, but to defend the state against the Pentagon, Washington lobbyists, and the U.S. Congress.

On a less grandiose scale, we shall examine the distribution of several other subsidies. Particularly irksome to some liberal members of Congress are subsidies aimed originally at promoting westward expansion — some dating back to the 1800s. These include subsidies for mining, timber, and other industries using public lands. The same conservative Republicans who oppose federal subsidies for the urban poor staunchly defend the practice of prosperous mining companies paying little to the federal government for extracting hard-rock minerals such as gold and silver from public lands in the West. They also support delivering free water to irrigate surplus crops on large western farms as well as giving free livestock feed to ranchers who overgraze their land and then claim they have no grass.

But these so-called drought subsidies are a drop in the pork-barrel bucket compared to the $150 billion spent on crop subsidies nationwide over the past decade. Kansas farmers, for example, typically receive $20,000 to $40,000 annually in crop subsidies, and their state netted a cool $8 billion in farm subsidies over the decade.

No institutions are more dependent on federal subsidies than large research universities, which receive $11.64 billion in R & D support annually from our government.

Until recently, federal welfare payments to the urban poor provided little incentive for them to break free of their inner-city hell. These payments indirectly lead to increased federal government expenditures for urban infrastructure, law enforcement, public education, and drug

---

Government Burden

Basically something is a burden when it is not for the rich, not for the merely affluent, but for the poor.

John Kenneth Galbraith

---

and alcohol rehabilitation. Also, by encouraging more people to move to big cities and to remain there, we inadvertently play into the hands of the big military spenders who use the size of our big cities to justify spending even more money for B-2 bombers and sophisticated antiballistic missile systems. Big cities require big military protection to keep them safe.

Cuban and Haitian immigrants to Florida cost state taxpayers $3.3 billion in services in one year, even though the state of Florida has no control whatsoever over U.S. immigration policies. This is but one of countless examples of U.S. government regulations imposed on the powerless states for which the states must bear the brunt of the cost of implementation. Numerous other examples can be found in such diverse areas as civil rights, environmental protection, public education, employee safety, prison reform, and social welfare.

Pork Barrel

President Clinton announced nearly $1 billion in shipbuilding contracts today, holding them up as the products of a Government effort to assist the struggling maritime industry.

Associated Press

In 1995 when Congress refused to approve a $40 billion U.S. loan guarantee for Mexico in the face of widespread opposition and opinion polls showing little public support, President Clinton ignored the will of Congress and used a special backdoor U.S. Treasury fund to provide Mexico with a $20 billion bailout. Washington bailouts are certainly nothing new. Two of the more notable above-the-table corporate bailouts were Chrysler and Lockheed. But at one time or another, government subsidies have kept inefficient airlines, railroads, truckers, and shippers afloat for years, not to mention the entire defense and aerospace industry. For years, the U.S. Department of Agriculture has spent hundreds of millions of dollars supporting the promotional efforts abroad of companies such as Pillsbury, McDonald's, and Campbell Soup. A consortium of the fourteen largest computer microchip manufacturers receives a $100 million annual subsidy from the Pentagon to support their foreign marketing efforts. To construct and upgrade roads through national forests used by Weyerhaeuser and Georgia-Pacific to haul lumber, the U.S. Forest Service spends $140 million a year. In 1994, the federal government provided American businesses with subsidies totaling $51 billion in corporate tax breaks.

According to the U.S. Justice Department, over thirty-five counties in Nevada, California, Idaho, New Mexico, and Oregon have adopted ordinances calling for county control of national forests and other federal lands and the ownership of the roads through them. In March 1995, the Justice Department filed a lawsuit seeking to halt Nye County, Nevada, from seizing control of federal lands and intimidating federal officials there. Could this be the beginning of a political war over control of public land in the West?

The federal government owns nearly 70 percent of all of the land in Alaska. The state of Alaska sued the federal government for $29 billion, claiming that nearly half of this land has been withdrawn from potential development, thus thwarting the state's plans for further oil and natural gas development, the piping of Alaskan water to California, and the construction of highways and railroads into wilderness tracts.

And then there is America's captive nation Puerto Rico, whose citizens have never been allowed to vote on whether they prefer independence, statehood, or continued commonwealth autonomy since being annexed by the United States from Spain in 1898. Not unlike the Baltic states, Puerto Rico was involuntarily acquired by a big neighbor.

Where Is the Glue?

In the first chapter we posed the question, Where is the glue that binds our fifty states together? Is it freedom, democracy, individualism, or the highly cherished American way of life? Alternatively, is it consumerism, hedonism, narcissism, or greed? Or is it perhaps something more subtle?

Bowling Alone

The most whimsical yet discomfiting bit of evidence of social disengagement in contemporary America that I have discovered is this: more Americans are bowling today than ever before, but bowling in organized leagues has plummeted in the last decade or so. Between 1980 and 1993 the total number of bowlers in America increased by 10 percent, while league bowling decreased by 40 percent. The rise of solo bowling threatens the livelihood of bowling-land proprietors because those who bowl as members of leagues consume three times as much beer and pizza as solo bowlers, and the money in bowling is in the beer and pizza, not the balls and shoes. The broader social significance, however, lies in the social interaction and even occasionally civic conversations over beer and pizza that solo bowlers forgo.[11]

After World War II, Moscow maintained tight control of the Soviet Union by providing the 250,000 or so self-perpetuating elites, known as the *nomenklatura* (who controlled the Communist Party, the KGB, and Soviet military), with a number of valuable perquisites, including high salaries, larger flats, dachas, private cars, trips abroad, and access to foreign goods and special state-run food stores. Although few Americans view our government as repressive, democratic it is not — at least not at the national level. Coercion is the rule, not the exception. Is the behavior of our *ruling class* — the military-industrial complex, corporate farmers, labor union leaders, major university presidents, and nationally known televangelists — any different from that of the *nomenklatura?* "The reason the United States Government cannot solve our pressing problems is because the United States Government is the *problem*," says the Washington-based citizens' lobby group Common Cause.

How much power do individual citizens wield at the state and local level when confronted by the force of the U.S. government? How much responsibility are they prepared to assume for the solution of local problems when big government is all too willing to step in whether invited to do so or not?

---

11. Robert D. Putnam, "Bowling Alone," *Journal of Democracy*, January 1995, p. 70.

The Ruling Class

The ruling class in our culture is our managers and executives. They are the class of people who drive much of what we do. They control the majority of our resources, they are the heroes of the American dream. We have no royalty, no powerful church. It is the executives of our organizations who have paved our streets with gold.

We have all created this ruling class. We have separated those who manage the work from those who do the work.[12]

Increased competition for federal block grants among the fifty states may lead to the further Balkanization of America:

There is constant and bitter competition between regions for defense contracts, army bases, public-works projects, R&D money, tax subsidies, agricultural supports, energy boondoggles; both public and private forces are at work to lure businesses, venture capital, conventions, book collections, academic superstars, conductors, advertising agencies, ballplayers, and a wide variety of other perceived attractions from one section to another. New England competes with the South over runaway companies, Appalachia with the Rockies over coal development, the Southwest with California over water allocation, the Northwest with the Rocky Mountains over water power, Hawaii with California over immigration, Alaska with the West Coast over oil shipments, the Southeast with the Northeast over natural-gas regulation, the Grainbelt with the East over beef prices, the Gulf States with the mid-Atlantic over offshore drilling — and on it goes, a display of divisiveness without parallel in this century.[13]

Given the feelings of separation, alienation, and powerlessness experienced by many Americans in relation to their government, is it any wonder that private, self-styled militias have sprung up in over thirty states? According to some estimates, as many as one hundred

---

12. Peter Block, *Stewardship* (San Francisco: Berrett-Koehler, 1993), p. 45.
13. Kirkpatrick Sale, *Human Scale* (New York: Coward, McCann & Geoghegan, 1980), pp. 437-38.

thousand Americans may be involved. Obsessed with guns and the FBI siege and burning of the Branch Davidian compound in Waco, Texas, on April 19, 1993, these secretive, paranoid militias often harbor far-fetched conspiracy theories. Many of these local militias such as the Michigan Militia, which claims twelve thousand members, are preparing to defend themselves against the U.S. government, "just in case."

But haven't we already tried the military approach to disunion, resulting in a national bloodbath in the 1860s? Over six hundred thousand soldiers died during the Civil War. Surely there must be an alternative to the military option? We believe that one alternative is planned, orderly, peaceful secession!

Tiny European States

Even though there are fewer than two hundred officially recognized countries in the world, there are approximately five thousand nations, if we define a nation as a group of indigenous people who share common language, culture, history, territory, and government institutions. In Africa, for example, there are several hundred tribes, each of which could be thought of as a minination. Thus the possibility exists for a significant increase in the number of countries or states worldwide as well as a reduction in their size. The United States is no exception to the rule.

> Instead of union, let us have disunion now. Instead of fusing the small, let us dismember the big. Instead of creating fewer and larger states, let us create more and smaller ones.[14]

In chapter 1, we briefly sketched out a picture of the high quality of life of small European nations such as Austria, Denmark, Finland, Iceland, Norway, Sweden, and Switzerland, four of which happen to be neutral — Austria, Finland, Sweden, and Switzerland.

We now consider one of them, Switzerland, in more detail. We

14. Leopold Kohr, *The Breakdown of Nations* (New York: E. P. Dutton, 1978), p. 51.

focus on Switzerland because it is the wealthiest, most democratic, and most market-oriented country in the world, with the weakest central government in the West.[15]

Over the past seven hundred years Switzerland has developed a unique social and political structure with a strong emphasis on federalism and direct democracy which brings together in its twenty-six cantons (tiny states) four languages and cultures — German, French, Italian, and Romansh. Its cantons enjoy considerable autonomy. Several cantons still follow the centuries-old traditions of *Landsgemeinde,* or open-air parliaments, each spring.

Ancient Greece

Greece was politically the most dismembered country on earth. Every city took zealous care lest its political independence be assailed; for this the inhabitants of even the smallest of them were in no mind to surrender. Each of these little city-republics had its own constitution, its own social life with its own cultural peculiarities; and this it was that gave to Hellenic life as a whole its variegated wealth of genuine cultural values.

It was this healthy decentralization, this internal separation of Greece into hundreds of little communities, tolerating no uniformity, which constantly aroused the mind to consideration of new matters. Every larger political structure leads inevitably to a certain rigidity of the cultural life and destroys that fruitful rivalry between separate communities which is so characteristic of the whole life of the Grecian cities.[16]

A petition signed by one hundred thousand voters can force a nationwide vote on a proposed constitutional change. The signatures of only fifty thousand voters can force a national referendum on any federal law passed by parliament. Although Switzerland has a strong military defense, it has remained neutral since 1815.

15. Thomas H. Naylor, "The Swiss Way to Run a Nation," *Journal of Commerce,* January 10, 1995, p. 8A.

16. Rudolph Rocker, *Nationalism and Culture* (Los Angeles: Rocker Publications, 1937), p. 362.

Scattered throughout the Swiss Alps and neighboring Austria, Bavaria, and northern Italy are dozens of small villages, all of which are several hundred years old — each possessing a strong sense of community.

> ### Little Comic-Opera States
>
> As long as the Italians and Germans were organized, or disorganized, in little comic-opera states, they not only gave the world the greatest masters of comic opera but, as in England during the time of Elizabethan political insignificance, an unrivaled string of immortal lyricists, authors, philosophers, painters, architects, and composers.[17]

When one gets up in the morning in a typical Swiss village, one does not drive across town to an impersonal shopping mall but rather walks to the village bakery to pick up freshly baked bread and pastries for breakfast. Later in the day one may walk to the market, the bank, the post office, and the farmer's house — in the latter case for milk, butter, and cheese. The market sells juicy Italian tomatoes — not tasteless plastic ones — and fresh drug-free chickens. The ice cream is so good it defies description. Although acid rain has taken its toll on Swiss forests, water pollution — with a few notable exceptions — is rare.

Although farming and tourism are important sources of village employment, it is not uncommon for some to travel twenty-five miles to work in nearby factories. In most Alpine villages, there is an inexorable commitment to the land. A gift of land from one's parents carries with it a moral obligation of continued stewardship. Few would think of selling their land and leaving the village.

The church is often the center of village spiritual life, as well as social life. Friends meet at the market, the pub, the inn, the post office, and the churchyard to catch up on village news. The harsh winters create an environment encouraging cooperation, sharing, and trust. The extraordinary beauty and the severity of the winters provide the glue which holds these communities together.

17. Kohr, p. 127.

> I love small nations
> I love small numbers
> The world will be saved
> By the few.
>
> André Gide

In these villages, in stark contrast to the rootless mobility that characterizes American life, one finds a sense of continuity where the generations are born, grow up, remain, and eventually die — a mentality which pervades all of Switzerland. Protective agricultural policies have made it financially viable for families to remain in the countryside. Conspicuously absent is the dilapidation, deterioration, and decay found, for example, throughout the American rural South. Since small Swiss farms use fewer nitrates, pesticides, and herbicides, wells and streams are much less likely to be contaminated than in the United States.

Geneva and Zurich are consistently ranked among the ten best cities in the world in which to live.

Despite their fierce independence, Swiss towns, villages, and cantons do cooperate on major projects involving the general public interest, including railroads, highways, tunnels, electric energy, water supply, and pollution abatement. Switzerland works because it is a tiny, hardworking, democratic country with a strong sense of community.

But the Swiss are not without their critics. Some view them as arrogant, narcissistic, racist, sexist, and xenophobic — concerned only about themselves. Unfortunately, Zurich, with Europe's biggest drug abuse and AIDS problems, has become an ignoble exception to the Swiss rule. Before it was closed by the police, the once-elegant Platzpitz had become an open drug market.

Swiss banks have recently come under attack for the way they handled unclaimed deposits of World War II Holocaust victims as well as Nazi gold deposits.

Another tiny, prosperous European country with close ties to Switzerland is Liechtenstein — tax haven to some sixty thousand corporations. With a population of only 28,800, Liechtenstein, an independent sovereign state, is within Swiss customs control, uses the Swiss postal system and the Swiss franc, and is a member of the European Economic Space.

Vermont: The Green Mountain Mystique

Driving through Vermont, one is struck not only by the majestic beauty of the Green Mountains, the classic red barns and covered bridges, but also by the picturesque patchwork patterns of small farms, villages, little rivers, ridges, hollows, and dirt roads, and the absence of billboards. Because they like it that way, Vermonters have the highest percentage of unpaved roads in the country. Roadside billboards were banned in 1968.

> **Vermont**
>
> The hills are still alive with the sound of town and village, of neighborhood, corner, and place.
>
> Frank Bryan and John McClaughry
> *The Vermont Papers*

From these initial impressions one suspects that Vermont may be different from most states — very different. And many of these differences can be traced back to the life and times of Vermont's folk hero Ethan Allen, when Vermont first became an independent republic on January 17, 1777, and remained independent until it joined the Union in 1791. In the eyes of some historians, Ethan Allen may have been the "most underrated" American revolutionary — a skilled military strategist, a patriot, a populist, a farmer, a businessman, a philosopher, and a writer — Vermont's equivalent of George Washington. But to others he was a belligerent, loudmouthed, heavy-drinking, rebellious rabble-rouser — a charismatic charlatan, a braggart, an atheist, and a scoundrel with a strong penchant for political incorrectness. Regardless of one's perspective, most agree that Ethan Allen was truly bigger than life!

> I was called by the Yorkers an outlaw, and afterwards, by the British, was called a rebel; and I humbly conceive, that there was as much propriety in the one name as the other.
>
> Ethan Allen, 1779

Whether Allen and his mythical Green Mountain Boys were outlaws, revolutionaries, or both, they seemed to have embodied a great deal of the frontier spirit of their time. The northern frontier of New England was simultaneously democratic yet autocratic, egalitarian yet unjust, communitarian yet individualistic, and nonviolent yet militaristic. These contradictions were all part and parcel of Ethan Allen as well as the independent republic of Vermont. But is it possible that some of what Ethan Allen was up to in the divisive late eighteenth century may be worthy of emulation by independent-minded Vermonters in the twenty-first century?

Ethan Allen's Rules of Warfare

To bring superior numbers quickly to bear, while leaving open lines of retreat and relying on threatening gestures rather than violence. More than a soldier, Allen was an actor.[18]

Living in Vermont is a little like living in a very small foreign country.

Nestled between Lake Champlain in the west and the Connecticut River in the east and between Massachusetts in the south and Canada in the north, Vermont ranks forty-third in size and forty-ninth in population among the fifty states.

Two important factors contribute to Vermont's uniqueness — its tiny size (one-fiftieth the population of California) and its rural nature.

With 67.8 percent of its 585,000 inhabitants living in the countryside, Vermont stands in sharp contrast to the nation as a whole, which is only 24.8 percent rural. Only West Virginia with a 63.9 percent rural population comes close to Vermont.

Although the Green Mountains pale in comparison with the Swiss Alps, Vermonters, as we noted previously, do share many common values with the Swiss. Even though Vermont may be too small to save our nation from the debilitating effects of separation, alienation, and spiritual emptiness, it can provide an alternative model of commu-

---

18. Michael A. Bellesiles, *Revolutionary Outlaws* (Charlottesville: University Press of Virginia, 1993), p. 128.

nity and democracy to combat the isolation and loneliness so prevalent in America.

A cursory glance at Vermont's history makes it obvious that it was not by chance that "Freedom and Unity" became the state's motto. Only Vermont and Texas were independent republics before joining the Union. Unlike other New England states, Vermont was never an English colony, thus avoiding a period of aristocratic oligarchy. Influenced by some of its earlier Iroquois and Yankee inhabitants, Vermont established an almost casteless society never to be replicated elsewhere in America.

Even though Vermont has the lowest percent of black population in the nation, it does have an exemplary civil rights record. No blacks were ever imported to pick cotton or anything else in Vermont. Nor were they ever shunted into urban industrial ghettos in Vermont as elsewhere. Indeed, there are no urban ghettos in Vermont.

Vermont was the first state to outlaw slavery in its constitution in 1777 and also the first to require universal manhood suffrage. By the 1830s, Vermont and Massachusetts had the strongest abolitionist sentiments of any states in America. Vermonters were active participants in the Underground Railroad, which helped runaway slaves find refuge in Canada. In 1858, in defiance of the Federal Fugitive Slave Law, Vermont freed all blacks who had been brought into the state. In 1861, Vermont became the first state to send troops to fight in the Civil War. Half of the eligible men in Vermont served in the Union Army.

Although few in number, several black Vermonters distinguished themselves as far back as the nineteenth century. For example, Alexander Twilight became the first black to earn a college degree when he graduated from Middlebury College in 1823. When he was elected to the Vermont legislature in 1836, Mr. Twilight became the first black legislator in America. He was followed by George Washington Henderson, who graduated from the University of Vermont in 1877 at the top of his class — the second black to become a member of the national honor society Phi Beta Kappa.

In spite of Vermont's liberal attitude toward blacks, few African Americans have been attracted to the Green Mountain State with its small industrial base. Idaho, Montana, North Dakota, South Dakota, and Wyoming also have few blacks for reasons similar to those found in Vermont. When the mass out-migration of blacks from the South began in the 1930s and continued into the 1970s, Southern blacks were drawn to large industrial cities in the North where the best jobs were.

If you were fleeing from the Mississippi Delta, low-paying agricultural jobs in predominantly rural states had little appeal.

Further evidence of Vermont's unique commitment to freedom and democracy is the way the state governs itself. By far the most important democratic institutions in Vermont are its 246 towns, in which the chief executive officer is a three- or five-member board and the legislative arm is the legendary town meeting. So important is Town Meeting Day, the first Tuesday in March, that it is a statewide holiday. Vermont is one of only two states which has a two-year term for its governor. There are only twelve lawyers in its 180-member, nonprofessional, citizen legislature. Montpelier, Vermont's tiny state capital with a population of 8,300, is the nation's smallest. There is no traditional governor's mansion in Montpelier.

Unfortunately, since the 1950s there has been a steady erosion of the political influence of Vermont's town meetings. Social welfare, public education, roads, taxation, and financial management, previously

Vermont Local Self-Government

The most distinguishing feature of life in Vermont just now is the determination of our people to do things for themselves and to learn how those things can be done better and more economically.

The first ideal that prompted the settlement of Vermont was the love of liberty. It was this ideal which prompted the founders of our state to forswear allegiance to any government or any other state or colony. It was that ideal which prompted the settlers of 1777 to set up their own form of government; to write their own Constitution without the aid of a lawyer . . . and it is this love of liberty that today prompts Vermont to revolt against the approach toward the type of centralized government which history has so often proved undesirable.

These principles of loving liberty, of self-reliance, of thrift, and of liberalism have inspired Vermonters to the greatest, most satisfying of all ideals — self-respect. We are not ashamed. We do not think it old-fashioned or reactionary to insist upon the principles of local self-government. We believe that remote control of government is antiquated and not progressive.

Governor George Aiken

Vermont's Virtues

I like Vermont because it is quiet, because you have a population that is solid and not driven mad by the American mania — that mania which considers a town of four thousand twice as good as a town of two thousand, or a city of one hundred thousand, fifty times as good as a town of two thousand. Following that reasoning, one would get the charming paradox that Chicago would be ten times better than the entire state of Vermont, but I have been in Chicago and have not found it so.[19]

---

controlled by the town meetings, are now increasingly the object of bureaucratic state control.

When the first moose hunting season in ninety-seven years was over in October 1993, the lead headline on the front page of the *Burlington Free Press* read "Moose Season Over; Hunters Kill More Than Experts Predicted." The sixteen most dangerous days in the Green Mountain State each year are the deer hunting season. Even though Vermont's gun control laws are among the most lax in the nation, Vermonters are much more into shooting moose and deer than other homo sapiens. Vermont and Alaska are among the very few states in which carrying a concealed weapon is not illegal.

Despite being ranked forty-second in the nation in per capita criminal justice expenditures, Vermont is forty-ninth in terms of violent crimes committed per one hundred thousand population. Although the average per capita criminal justice expenditure for the country is $299, Vermont spends only $185 per capita on law enforcement — thus casting some doubt about the popular American myth that the only way to fight crime is through tougher law enforcement and increased criminal justice expenditures. No one has been executed by the State of Vermont since 1958. Furthermore, the percentage of the Vermont population incarcerated in correctional institutions is the lowest in the nation.

During 1994, the year Richmond, Virginia, had 160 homicides, Vermont, which has a population nearly three times the size of Richmond, had only 5 homicides.

19. Sinclair Lewis, "Vermont's Virtues," cited in *The Vermont Experience,* ed. Susan Bartlett Weber (Montpelier: Vermont Life, 1987), p. 41.

Ethan Allen's Leadership Style

Allen's leadership rested on the personalization of political authority. His power did not emerge from elected office, and his sole official position was commander of the state militia. But this rank proved sufficient, especially as he freely sat in on any governmental body he chose, from the council to the courts. Command of the Green Mountain Boys made Allen the defender of the frontiers and the stability of Vermont while supplying him with the requisite force for coercing Yorkers and other hesitant citizens.[20]

Although Vermont was until recently a Republican state, it was never the mean-spirited Republicanism one finds in New Hampshire or the racially based Republicanism so common to the South. Vermont politics is more a politics of reason than one finds in most states. It avoided the anticommunist hysteria generated by McCarthyism in the 1950s. It has been spared the destructive consequences of the politics of race.

Vermont's democratic ways show up in many areas other than town meetings. For example, 67.5 percent of Vermont's voting age population voted in the 1992 presidential election, in contrast to the 55.2 percent for the country as a whole.

Vermonters have traditionally been willing to tax themselves heavily to provide high-quality public schools, child care, early childhood education, medical care, mental health services, and social welfare services. One measurable benefit of Vermont's commitment to the health and welfare of its citizens is the fact that it has the second lowest infant mortality rate in the country.

There are threats to Vermont's way of life. In June of 1993, the National Trust for Historic Preservation designated the entire state as one of America's eleven most "endangered historical places." It was the first time a state had ever been placed on the list. That Vermont, of all states, would end up on the endangered species list took many people by surprise. A proposed $40 million shopping mall in Rutland and Wal-Mart's attempt to open stores in Saint Albans and Williston contributed to Vermont being placed on such an inauspicious list.

20. Bellesiles, p. 163.

Green Mountain Politics

A politics of human scale [which] can give expression to humankind's longed-for ideals of liberty and community, freedom and unity.

Frank Bryan and John McClaughry
The Vermont Papers

Suburban sprawl has turned the ten-mile stretch of Route 7 south of Burlington into the most unsightly ten miles of highway in the entire state. What was once a scenic drive near Lake Champlain to the quaint village of Shelburne has become a grotesque strip mall of fast-food restaurants, automobile dealerships, discount stores, and shopping malls. During most of the day there is bumper-to-bumper traffic between Burlington and Shelburne.

By 1970 real estate development had already produced such adverse effects in Vermont that the legislature passed an unprecedented law aimed at controlling the abuse of Vermont's natural heritage — Act 250. According to Act 250, any substantial public or private real estate development project must obtain a permit certifying that the project will not adversely affect air and water quality, water supplies, roads and transportation, public schools, municipal services, scenic beauty, historic sites, wildlife, and irreplaceable natural areas.

Poet Robert Frost, who spent his summers in a cabin near Middlebury College's Bread Loaf Campus, captured the essence of Vermont in his poem "The Road Not Taken."[21]

> Two roads diverged in a wood, and I —
> I took the one less traveled by,
> And that has made all the difference.

Ten percent of Vermont's population speaks French as a first language. In 1985 Vermonters elected a Jewish woman, Madeleine M. Kunin, who was born in Switzerland, governor of their state. Interestingly enough, Ms. Kunin is now American ambassador to Switzerland.

---

21. Robert Frost, "The Road Not Taken," in *The Road Not Taken,* by Robert Frost (New York: Henry Holt, 1971), p. 271.

Vermont was one of two states which did not experience bank closures during the early 1930s.[22] Vermont dairy farmers refuse to use bovine somatotropin growth hormone to increase milk production. And for nearly twenty years, Cavendish, Vermont, was the home of eccentric Russian Nobel Prize–winning novelist Alexander Solzhenitsyn.

Vermont Wants Out

For two centuries Vermonters have put up with a lot from America. Too much. Our association with the United States has caused an accumulation of offenses matched only by our capacity to forgive, to accept hollow apologies, and to begin (we are ashamed to admit) to question our own principles in an attempt to go halfway and look at things through others' eyes.[23]

Yes, Vermont is indeed different, but not unlike most places, it too has a dark side, perhaps related to its long winters. Vermont ranks second in the nation in the percentage of people who get extremely drunk and tenth in the percentage of those who get drunk regularly. In addition, it consistently ranks among those states with the highest rate of alcohol-related automobile fatalities. A particularly obnoxious and dangerous habit of some young, male Vermonters — often inebriated — is driving down country roads shooting at road signs.

Only eleven states have a higher suicide rate than Vermont — most notably Rocky Mountain states such as Montana, Idaho, and Wyoming, which experience winters similar to those in Vermont. However, Vermont's suicide rate is considerably lower than that found in Nordic countries like Finland, Denmark, and Sweden, which have much longer periods of winter darkness than Vermont.

Not everyone who is fed up with the crime, drug abuse, traffic, urban sprawl, and deteriorating quality of life in urban America can pack up and move to Vermont. But we can all learn from Vermont's experience.

For example, in 1990 seven of seven independent-minded Ver-

---

22. Charles T. Morrissey, *Vermont* (New York: W. W. Norton, 1984), p. 64.
23. Frank Bryan and Bill Mares, *Out! The Vermont Secession Book* (Shelburne, Vt.: New England Press, 1987), p. 29.

mont communities voted overwhelmingly to secede from the Union in their annual town meetings. Just a few years earlier, when many Americans thought President Ronald Reagan could walk on water, 150 Vermont towns defied Reagan and demanded a nuclear freeze.[24] By way of explanation of Vermont's contrariness, University of Vermont political scientist Frank Bryan once said, "Vermont is just obstinate. We'll do anything to be on the wrong side."

As part of Vermont's bicentennial celebration in 1991, Bryan and Vermont Supreme Court justice John Dooley traveled around the Green Mountain State debating the pros and cons of Vermont seceding from the Union.

Vermonters Can Do It Better

Vermonters can do it better themselves. We are better at education, welfare, building roads, catching crooks, dispensing justice, and helping farmers. We report our own news better. Vermonters know much more about what's happening in Vermont than Americans know about what's happening in America. We're better at democracy, too, much better. We can balance our budget! We've watched as Congress pitters and patters, dillies and dallies, postures, poses, and primps. If that's America's idea of democracy, we want out![25]

Bryan coauthored with Vermont state representative Bill Mares a provocative little book entitled *Out! The Vermont Secession Book*. In this fantasy about the discovery of the Moscow Covenant — signed by George Washington and Ethan Allen — the authors lead you to the realization that Vermont never joined the Union, rather the Union joined Vermont and, "after two hundred years of bureaucracy, federal mismanagement, and un-Vermont-like actions, Vermont wants out."

Most readers assumed that *The Vermont Secession Book* was written tongue in cheek. It was not!

24. Bryan and Mares, p. 30.
25. Bryan and Mares, p. 33.

The Alaskan Independence Party

> Dedicated to the peaceful and lawful separation of Alaska
> from the United States.

Alaska's six hundred thousand residents not only have the sixth highest per capita income in the country and pay no state taxes whatsoever, but they also have the most vocal secessionist movement of any state in the Union.

Alaska's best-known secessionist was Joe Vogler, who founded the Alaskan Independence Party (AIP) in 1973 and headed it for twenty years until he was murdered in 1993. Vogler ran for governor under the party's banner in 1974, 1982, and again in 1986, when he took 5.8 percent of the statewide vote and 17.3 percent of the vote in his hometown of Fairbanks.[26]

The main thrust of the AIP's challenge to an Alaskan statehood is based on the party's claim that the 1958 statehood election was deliberately manipulated by the U.S. government, which wanted to assure an affirmative vote because of Alaska's strategic military importance in the Cold War. Specifically, the AIP questions the legality of granting voting rights to forty-one thousand military personnel as well as thirty-six thousand of their dependents without forfeiting their overseas financial allowances. Furthermore, many indigenous Americans were disqualified from voting because they could not read or write English.

In 1990, the AIP moved from the political sidelines to center stage when it allowed former Governor Walter J. Hickel to run for governor under the AIP label even though he was a Republican who distanced himself from secession. Hickel won the three-way race by capturing 39 percent of the vote.

Shortly before Vogler's disappearance in May 1993, the AIP petitioned the United Nations complaining of abuses by the United States government toward Alaska. The complaint accused the United States of denying the Alaskan people their fundamental right to "political self determination" and their right to "use and exploit" the state's wealth and natural resources. The petition requested that the United Nations vote on whether Alaska should remain a state or become an independent nation or a commonwealth.

26. Nate Ripley, "Gone without a Trace," *Alaska*, March 1994, pp. 34-39.

Joe Vogler — Alaskan Secessionist

Joe Vogler, a miner, land developer, and founder of the Alaskan Independence Party, was 80 years old when he disappeared in May 1993. After 16 months of investigation, his body was unearthed from a shallow grave near Fairbanks on October 12, 1994. A Fairbanks man was indicted for his murder.

Vogler was an outspoken critic of government and advocated Alaska's secession from the Union. He made war on his neighbors, local government and the state, sometimes appearing in court as his own lawyer. He saved his most spectacular verbal volleys for federal officials, especially those of the Park Service who imposed control on his mining and land development activities.

Vogler made three unsuccessful bids for governor under the Alaskan Independence banner. His last appearance on Alaska's political stage was in 1990, when he lent the Alaskan Independence Party to former Gov. Wally Hickel so Hickel would have a spot on the general election ballot. At his request, Vogler will be buried in Canada, beyond the reach of Washington bureaucrats.

Anchorage Daily News

The Independent Nation-State of Hawaii

In November 1993, President Clinton signed Public Law 103-150 apologizing to the 140,000 Native Hawaiians, who call themselves *Kanaka Maoli,* for the January 17, 1893, U.S. Marine invasion of Hawaii deposing Queen Liliuokalani which led to Hawaii's annexation by the United States and ultimately statehood in 1959.

Public Law 103-150

The Congress apologizes to Native Hawaiians on behalf of the people of the United States for the overthrow of the kingdom of Hawaii on January 17, 1893 with the participation of agents and citizens of the United States and deprivation of the rights of Native Hawaiians to self-determination.

Proclamation Restoring the Independence of the Sovereign Nation State of Hawaii, January 16, 1994

Today the Kanaka Maoli proclaim our Right of self-determination as a People in accordance with Article 1 (2) of the United Nations Charter, and join the World Community of States as an independent and Sovereign Nation state. We hereby re-establish our Independent and Sovereign Nation State of Hawaii, that was illegally taken from the Kanaka Maoli on January 17, 1893.

By virtue of our right to self-determination the Kanaka Maoli claim the Right to freely determine our political status and freely pursue our economic, social and cultural development in accordance with common Article 1 of the International Covenant on Economic, Social and Cultural Rights.

The Kanaka Maoli claim the Right, for our own ends, to freely dispose of our natural wealth and resources . . . including our lands and our waters without prejudice to any obligations arising out of international economic cooperation, based upon the principle of mutual benefit and international law.

We the Kanaka Maoli, claim all the Land, and Natural Wealth, Resources and Minerals, and Waters, which has always resided and will always reside within the Hands of the Kanaka Maoli, to be ours forever, originally under communal land tenure.[27]

Whether it was his intention or not, President Clinton clearly raised the expectations of the *Kanaka Maoli* that one day Hawaii might once again become an independent nation-state. The downtrodden *Kanaka Maoli*, who make up more than 12 percent of Hawaii's population, "die younger, earn less, go to jail more frequently, and are more likely to be homeless than any other ethnic group in the islands," according to the *Honolulu Weekly*.

On January 16, 1994, the *Kanaka Maoli* proclaimed the independence of the Sovereign Nation State of Hawaii.

In a 1996 state-sponsored plebiscite, 30,000 descendants of Hawaii's original Polynesians voted 3 to 1 in favor of creating some

27. Francis Anthony Boyle, "Restoration of the Independent Nation State of Hawaii under International Law," *St. Thomas Law Review,* summer 1995, p. 751.

form of Native Hawaiian government — paving the way for a 1998 constitutional convention to decide what kind of Native government they want. Proposals range from full independence to Indian reservation–like status.

Other Secession Movements

The decentralists we have described in Alaska, Hawaii, and Vermont all want their respective states to secede from the United States and go it alone as independent nations. On the other hand, decentralists in West Kansas, New York, and California are more interested in breaking up their states into smaller regions. The last time a new state was created by splitting from another was back in 1863 when West Virginia was sliced from Virginia.

Splinter States

New states may be admitted by the Congress into this union; but no new state shall be formed or erected within the jurisdiction of any other state; nor any state be formed by the junction of two or more states, or parts of states, without the consent of the legislatures of the states concerned as well as of the Congress.

U.S. Constitution

Agitated by then-Governor Joan Finney's plan to impose statewide property tax levies and state-controlled per pupil expenditures for each school district in Kansas, country lawyer Don Concannon petitioned the Stevens County Board of Commissioners on January 27, 1992, to call a special countywide election to consider the following question:

> Should the Stevens County Commissioners, as the duly elected governing body of all the citizens of Stevens County, pursue the steps necessary to immediately disassociate Stevens County from the authority of the State of Kansas for the purpose of establishing a new state or other independent republic to be separate and distinct

from the State of Kansas and to pursue statehood either individually or in cooperation with adjacent and contiguous areas whose citizens are being taxed disproportionately to the benefits received from the state government.

Later that spring the people of Stevens County voted 1,467 to 73 to split with Kansas. Other western counties soon voted overwhelmingly to join Stevens.

In chapter 3 we outlined some of the arguments put forth by secessionists who favor a divorce between New York City and upstate New York.

Home Rule

We are a nation born in secession, consecrated to the right of a free people to rule themselves, and our inherited desire for local control flickers on. With every passing day, the antipathy of the outland for the imperious capitals — be they Washington, Albany, Sacramento, or Topeka — grows fiercer. Independence for regions such as the Oklahoma panhandle, eastern Colorado, Michigan's Upper Peninsula, northwest Texas, and southern Oregon may strike worldly ears as a delusion of romantics clinging stubbornly to principles long ago entombed in the foundation of centralized empire. But home rule is an old American story, and may be due for a revival by some band of cowlick Jeffersons. For when in the course of human events it becomes necessary for one People to dissolve the Political Bands that have tied them to another, self-evident truths have a funny way of asserting themselves.[28]

Former nine-term California assemblyman Stan Statham has called for dividing California into three parts. Other states where secession is being seriously debated include Colorado, Idaho, Louisiana, Montana, Nevada, New Mexico, Oregon, and Washington.

---

28. Bill Kauffman, "Smaller Is Beautiful," *American Enterprise,* March/April 1995, p. 41.

Logland, Smogland, and Fogland

The woodsy north, with 2.3 million residents; the sprawling urban-suburban south, home to 17.5 million; and central California from the San Joaquin Valley to San Francisco, encompassing Silicon Valley, Santa Barbara, and 10.5 million people between.[29]

What a Great Splish-Splash!

> If all the seas were one sea,
> What a great sea that would be!
> If all the trees were one tree,
> What a great tree that would be!
> And if all the axes were one axe,
> What a great axe that would be!
> And if all the men were one man,
> What a great man that would be!
> And if that great man took the great axe,
> And cut down the great tree,
> And let it fall into the great sea,
> What a splish-splash that would be!

> English Nursery Rhyme

Margaret Wheatley affirms the primacy of the small and the local as the place to begin the transformation of any system, no matter how large: "Acting locally is a sound strategy for changing large systems. Instead of trying to map an elaborate system, the advice is to work with the system that you know, one you can get your arms around."[30]

The modern, Newtonian worldview says that by working with small segments of a larger system, we affect the total system by degrees, incrementally. Eventually, enough small changes will affect the larger system.

The quantum view, however, stresses that each small segment

---

29. Kauffman, p. 41.

30. Margaret Wheatley, *Leadership and the New Science* (San Francisco: Berrett-Koehler, 1992), p. 42.

of a system shares certain characteristics with the larger whole. Events occur simultaneously, at different locales through the entire system, and eventually impact the whole. The smaller units share an unbroken whole with a larger system. We begin to work where we are in a system, where change is possible, such as in the state of Vermont, confident that other segments of the larger system are awaiting change. Vermont is surprised that, in seeking its well-being as a state, it connects with other places where change is needed.

The Idolatry of Giantism

You do not make non-viable people viable by putting large numbers of them into one huge community, and you do not make viable people non-viable by splitting a large community into a number of smaller, more intimate, more coherent and more manageable groups.[31]

We believe small is not only beautiful as the final form of institutions; small is also the place to begin to change our institutions. All good global solutions are local in origin and intent. It is toward a local strategy for dissolution that we now turn.

Strategies for Empowering and Downsizing States

1. Repeal most federal regulations of states.
2. Eliminate most federal financial subsidies to states.
3. Allow megastates such as California, Florida, New York, and Texas to split up into smaller states.
4. Allow megacities such as New York, Chicago, and Los Angeles to become separate states.

---

31. E. F. Schumacher, *Small Is Beautiful* (New York: Harper & Row, 1973), p. 76.

11 Dissolution, Not Devolution

When, in the course of human events, it becomes necessary for one people to dissolve the political bands which
have connected them with another, and to assume, among
the powers of the earth, the separate and equal station to
which the laws of nature and of nature's God entitle them,
a decent respect to the opinions of mankind requires that
they should declare the causes which impel them to the
separation.

We hold these truths to be self-evident, that all men
are created equal; that they are endowed by their Creator
with certain unalienable rights; that among these, are life,
liberty, and the pursuit of happiness. That, to secure these
rights, governments are instituted among men, deriving
their just powers from the consent of the governed; that,
whenever any form of government becomes destructive
of these ends, it is the right of the people to alter or to
abolish it, and to institute a new government, laying its
foundation on such principles, and organizing its powers
in such form, as to them shall seem most likely to effect
their safety and happiness.

The Declaration of Independence
July 4, 1776

Control, Chaos, or Creative Change?

Our present form of government, like our present form of death-deny-ing health care, is founded upon fear. Our national government is a by-product of Hitler and Stalin, the Great Depression, and the urban riots of the sixties. If we seem overstructured in our government, it is due to our belief that only strong, complex structures, some new tower of Babel, can protect us from chaos. It's a dark, destructive world out there; only a strong, well-organized state will protect us.

It is our job to hold the world together, collectively to fight our feelings of fear and fragility. This view of government originated in the emerging worldview of the seventeenth and eighteenth centuries. Nas-cent science gave us a world without God or, at the least, a world where God no longer mattered. The world is a great, free-standing machine, a closed clockwork system set in motion, left to run on its own.

The world therefore is not magic. It is a machine. If there is any change or progress, it's up to us to provide the energy by sheer force of will — but we better be careful. In any interlocking machine, one broken part causes the whole mechanism to quit. Every part must be attached to every other part for the machine to work.

But what if our world is more organic than mechanistic? What if systems, like the United States, are not machines but rather living, breathing organisms always renewing themselves, always moving, changing shape in order to survive?

Margaret Wheatley has shown that the old mechanistic view of the universe is giving way to a more organic, interconnected view of the universe as a place of constant growth and change, constant reinte-gration and movement.

"New science is . . . making us aware that our yearning for simplicity is one we share with natural systems. In many systems, scientists now understand that order and conformity and shape are created not by complex controls, but by the presence of a few guiding formulae or principles."[1]

Alas, in too many of our social systems, as we have noted in this book, we have confused hierarchical control with order. It was Lenin who said, "Freedom is good, but control is better."[2] If our social organi-

---

1. Margaret J. Wheatley, *Leadership and the New Science* (San Francisco: Ber-rett-Koehler, 1992), p. 11.
2. Wheatley, p. 22.

zations, like our nations, are no more than machines, then control makes sense. But what if we seek order rather than control? What if we seek those means whereby our diversities and our regional differences might be connected rather than controlled?

One of us recently said to a friend who is an expert on Russia, "Things have really become messy over there since the demise of the Soviet Union, what with the breakaway republics, the rebellions, and difficulties."

He replied, "No. Things were always messy, interesting, and conflicted there, though for a time Soviet tanks made it seem unified and coherent."

The modern lust for unity, for a center, for coherence and cohesiveness produced not only perhaps the most violent century the world has ever known but also some of the most dreary centralized governments and collectivist schemes, to say nothing of some of the ugliest architecture, ever. The delightful differences which make us human are suppressed, coerced into stifling conformity which produces inhumanity. Anyone who admires New York's World Trade Center or the Atlanta airport will disagree with what we say in these pages.

In her book *Leadership and the New Science,* Margaret Wheatley uses the term *autopoiesis* (from the Greek, meaning "self-production") to describe "The characteristic of living systems to continuously renew themselves and to regulate this process in such a way that the integrity of their structure is maintained."[3]

She says that "Every living thing expends energy and will do whatever is needed to preserve itself, including changing. Every living thing exists in form and is recognizable as itself." Systems never are at rest; they constantly seek self-renewal.

> In a dissipative structure, things in the environment that disturb the system's equilibrium play a crucial role in creating new forms of order. As the environment becomes more complex, generating new and different information, it provokes the system into a response. New information enters the system as a small fluctuation that varies from the norm. If the system pays attention to this fluctuation, the information grows in strength as it interacts with the system and is fed back on itself. . . . Finally, the information grows to such a level of disturbance that the system can no longer ignore it. At this point,

3. Wheatley, p. 18.

jarred by so much internal disturbance and far from equilibrium, the system in its current form falls apart. But this disintegration does not signal the death of the system. In most cases the system can reconfigure itself at a higher level of complexity, one better able to deal with the new environment.[4]

Disorder can therefore be a creative source of new order. Defenders of the old order will cry that chaos threatens, that disorder will lead to destruction. We believe chaos can be a source of creativity.

John Stuart Mill on the Importance of the Local

The only security against political slavery is the check maintained over governors by the diffusion of intelligence, activity and public spirit among the governed. . . . It is . . . of supreme importance that all classes of the community . . . should have much to do for themselves; that as great a demand should be made on their intelligence and virtue as it is in any respect equal to; that the government should . . . encourage them, to manage as many as possible of their joint concerns by voluntary co-operation.

We began this book with a chronicle of the many signs of dysfunction and disorder in our society. Yet might these also be seen as new information indicating that our society is overdue for reconfiguration? When we call for dissolution, it is not a call to go back to some allegedly "good old days," when life was more simple, less complicated and serene. Rather, it ought to be seen as a call to admit how much of our modern regimentation, organizational complexity, and lust for control has lied about the real differences which exist among us, has given the illusion of serenity behind a mask of government control. And then it ought to be seen as an invitation to restructure ourselves so that our national structures are more faithful to the complexity among us. Disorder need not be seen as a threat, but rather as a source of new order. Our view is therefore at odds with Arthur Schlesinger's *The Disuniting of America,* in which disunity and a diversity of voices is equated with weakness. We say that Schlesinger's

4. Wheatley, pp. 19-20.

imposition of false unity ought to be recognized as one of the major causes of civil strife.

The Case for Dissolution

With the collapse of communism in Eastern Europe and the Soviet Union, secession fever has spread all over Europe. The Soviet Union split into fifteen independent republics, many of which have their own internal secessionist groups which are striving for independence as well. Bulgaria, Hungary, Poland, and Romania are all separate, independent countries beholding to no one. Czechoslovakia peacefully divided itself into the Czech and Slovak republics. As a result of the dissolution of Yugoslavia, Slovenia, Croatia, Serbia, and Bosnia are all independent nations as well. Throughout Europe there are dozens of other independence movements in such diverse countries as Belgium, Bulgaria, England, Italy, Poland, Romania, Serbia, and Spain.[5] And in our own backyard, the Quebecois seem more determined than ever before to split with English-speaking Canada.

We believe the time has come to reconsider secession as a viable option for dealing with our own problems of big government, big military, big business, big labor, and big cities. America has become an unworkable meganation which defies central management and control. We must begin downsizing our nation, including our government, our military, our corporations, our labor unions, our cities, our farms, our schools, and our universities. Our states should be allowed to secede from the Union; megastates such as California, Texas, and New York should be permitted to break up; and megalopolises such as Chicago, Houston, Los Angeles, and New York should be encouraged to downsize and possibly even split with their respective states. Decentralization and devolution are pretend solutions to problems which require radical surgery, not just more political rhetoric.

In response to the question, "Is there a size limit below which it is not feasible for a political unit to secede?" Robert W. McGee argues that

> there appears to be no size that is too small. Many independent nations are smaller than New York City, yet are viable: Consider

5. Hans-Hermann Hoppe, "Against Centralization," *Salisbury Review,* June 1993, p. 26.

The Paradox of Size

Secessions are alarming to us if we think that making small things from bigger things is a step backward or downward. Is it? Does progression from bigger to smaller signify deterioration?

Jane Jacobs
The Question of Separatism

Andorra, Antigua and Barbuda, Bahrain, Barbados, Dominica, Grenada, the Republic of Kiribati, Liechtenstein, the Republic of Maldives, Malta, Monaco, the Republic of Nauru, St. Kitts and Nevis, Saint Lucia, Saint Vincent and the Grenadines, San Marino, the Republic of Seychelles, Tonga, Tuvalu, and Vatican City. Two nations, Monaco and Vatican City, are actually smaller than New York City's Central Park. Another nation, Hong Kong, is one of the world's economic giants, and is only slightly larger than New York City.[6]

We believe that not only is secession morally justifiable but that it is completely consistent with the U.S. Constitution.

The Right to Band Together

Any group of free individuals has the fundamental right to band together to form a voluntary association to promote the common good whether it be a nation, a state, a town, or a district.

The Right to Secede

Just as a nation, a state, a town, or a district has a right to form, so too does it have a right to disband, subdivide itself, or secede from a larger unit.

Naylor & Willimon

6. Robert W. McGee, "Secession Reconsidered," *Journal of Libertarian Studies*, fall 1994, p. 13.

The Morality of Secession

Early in his political career Abraham Lincoln supported the right to secede:

> Any people anywhere being inclined and having the power have the right to rise up and shake off the existing government, and form a new one which suits them better. This is a most valuable, a most sacred right — a right which we hope and believe is to liberate the world. Nor is this right confined to cases in which the whole people of an existing government may choose to exercise it. Any portion of such people that can may revolutionize and make their own so much of the territory as they inhabit.[7]

Later he had a change of heart and made preservation of the Union *the* moral imperative of the United States. Lincoln said clearly that the war was about preservation of the Union and "If I could save the Union without freeing *any* slave I would do it, and if I could save the Union by freeing some and leaving others alone I would also do that. What I do about slavery, and the colored race, I do because I believe it helps to save the Union."[8] Later, when it seemed politically expedient, Lincoln freed the slaves. Yet not before he had enshrined in the American heart the notion that the main job of being an American is to ensure the survival of the Union in its present form. We do this not only for ourselves, but for the entire world, to ensure that "government of the people, by the people, and for the people will not perish from the earth." When one can accept even slavery as subordinate to the Union, one has claimed a very large moral stake for the Union.

We believe that it is time to consider secession and dissolution as moral acts designed to preserve the integrity of ethnic and minority interests from domination and suppression by the larger culture, as a way of returning power to the local community whereby our most pressing social problems can be solved, and as a legitimate development within our evolving national political life. We do so, not as many liberals have done in the past, seeing national government as a menace

7. Abraham Lincoln's speech "If You Can Secede You May," cited in Rupert Emerson, *From Empire to Nation* (Cambridge: Harvard University Press, 1960), p. 450.
8. Abraham Lincoln, *Speeches and Writings*, ed. Don E. Fehrenbach, vol. 2 (New York: Literary Classics of America, 1989), pp. 357-88.

Jefferson on Secession

The future inhabitants of [both] the Atlantic and Mississippi states will be our sons. We think we see their happiness in their union, and we wish it. Events may prove otherwise; and if they see their interest in separating why should we take sides? God bless them both, and keep them in union if it be for their good, but separate them if it be better.[9]

---

to the individual (which it indeed may be), but rather out of our continuing concern for the loss of community within our society.

Liberalism has always stressed *individual* rights and the need of government to protect those rights. A subtheme of this book has been our advocacy of *group* rights, the rights of whole communities to assert themselves and to be empowered to pursue their own future. One of the great failures of philosophical and political liberalism has been its denial of the efficacy of community, neighborhood, tribe, family, church, and group in its creation of and exaltation of the sovereign individual. Our government, for instance, has attempted to address the evil of racism as an individual human rights problem rather than a minority rights problem, perhaps fearing that to deal with racism as a group problem would be to recognize a distinct group with distinct political needs, and this our government has been loath to do. Whenever we become more attentive to the rights of the group, then the right of a group to withdraw from those political configurations which are injurious to the survival and sustenance of the group will be an option.

Many base their belief in our present constitutional government upon some idea of a hypothetical *social contract*. In the United States, it is argued, individuals are bound together in a "social contract" whereby we give over certain individual rights to the government in exchange for the government giving us certain goods we could not otherwise have on our own as individuals — military protection, civic order, welfare in time of distress, etc.

Yet there is in fact no such contract. None of us were ever asked to sign such a contract. Liberalism, growing out of the Enlightenment,

---

9. Merrill D. Peterson, *Thomas Jefferson and the New Nation* (New York: Oxford University Press, 1970), p. 772.

thought there was some universal agreement on what basic rights are and how a government which honored those rights would look. Such arrogant claims to universalism are now discredited by the cacophony of voices whose words demonstrate that different groups see these matters quite differently. The social contract theory assumes that all of us are agreed upon which rights are worth having and which goods dispensed by government are worth having at the expense of which freedoms. For instance, the government is said to give us "freedom of religion." Yet to have this "freedom of religion," religious groups must agree that they are not free to practice their faith in ways that are repugnant to the larger majority. Religion is free so long as it is personal and private. No wonder, then, that a number of religious communities have experienced our "religious freedom" not as freedom, but as a brand of tyranny.

Yet defenders of "the social contract" have said governments can only be dissolved when they are guilty of gross injustices. Then, and only then, can we make the contract invalid. This was the argument used by Jefferson and others in the American Revolution. But even as "the social contract" view of government makes government sound terribly rational and natural, it also makes dissolution terribly serious and rare. Despite the claims of the American revolutionaries, England was high-handed with its colonies, or insensitive, but was not terribly, irrevocably unjust in its dealings with the Americans. Yet is injustice the only possible cause for secession?

We like the analogy used by Allen Buchanan in his fine book on secession. Government is not based on some God-given or humanly devised "social contract" handed down from on high forever and ever. Government, even a democratic government, is not a natural fact. It is a human construction designed to suit the needs of the people. Buchanan says that government is more like marriage than a social contract. Marriages are dissolved for a variety of reasons, sometimes rather vague, but nevertheless important to the parties. Cannot governments also be dissolved for reasons other than gross injustice on the part of the government?[10]

When the Quebec separatists argue that they should be separated from the government in Ottawa, they may argue that government is insensitive, or dull, but it is not terribly unjust. However, to the

10. Allen Buchanan, *Secession: The Morality of Political Divorce from Fort Sumter to Lithuania and Quebec* (San Francisco: Westview, 1991), p. 7.

The Secessionist

Unlike the revolutionary, the secessionist's primary goal is not to overthrow the existing government, not to make fundamental constitutional, economic, or sociopolitical changes within the existing state. Instead, she wishes to restrict the jurisdiction of the state in question so as not to include her own group and the territory it occupies. . . . The secessionist does not deny the state's political authority as such, but only its authority over her and the other members of her group and the territory they occupy. Further, to attempt to secede . . . need not be an attempt to achieve complete political independence. In some cases a group may endeavor to secede from one state in order to become part of another.[11]

---

separatists, the cause of French Canadian cultural preservation may be cause enough.

At a minimum, our government must be willing to experiment with forms of semiautonomy or limited sovereignty for certain areas and groups. Secession does not necessarily mean complete political independence, and it certainly does not mean the overthrow of the existing government; it does mean greatly increased political sovereignty for a separated area. Secession, as a morally defensible idea, is a limited, diverse, necessarily vague idea because a group's or state's need for "self-determination" is also diverse and particular, specific and local. And that is part of the difficulty we have in thinking about these matters. We tend to be modern people who assume that the only valid political solutions are those which are allegedly universal, general, and which apply to all contexts. In this book we are urging a postmodern political imagination which is specific, local, contextual, and particular.

If people love the liberal democratic state, then they ought to honor secessionism because it may be the last hope of preserving that state. Any state which can only be maintained through a rigid, uniform, state-run educational system (as some claim the United States to be) is a state in great danger in the future. America must show how democratic it is willing to be in the cause of democracy, must demonstrate its ability to hold a maximum number of groups together, giving

11. Buchanan, p. 10.

them the maximum amount of freedom, or it is in peril. New democracies will find their formative tasks easier if they include the right to secede in their constitutions (the only government, to our knowledge, to include such a right is the old Soviet Union). Just as Roosevelt's New Deal, far from being an attack upon capitalism, may have saved capitalism from extinction, so secessionism may be the last best hope for the preservation of the old liberal democracy.

Secessionism claims that governments are limited arrangements, that the union effected in government tends to be limited and quite specific, and that it is permissible for a group to withdraw itself from that political union.[12] A constitutionally guaranteed right to secede is therefore a mark of good and just government.

> Good fences make good neighbors.
>
> Robert Frost

The Constitutionality of Secession

Although conventional wisdom holds that the eleven Confederate States of America acted illegally when they seceded from the Union in the 1860s, in a carefully prepared legal analysis, Pepperdine University law professor H. Newcomb Morse argues convincingly that the Confederate States did indeed possess the right to secede and that they exercised this right in a proper manner.[13]

First, no less than seven states had engaged in acts of *nullification* of the U.S. Constitution long before South Carolina announced its plans to secede on December 20, 1860 — Kentucky (1799), Pennsylvania (1809), Georgia (1832), South Carolina (1832), Wisconsin (1854), Massachusetts (1855), and Vermont (1858). According to Professor Morse, "Nullification occurs when the people of a state refuse to recognize the validity of an exercise of power by the national government which, in the state's view, transcends the limited and enumerated delegated powers of the national constitution."[14] Those instances where national

12. Buchanan, p. 35.
13. H. Newcomb Morse, "The Foundations and Meaning of Secession," *Stetson Law Review* 15 (1986): 419-36.
14. Morse, p. 420.

laws had been nullified by Northern states gave credence to the view that the compact forming the Union had already been breached and that the Confederate states were morally and legally free to leave.

The Constitutionality of Secession

Contrary to popular belief, the War Between the States did not prove that the Southern States had no legal right to secede. In fact, many incidents both preceding and following the War support the proposition that the Southern States did have the right to secede from the Union. Instances of nullification prior to the War Between the States, contingencies under which certain states acceded to the Union, and the fact that the Southern States were made to surrender the right to secession all affirm the existence of a right to secede.

In addition, the national Constitution's failure to forbid secession and the various amendments concerning secession that were proposed while the Southern States were seceding each strengthen the proposition: that the Southern States had an absolute right to secede from the Union prior to the War Between the States.[15]

Second, and most importantly, the U.S. Constitution does *not* forbid secession. According to the Tenth Amendment to the Constitution, "The powers not delegated to the United States by the Constitution, nor prohibited by it to the States, are reserved to the States respectively, or to the people." Stated alternatively, that which is not expressly prohibited by the Constitution is allowed.

Third, while the Confederate States were in the process of seceding, three amendments to the Constitution were presented to the U.S. Congress placing conditions on the rights of states to secede. Then on March 2, 1861, after seven states had already seceded, an amendment was proposed which would have outlawed secession entirely. Although none of these amendments were ever ratified, Professor Morse asked, "Why would Congress have even considered proposed amendments to the Constitution forbidding or restricting the right of secession if any such right was already prohibited, limited or non-existent under the Constitution?"

15. Morse, p. 420.

> ### The Articles of Confederation
>
> Each state retains its sovereignty, freedom and independence, and every Power, Jurisdiction and right, which is not by this confederation expressly delegated to the United States, in Congress assembled.
>
> The said states hereby severally enter into a firm league of friendship with each other, for their common defense, the security of their Liberties, and their mutual and general welfare, binding, themselves to assist each other, against all force offered to, or attacks made upon them, or any of them, on account of religion, sovereignty, trade, or any another pretense whatever.

Fourth, three of the original thirteen states — Virginia, New York, and Rhode Island — ratified the U.S. Constitution only conditionally. Each explicitly retained the right to secede. By the time South Carolina seceded in 1860, a total of thirty-three states had acceded to the Union. By accepting the right of Virginia, New York, and Rhode Island to secede, had they not tacitly accepted the doctrine of secession for the nation as a whole?

Fifth, according to Professor Morse, after the Civil War the Union occupational armies were removed from Arkansas, North Carolina, Florida, South Carolina, Mississippi, and Virginia "only after those

> ### South Carolina Secedes
>
> We, the people of the State of South Carolina, in Convention assembled, do declare and ordain, and it is hereby declared and ordained that the ordinance adopted by us in Convention, on the 23rd day of May, in the year of our Lord 1788, whereby the Constitution of the United States of America was ratified, and also all Acts and parts of Acts of the General Assembly of this State ratify the amendments of the said Constitution, are hereby repealed, and that the union now subsisting between South Carolina and other States under the name of the United States of America is hereby dissolved.
>
> December 20, 1860

former Confederate States had incorporated in their constitutions a clause surrendering the right to secede."[16] Mr. Morse has also noted that, "under this premise, all of the Northern States and any other states not required to relinquish the right to secede in their constitutions would still have the right to secede at present."[17]

Sixth, Morse argues that the proper way for a state to secede from the Union is through a state convention elected by the people of the state to decide one and only one question, namely, secession. "Every seceding state properly utilized the convention process, rather than a legislative means, to secede."[18] This is as it should be.

Perpetual Union

The Articles of this confederation shall be inviolably observed by every state, and the union shall be perpetual; nor shall any alteration at any time hereafter be made in any of them; unless such alteration be agreed to in a congress of the united states, and be afterwards confirmed by the legislatures of every state.

Articles of Confederation, 1777

Others, most notably Abraham Lincoln, argue that the Union is perpetual and that secession is tantamount to an unlawful form of anarchy. In March 4, 1861, after seven states had already seceded, Lincoln said:

The Union is much older than the Constitution. It was formed, in fact, by the Articles of Association in 1774. It was matured and continued by the Declaration of Independence in 1776. It was further matured, and the faith of all the then thirteen States expressly plighted and engaged that it should be perpetual, by the Articles of Confederation, in 1777. And, finally, in 1787, one of the declared objects for ordaining and establishing the Constitution was "to form a more perfect Union."

16. Morse, p. 431.
17. Morse, p. 433.
18. Morse, p. 435.

Notwithstanding the conditions imposed on the six former Confederate States requiring them to incorporate clauses in their constitutions forbidding secession, the ultimate test of sovereignty lies with the people themselves. We believe that all American states have a moral and legal right to secede. The Tenth Amendment; the history of nullification; the contingencies under which Virginia, New York, and Rhode Island acceded to the Union; and constitutional amendments proposed while the Confederate States were seceding all support the proposition that secession is indeed legal.

The Economics of Secession

Whether a state will be motivated to leave the Union or not may depend in part on whether it receives more or less in benefits from the federal government than it pays in federal taxes. Alternatively, the Union's willingness to let a state go may be influenced by whether federal tax collections from that state exceed federal government expenditures.

Considerable light may be shed on this subject from information gleaned from the following table, which shows per capita federal expenditures to each state, per capita federal taxes paid by each state, and federal expenditures per dollar of federal taxes by state. A state with a ratio of federal expenditures to federal taxes that is greater than 1.00 is a net winner. At least in theory, for every dollar it sends to Washington it is getting back more than it spends. States which receive federal benefits which are less than their federal taxes are net losers and have a ratio that is less than 1.00.

Thirty states and the District of Columbia are winners in the sense that they each receive more per capita from the federal government than they pay in federal taxes. New Mexico and Mississippi have the highest ratio of federal expenditures to federal taxes paid — 1.86 and 1.61 respectively. In the case of New Mexico this means that for every dollar paid to Washington, the state receives $1.86 in federal benefits — not a bad return on its federal investment. The District of Columbia, which is a special case, receives $5.26 from the U.S. government for every dollar it pays in federal taxes.

Connecticut and New Jersey have the lowest ratio of federal expenditures per dollar of federal taxes, followed closely by Illinois, New Hampshire, Minnesota, Delaware, Michigan, and Nevada. For every dollar paid in federal taxes, New Jersey receives only $.68 back

Federal Expenditures and Taxes by State, Fiscal Year 1995[a]

	Federal Expenditures Per Capita[b]	Federal Taxes Per Capita	Expenditures Per Dollar of Taxes
United States	$5,006	$5,006	1.00
Alabama	5,291	3,919	1.35
Alaska	6,827	5,786	1.18
Arizona	5,022	4,256	1.18
Arkansas	4,696	3,818	1.23
California	4,788	5,040	0.95
Colorado	5,168	5,328	0.97
Connecticut	5,235	7,699	0.68
Delaware	4,566	5,930	0.77
Florida	5,316	5,063	1.05
Georgia	4,623	4,577	1.01
Hawaii	6,265	5,135	1.22
Idaho	4,638	4,104	1.13
Illinois	4,252	5,746	0.74
Indiana	3,907	4,596	0.85
Iowa	4,483	4,439	1.01
Kansas	4,782	4,735	1.01
Kentucky	5,140	3,836	1.34
Louisiana	5,097	3,891	1.31
Maine	5,193	4,057	1.28
Maryland	7,261	5,717	1.27
Massachusetts	5,797	6,102	0.95
Michigan	4,056	5,267	0.77
Minnesota	4,037	5,312	0.76
Mississippi	5,244	3,257	1.61
Missouri	5,817	4,617	1.26
Montana	5,532	3,980	1.39
Nebraska	4,631	4,631	1.00
Nevada	4,524	5,875	0.77
New Hampshire	4,210	5,614	0.75
New Jersey	4,638	6,821	0.68
New Mexico	7,003	3,765	1.86
New York	5,074	6,041	0.84
North Carolina	4,246	4,289	0.99
North Dakota	5,813	4,212	1.38
Ohio	4,442	4,828	0.92

Oklahoma	4,848	3,817	1.27
Oregon	4,385	4,715	0.93
Pennsylvania	5,228	5,076	1.03
Rhode Island	5,649	5,183	1.09
South Carolina	4,762	3,840	1.24
South Dakota	5,185	4,357	1.19
Tennessee	4,979	4,406	1.13
Texas	4,478	4,523	0.99
Utah	4,395	3,693	1.19
Vermont	4,521	4,476	1.01
Virginia	7,692	5,128	1.50
Washington	5,325	5,325	1.00
West Virginia	5,361	3,504	1.53
Wisconsin	3,845	4,806	0.80
Wyoming	5,145	4,854	1.06
District of Columbia	37,293	7,090	5.26

a. Source: "1996 Federal Tax Burden by State," Tax Foundation, Washington, D.C., July 1996.
b. Raw Bureau of Census expenditure data have been adjusted downwards reflecting the fact that the federal government finances a large portion of spending through annual borrowings. Expenditures for each state have been adjusted so that average U.S. spending per capita is equal to average U.S. taxes, i.e., $5,006.

from the federal government in the form of federal expenditures. Nebraska and Washington are neither winners nor losers since each receives an amount in federal expenditures approximately equal to what it pays in federal taxes.

Of the thirteen original states only Georgia, Maryland, Pennsylvania, Rhode Island, South Carolina, and Virginia have federal expenditure-tax ratios which are greater than one. Nine of the eleven former Confederate States of America are net gainers from their relationship to the United States government. Only North Carolina and Texas are losers. Three New England states are net winners — Maine, Rhode Island, and Vermont. The others — Connecticut, Massachusetts, and New Hampshire — are all losers. Finally, Connecticut has the highest per capita federal tax burden in the nation and Mississippi the lowest.

But why would a state like Alaska consider secession, if for every dollar it pays the U.S. government it receives $1.18 in return? That sounds like a very good deal for Alaska. It is not! Most of the federal expenditures in Alaska go for military defense and the "protection" of the 250 million acres of government land in the state. It is no secret that Alaska was annexed in 1959 primarily as a Cold War strategy. The military bases built there were to protect the lower forty-eight states — not Alaskans. Although some Alaskan state government officials may sleep better at night knowing that the state's cash cow, the Prudhoe Bay oil field, is under the watchful eye of the Pentagon, it's hard to imagine why small towns like Anchorage, Fairbanks, and Juneau would ever be subjected to military attack.

Most federal funds are spent in Alaska enforcing government regulations linked to the management of public lands. Not unlike the Swiss, most Alaskans feel they could do a better job of managing their abundance of natural resources than some group of Washington bureaucrats.

States such as Vermont whose ratio of federal expenditures to the federal taxes is close to 1.00 have even less incentive to stay in the Union. Many of the alleged benefits Vermont receives from the federal taxes it pays are not benefits at all. Consider the four hundred million dollars spent on the twenty F-16 fighter jets flying out of the Burlington airport. Other than providing a handful of Air National Guard pilots with part-time employment, these fighters are of no military significance to Vermont. Furthermore, they are a public nuisance and a risk to commercial air travelers.

Other federal funds are spent in Vermont enforcing a plethora of environmental, civil rights, education, and social welfare regulations which few Vermonters asked for and would be delighted to end. Most federal programs are so inefficient that Vermonters would be much better off assuming the full responsibility for these programs themselves without any federal money (or extra federal taxes) whatsoever. In some cases the sheer hassle involved in writing federal grant applications and proposals is not worth the effort.

Vermonters have always taken pride in self-sufficiency, individualism, and hard work. Fifty years ago small Vermont towns and villages took care of their own poor and were not dependent on a costly, rigid, inefficient federal social welfare system. Some Vermonters would like to see a return to local control and responsibility for social welfare.

Connecticut and New Jersey have a particularly strong financial incentive to secede, since they are the biggest losers in the federal tax-and-spend game.

The thirty states that contribute less to the federal government than they receive in benefits may encounter less resistance to secession from Washington than the eighteen net contributors. One obstacle to secession the federal government will surely employ will be to hold a seceding state responsible for its share of the national debt. However, Washington may be more inclined to discount a state's share of the federal debt if the state is a net spender, such as Alabama, rather than a net contributor, such as Indiana. The extra $.18 Alaskans receive for every dollar they send to Washington increases the federal deficit, thus potentially raising the price of secession for Alaska and every other state.

Secession Justice

Some people ask: "What happens when a country, composed of one rich province and several poor ones, falls apart because the rich province secedes?" Most probably the answer is: "Nothing very much happens." The rich will continue to be rich and the poor will continue to be poor. "But if, before secession, the rich province had subsidized the poor, what happens then?" Well then, of course, the subsidy might stop. But the rich rarely subsidize the poor; more often they exploit them.[19]

Settlement Costs

But the real question is not whether secession is legal or not, but rather how Washington would respond if a state actually tried to secede. Would our government's reaction be any different from Moscow's heavy-handed response to Chechnya's ill-fated attempt to secede from Russia? Even if the U.S. Supreme Court were to rule that secession is legal, it is not a foregone conclusion that the White House and Congress would allow a state to leave the Union peacefully.

We believe that Washington's response to a specific state's secession initiatives will depend in part on how that state deals with four complex economic issues: (1) compensation for U.S. government-

19. E. F. Schumacher, *Small Is Beautiful* (New York: Harper & Row, 1973), pp. 76-77.

owned property within the state, (2) payment of relocation costs for citizens who want to leave the state but remain in the United States, (3) disposition of the state's share of the federal debt, and (4) settlement of the state's pro rata claim on the total net worth of the United States taken as a whole.

U.S. Government Property

Whether a state is allowed to depart peacefully may be influenced by the extent to which it is willing to compensate the United States for government-owned property within its territory, including land, highways, buildings, dams, power plants, and military bases.

The U.S. government owns nearly 650 million acres — 28.6 percent of the land within its territorial boundaries. The greatest concentrations of government-owned land lie in the Rocky Mountain and Pacific states. Public land accounts for 82.9 percent of Nevada's territory, 67.9 percent of Alaska, 63.9 percent of Utah, and 61.6 percent of Idaho. Over 90 percent of this government-owned land was already in the public domain when the respective states acceded to the United States. Only 8.7 percent of it was acquired by the United States by direct purchase after accession. Clearly the U.S. government's claims for compensation from seceding states are much stronger for acquired lands than for land which has always been in the public domain. No doubt a seceding state will argue that land which was in the public domain before it joined the Union still belongs to it after secession.

When the Soviet Union broke up in 1991, compensation for Soviet-owned property became a moot point, since the Soviet Union no longer existed. Since it is quite unlikely that the entire United States will dissolve simultaneously, those states remaining in the Union may expect to be compensated for government property by departing states. Establishing a price for, say, an abandoned military base may not be easy. With whom will a state negotiate — the U.S. State Department, the Pentagon, the Department of the Interior, or perhaps several different agencies?

Relocation Costs

Suppose that Vermont decides to leave the Union. Some "flatlanders" (people not born in Vermont) living in Vermont may prefer not to remain in a completely independent Vermont. They may opt to move

U.S. Government-Owned Land, 1991		
	Million Acres	*Percent*
United States	649	28.6
Rocky Mountain States	265	48.3
Arizona	34	47.2
Colorado	24	36.3
Idaho	33	61.6
Montana	26	28.0
Nevada	58	82.9
New Mexico	25	32.4
Utah	34	63.9
Wyoming	30	48.9
Pacific States	338	58.8
Alaska	248	67.9
California	45	44.6
Oregon	32	52.4
Washington	12	28.3

to Florida or some other state which stays in the Union. Vermont may be obliged to pay part of the relocation costs for these loyal Americans. If reason prevails, one would hope that these relocation costs along with Vermont's share of the cost of U.S. government property and the federal debt would all be negotiable.

Federal Debt

One of the stickiest questions may involve the settlement of a seceding state's share of the nation's $5 trillion debt. In 1995 the per capita federal debt stood at a whopping $19,157 for every man, woman, and child in the United States. At face value, Vermont's share of the federal debt would amount to $11 billion, while Texas's share would be a staggering $350 billion.

At first blush these numbers are quite intimidating — enough to make even the most ardent secessionist step back and take note. If a state were obliged to pay its full share of the national debt as part of its secession price, then few if any states would choose the secession option. By allowing the federal debt to grow without limits, have we not created the illusion that secession is completely unaffordable? Sadly, our national debt appears to be part of the glue that holds our fifty states together.

But there is another important piece of the secession puzzle which we have not yet considered — the total value of the net worth of the entire United States to which every state has a pro rata claim.

U.S. Net Worth

The extent to which a seceding state is responsible for covering the aforementioned exit costs will no doubt become an integral part of the debate between the U.S. government and any state which attempts to leave the Union. The government will surely argue vigorously in favor of requiring a seceding state to cover some or all of these costs. If the government wants to block the secession attempt, it will try to impose as high a cost as possible on the departing state.

However, the seceding state is not without some economic bargaining power, since it has a pro rata claim on *all* of the assets of the United States, including land, forests, mineral reserves, waterways, highways, buildings, military bases, military hardware, gold reserves, foreign currency reserves, U.S. government loans, etc. Assuming the net worth of the United States is greater than $5 trillion, which seems quite likely, then the claim that a state must cover its share of the national debt becomes moot. Indeed, depending on how much greater than $5 trillion the nation's net worth actually is, then the United States should compensate a departing state for forgoing its share of the nation's wealth.

Ultimately, whether or not a state is allowed to secede will depend on the political power and the political will of the state compared to the federal government. Economics is sometimes an important surrogate for political power.

12 Empowering the Powerless

The time has come . . . when we must actively fight bigness and overconcentration, and seek instead to bring the
engines of government, of technology, of the economy,
fully under the control of our citizens.

Robert F. Kennedy

Anarchy

What we are advocating here could be described as a form of anarchism.
Anarchy, a belief that government tends to be harmful and unnecessary,
has a long and circuitous history. Although Tolstoy refused the title
anarchist, on the basis of his Christian faith he developed a form of
pacifist radicalism which rejected the idea of the state as well as all
forms of government as unchristian. Tolstoy called for the simplification
of life and for national moral regeneration, frequent themes in anarchist
thought. Oscar Wilde's libertarian essay "The Soul of Man under Socialism" (1891) typifies the romantic, aesthetic tendencies of nineteenth-
century anarchism. The murders of President McKinley and King Um-
berto I of Italy typified the violent, insurrectionist tendencies of
anarchism and account for the linkage, in the popular mind, of anarchy
and terrorism. Eventually, the anarchist movements of the nineteenth
and early twentieth centuries proved to be no match for communism,

259

which captured the revolutionary imagination, seeking to redress class injustice by the imposition of the allegedly proletarian centralized state.

Mahatma Gandhi based much of his nonviolent strategy, as well as his plan for a decentralized society through autonomous village communes, on anarchist thought. While Gandhi's idea of *gramdan* — village ownership of land — has never been put into full effect in India, the hundreds of Indian villages which have adopted the practice, or which still claim to be working toward this ideal, represent a widespread realization of an anarchist principle.

W. B. Yeats on Anarchy

Things fall apart; the centre cannot hold;
Mere anarchy is loosed upon the world.

In 1932, Aldous Huxley's *Brave New World* was a warning about the sort of world modern technological infatuations might produce. In the foreword to the 1946 edition, Huxley stated his belief that only by radical decentralization and simplification could the dark dangers posed by the modern state be avoided. Sixties radicalism, as well as the civil rights movement, reawakened interest in anarchist thought as a way of resisting the unjust states derived from both communism and capitalism.

Anarchy tends to be a spirit of rebellion rather than an organized movement or a coherent body of thought. Like this book, anarchy stresses the need for direct action rather than theory, honors simplicity over complexity, and moral renewal as integrally related to political change. Anarchy is sometimes dismissed as utopian pursuit of an impossible ideal. A more positive reading of anarchy is that it is a vision which enables us to keep revolutionary hope alive. Without a vision, the people perish, says the biblical prophet. State regimentation in its various forms and collectivist and totalitarian thought are too easily accepted as normal without some visionary, apocalyptic expectation that human beings are destined for something better than present arrangements.

In a decaying Roman Empire, sick unto death, Augustine wrote of a different city, the "City of God," that New Jerusalem which is not congruent with the human city we have created. Augustine felt that the first step in political renewal is to remind ourselves that God did not create Rome, we did. Therefore, Rome can and should be changed. Secondly, Augustine asserted that Rome was not a true commonwealth because, like all pagan states, Rome achieved unity and "peace" only through military coercion.[1] Augustine's thought may be dismissed as escapist, other-worldly to the point of being irrelevant, or it may be seen as a visionary source for truly revolutionary action. We can only act in a world we can see.

Anarchy for the Rich — Government for the Poor

The poor have been rebels but they never have been anarchists; they have more interest than anyone else in there being some decent government; the poor man really has a stake in the country. The rich man hasn't; he can go away to New Guinea in a yacht. The poor have sometimes objected to being governed badly; the rich have always objected to being governed at all.

G. K. Chesterton
The Man Who Was Thursday

One of the trenchant criticisms of the anarchy advocated by intellectuals like Wilde was that anarchism exalted individualism at the expense of any concern for the good of community. You will note that, in this book, our concern for the harmful effects of large institutions arises not so much from our concern for individual freedom but rather out of our concern for the well-being of the community. Governments, as we have known them in this century, have a nasty habit of bringing order but destroying community, of forcefully yoking people together, but of destroying interconnectedness.

While there is much that we like in Robert Nozick's *Anarchy, State, and Utopia*,[2] Nozick, like many anarchists before him, depicts society as a collection of individuals who, from time to time, out of their own self-interest come together to cooperate with one another. In an odd sense, there is a connection between modernity's much-praised free individual and the totalitarian states which have made this century infamous.

1. John Milbank, *Theology and Social Theory: Beyond Secular Reason* (Cambridge: Basil Blackwell, 1991), pp. 400-406.
2. Robert Nozick, *Anarchy, State, and Utopia* (New York: Basic Books, 1974).

A great deceit fostered by modern society is that modern government treats us as "individuals" — sovereign, isolated persons. Modern democracy found that by rendering all of us into "individuals" — freestanding, isolated, autonomous units detached from community, tribe, and neighborhood — we were easier to manage and manipulate. The isolated individual, standing alone, disconnected from tribe, neighborhood, or family, proved to be no match for the totalitarian tendencies of the modern state.[3]

In his provocative 1979 essay "The Power of the Powerless" portraying life in communist Czechoslovakia, Václav Havel describes life in liberal democracies such as the United States:

> It would appear that the traditional parliamentary democracies can offer no fundamental opposition to the automation of technological civilization and the industrial-consumer society, for they, too, are being dragged helplessly along by it. People are manipulated in ways that are infinitely more subtle and refined than the brutal methods used in the post-totalitarian societies. But this static complex of rigid, conceptually sloppy and politically pragmatic mass political parties run by professional apparatuses and releasing the citizen from all forms of concrete and personal responsibility; and those complex foci of capital accumulation engaged in secret manipulations and expansion; the omnipresent dictatorship of consumption, production, advertising, commerce, consumer culture, and all that flood of information: all of it, so often analysed and described, can only with great difficulty be imagined as the source of humanity's rediscovery of itself. In his June 1978 Harvard lecture, Solzhenitsyn describes the illusory nature of freedoms not based on personal responsibility and the chronic inability of the traditional democracies, as a result, to oppose violence and totalitarianism. In a democracy, human beings may enjoy many personal freedoms and securities that are unknown to us, but in the end they do them

---

3. The most popular analysis of our current situation in an individualistic culture is Robert N. Bellah et al., *Habits of the Heart* (Berkeley: University of California Press, 1985). When asked, What is the good of our society? Bellah and his colleagues hear us Americans respond that "the ultimate ethical rule is simply that individuals should be able to pursue whatever they find rewarding because there is no moral common ground and therefore no common public relevance of morality outside the sphere of minimal procedural rules and obligations not to injure. . . ." They say, "Such a nation is not a family or a *communitas* but a well-regulated marketplace" (p. 237).

no good, for they too are ultimately victims of the same automatism, and are incapable of defending their concerns about their own identity or preventing their superficialization or transcending concerns about their own personal survival to become proud and responsible members of the *polis*, making a genuine contribution to the creation of its destiny.[4]

We have therefore discovered the irony that *true freedom is dependent upon community*. I know what I want, what wants are worth having, only in community where I receive the training, acquire the habits, learn the history, and gain self-knowledge to the point whereby I can lay hold of my life and name who I am and where I am going. My "I" is not an individual achievement but rather the gift, the product of a community which helps to name me, place me, value me, and tell me who I am.[5]

Liberal democracies have been willing to tolerate great economic inequalities in exchange for their protection of individual "freedom."[6] Liberty may mask other forms of domination. The question is not so much, Are we free? but rather, What is the purpose, the end, of our freedom? We have thought it possible to have a society where people are given freedom to exercise their "rights," without an argument about which rights are worth having and toward what end the exercise of our various rights is moving us.

In *The Needs of Strangers*, Michael Ignatieff argued that most contemporary political philosophy speaks of "justice" as an individual problem. The needs of groups and communities are subordinated to sets of individual needs. Yet more than this, Ignatieff says contemporary political philosophy is worse than too individualistic. In lacking any account of the good, we are led to believe that all of our individual

4. Václav Havel, "The Power of the Powerless," in *The Power of the Powerless,* ed. John Keane (Armonk, N.Y.: M. E. Sharpe, 1985), p. 91.

5. This insight was first brought home to us in our observation of college students. Those students who were most recognizably free individuals, self-confident, able to name themselves and where they were going, tended to be lodged most happily in some group that gave them the self-confidence they needed to move into the world as individuals. William H. Willimon and Thomas H. Naylor, *The Abandoned Generation: Rethinking Higher Education* (Grand Rapids: Eerdmans, 1995), pp. 89-91. The group as basis for individual freedom is also stressed by Will Kymlicka, *Liberalism, Community, and Culture* (New York: Oxford University Press, 1989).

6. This has been a persistent criticism of recent defenses of liberal democracies such as that of John Rawls, *A Theory of Justice* (Cambridge: Harvard University Press, 1961).

needs are worth meeting, that all of our desires are our rights. If I feel a desire, then that desire is elevated to the level of a need, which is further elevated to the level of an essential right.

The societies created by this account of human beings as bundles of boundless needs to be met tend to be societies free of constraints upon the needs of individuals within them. Both liberal-capitalistic and Marxist societies tend to be imperialistic, telling members of those societies that the government can deliver all that the individuals' hearts desire. Government exists to reward our unrealistic expectations. Thus, government has become our God.

> The best laid schemes o' mice and men.
>
> Robert Burns

Bureaucracy

Hannah Arendt, in her book *The Human Condition*, noted that Western, industrialized society had lost its "teleological view," that is, any sense that there is some purpose to society, that we are moving toward any common goal.[7] (*Telos* is the Greek word for "end" or "purpose.") We live in a self-operating, free-standing Newtonian universe. Economics, in this scheme, is no longer a discussion about how to alleviate human misery or how to better the human condition, but rather how to uncover the workings of the market so that the market might be better used to achieve greater wealth, without a discussion of where such activity might be leading us.

The abandonment of the teleological view, says Arendt, led to the split between private and public life. In an agricultural society,

---

7. "Liberalism assumes . . . that it is a natural condition of a free democratic culture that a plurality of conceptions of the good is pursued by its citizens." John Rawls, "Social Utility and Primary Goods," in *Utilitarianism and Beyond,* ed. Amartya Kumar Sen and Bernard Williams (Cambridge: Cambridge University Press, 1982), p. 160.

Michael Walzer writes that "A liberal nation can have no collective purpose." The liberal state can never be "a home for its citizens; it lacks warmth and intimacy." *Radical Principles: Reflections of an Unreconstructed Democrat* (New York: Basic Books, 1980), p. 69.

which we extolled in chapter 4, each person was interconnected to others by the nature of the labor itself. In such an economy, each person has a fixed, well-established identity given as a by-product of the connectedness of farm, home, church, town. The modern city, as opposed to a rural economy, is a huddle of interchangeable operatives, like interchangeable parts of a machine, each specialized and disposable, connected only to a narrow network of people to whom he or she chooses to connect. Our grandest goal is to be left alone.

Human behavior is now described in terms of cause-effect rather than purpose. We want to know what works and why, rather than the good or the ultimate value in what works. Modern science methodologically eliminated the notion of purpose from its investigations. Any explanation worthy of the term "scientific" is that explanation which carefully avoids any interest in the question, Where is all of this taking us? Declarations of what is are privileged over any consideration of what ought to be.

The demise of teleology accounts, in part, for the inherently conservative attitude we have encountered when questioning large bureaucratic organizations about themselves. These big organizations are based upon the assumption that they are the creation of the "facts," an organizational response to "the way things are," merely an efficient means of getting the job done in "the real world." Any other scheme of organization will be dismissed as inefficient, idealistic, unrealistic. Our imaginations become monopolized by one form of human organization — big is better — to the exclusion of alternative forms.

Politics, said Aristotle, is free people arguing, How ought we order our life together? What are the ends, the goal of our societies?

In *After Virtue* Alasdair MacIntyre charges that "Modern society is indeed often . . . nothing but a collection of strangers, each pursuing his or her own interests under minimal constraints. We still . . . find it difficult to think of families, colleges, and other genuine communities in this way; but even our thinking about those is now invaded to an increasing degree by individualist conceptions, especially the law courts."[8] As Robert Bellah and his colleagues write, we have created a world which has suspended each of us "in glorious, but terrifying isolation."[9]

8. Alasdair MacIntyre, *After Virtue* (Notre Dame, Ind.: University of Notre Dame Press, 1984), pp. 250-51.
9. Bellah et al., p. 6.

Loneliness

An ache
Dull as icewater.
Stays beneath
My stubborn wait.
Hides
In day rages,
Spasmodic laughter;
Curls around the corners
At the edge of sleep;
Threatens
Then disappears
Behind junk mail and catalogs,
A telephone's belled announcements,
The sizzle of pork chops
In a frying pan.
The refrigerator door opens
Then closes:
Milk and ice cream
Beer and cold beef gravy
Sit in darkness.
And I,
Toward the end of the day,
Wonder for whom it is I wait
And what for
In this half light.

John A. De Loyht

The absence of any notion of the common good other than my personal pursuit of my private good also accounts for the growth and power of bureaucracy in the modern state. Liberal societies, MacIntyre's "collection of strangers," require bureaucracies which are designed to function like machines with elaborate division of labor, specialization, uniformity, and anonymity, all in service to the great modern value — *efficiency.*

Each individual acquires freedom in the bureaucratic state by being guaranteed equal, anonymous treatment; that is, bureaucracy is the rule of nobody, nameless, faceless, just following the rules.[10] Ironically, we wonder why we feel less rather than more free under such an arrangement. We feel caught in a tyranny of impersonal, computerized technocrats. Our legal debates tend always to be about procedures rather than purpose.

These bureaucrats promise to be fair, efficient, and evenhanded in their application of the rules. They promise to have no feelings, no commitment to any larger purpose or goal other than efficiency in the application of procedure, no membership in any community other than bureaucracy. The great high priest of this hierarchy is the manager who rules only according to the rules, supported by the data provided by the social scientists.

Managers claim to rule us by facts, rather than by values or personal opinions, a distinction modern philosophy now knows is impossible to sustain. There are no free-standing "facts" about anything human. All our "facts" are produced by, privileged by, and in service to some social order.

The modern democratic state claims to be noncoercive, having no opinions about why life is worth living, or what ends each of us ought to be pursuing. The only function of government, it is claimed, is to administer the rules in a fair, nondiscriminatory, neutral way. Yet to do this, says Stanley Hauerwas, "it is necessary to create a bureaucracy that is more intrusive than the most absolute monarch."[11]

This book seeks dissolution not simply because "small is beautiful" (which it often is) but because we believe that our cherished goals of community are impossible within the current framework.

The theologian Wolfhart Pannenberg has noted where our institutional embodiment of the sovereign individual has gotten us:

> The dissolution of the traditional institutions of social life including family and marriage for the sake of promoting the emancipation of the individual leaves the individual to be victim of increasing loneliness in the midst of a noisy machinery of "communication." It is not likely that secular societies will be able in the long run to survive the consequences of the much-touted emancipation of the in-

10. Here we are indebted to the wonderful analysis of Lesslie Newbigin, *Foolishness to Greeks: The Gospel in Western Culture* (Grand Rapids: Eerdmans, 1986).
11. Stanley Hauerwas, *After Christendom?* (Nashville: Abingdon, 1991), p. 66.

The Power Brokers

The managers of our major tools — nations, corporations, parties, structured movements, professions — hold power. This power is vested in the maintenance of the growth-oriented structures which they manipulate. These managers have the power to make major decisions; they can generate new demands for the output of their tools and enforce the creation of new social labels to fit them. But they have no power to reverse the basic structure of the institutional arrangements which they manage.[12]

---

dividual. . . . Our cultural world, it seems, is in acute danger of dying because of the absence of God, if human persons continue to seek in vain for meaning in their personal lives, if increasing members fail to develop a sense of their personal identity, if the flood of neurosis continues to rise, if more and more people take refuge in suicide or violence, and if the state continues to lose its legitimacy in the consciousness of the citizens, while the cultural tradition functions according to the rules of supply at the discretion of individual demand. All these are the consequence of the absence of God. But far from indicating the death of God, they suggest, rather, that God is not neglected with impunity.[13]

We believe that built into the nature of reality is a divine concern for the powerless, the oppressed, and a divine predisposition against the powerful and the oppressive. Our view partly derives from our religious commitments, and partly from our reading of history. This book, if it is a reworking of anarchist themes, is in service to the empowerment of the powerless and in struggle against the injustice which our modern institutions have done to our beloved human communities.

12. Ivan Illich, *Tools of Conviviality* (Berkeley, Calif.: Heyday Books, 1973), p. 16.

13. Wolfhart Pannenberg, *Christian Spirituality* (Philadelphia: Westminster, 1983), pp. 89-91.

The Power of the Powerless

Within a matter of a few weeks in 1989, the iron-fisted communist regimes in Bulgaria, Czechoslovakia, East Germany, Hungary, and Poland were replaced by more democratic governments with little or no violence involved in the transition. Only Romania was a bloody exception to this rule.

The 1989 election of Solidarity leader Lech Walesa was the climax of a bitter, eight-year struggle to bring down the repressive Polish communist government which involved repeated confrontation and engagement and eventually complex negotiations. During marshal law, several hundred Solidarity leaders were imprisoned for relatively short periods of time, but amazingly only a handful of Poles were actually killed. Czechoslovak playwright Václav Havel played a similar role in the nonviolent demise of communism in Czechoslovakia. Four years later his country split peacefully into two independent nations — the Czech Republic and Slovakia.

Conventional wisdom among American conservatives gives Ronald Reagan credit for ending the Cold War by outspending the Soviets militarily, driving their economy into the ground, and forcing Gorbachev to "cry uncle." We don't buy this self-serving interpretation of the end of the Cold War.

We believe the Cold War ended because it didn't pay anymore for either side. Just as Stalinism had taken its toll on the Soviet Union and Eastern Europe, so too had Reagan-style anticommunism inflicted

Satyagraha

Its root meaning is "holding on to truth," hence "force of righteousness." I have also called it love force or soul force. In the application of *Satyagraha*, I discovered in the earliest stages that pursuit of truth did not permit violence being inflicted on one's opponent, but that he must be weaned from error by patience and sympathy. For what appears truth to the one may appear to be error to the other. And patience means self-suffering. So the doctrine came to mean vindication of truth, not by infliction of suffering on the opponent, but on one's self.

Mahatma Gandhi

enormous costs on the United States. We had spent so much time, energy, and other valuable resources fighting the threat of communism that we diverted our attention, our energy, and our resources from improving the working of our own capitalistic system.

Neither we nor the Soviets could afford a continuation of the military madness. It was no longer in the self-interest of either superpower to continue perpetuating the myths, the half-truths, and outright lies that had fueled the Cold War since the late 1940s. For years Americans had condescendingly criticized virtually every aspect of Soviet life. Yet when we looked into the tired eyes of our foremost adversary, we saw a reflection of ourselves. American capitalism and Soviet communism shared far more common problems than most Americans cared to admit — not the least of which was the fact that they both were too big.[14]

In our futile attempts to convince each other and the rest of the world of our superiority, the United States and the Soviet Union managed to become more nearly alike. That's what the Cold War endgame was all about.

Since the beginning of World War II, national security had been the driving force of the domestic and foreign policies of the United States and the Soviet Union. It was as though little else mattered. In the name of national security; foreign trade, improved health care, economic security, and education and the struggles against drug abuse, environmental pollution, poverty, and hunger were all given short shrift. In the absence of a strong consensus in either country supporting alternative national objectives, the Soviet and American superhawks controlled the foreign-policy agendas in our respective countries for fifty years.

In addition to the fact that the Cold War didn't pay anymore, there was another critical factor contributing to its end — Mikhail S. Gorbachev. With his strategies of tension reduction and power sharing, Gorbachev changed not only all of the political ground rules within the Soviet Union but the entire basis for U.S.-Soviet relations. He repeatedly employed tension reduction to reduce conflict at home and abroad. He

14. In his book *The Cold War Legacy* (Lexington, Mass.: Lexington Books, 1991), Thomas H. Naylor discusses nine common problems shared by the United States and the former Soviet Union: alienation, injustice, Cold War paranoia, excessive militarization, economic uncertainty, lack of competitiveness, declining international influence, global development, and leadership gap.

consistently pursued a nonconfrontational problem-solving approach to political problems based on open discussion, negotiation, and mutual trust. Ronald Reagan soon discovered that it's not much fun to pick a fight with someone who doesn't fight back.

The other linchpin of Gorbachev's leadership style was power sharing. Soviet enterprise managers, labor unions, local government and party officials, ethnic minorities, Soviet republics, religious groups, Eastern European nations, and Third World allies were among the groups with whom Gorbachev shared power. But power sharing is risky business, as Gorbachev learned. The leader can lose complete control, as did he.

For over six years Gorbachev's radical political and economic reforms were implemented in the Soviet Union with virtually no violence. He repeatedly confronted the all-powerful Soviet *nomenklatura* — the party leaders, the KGB, and the military. Then in December 1991 the Soviet Union disintegrated before our eyes, splitting nonviolently into fifteen independent republics.

Jesus Christ, Mahatma Gandhi, Martin Luther King Jr., Lech Walesa, Václav Havel, and South African leaders F. W. de Klerk and Nelson R. Mandela all employed nonviolent means to empower otherwise powerless people.

Nonviolence

Nonviolence is the answer to the crucial political and moral questions of our time; the need for man to overcome oppression and violence without resorting to oppression and violence.

Man must evolve for all human conflict a method which rejects revenge, aggression, and retaliation. The foundation of such a method is love.

Martin Luther King Jr.
Nobel Peace Prize Speech
December 11, 1964

Nonviolence is not a passive approach to conflict resolution but rather a proactive approach that goes right to the crux of power relationships. It can undermine power and authority by withdrawing the approval, the support, and the cooperation of those who have been dealt an injustice. It demands strength and courage and not idle pacifism. Nonviolence derives its strength from the energy buildup and very real power of powerlessness.

Ethan Allen and the Power of the Powerless

Ethan Allen used his oratorical skill to link local concerns and cultural values to larger translocal issues, making the Green Mountains conflict part of a general revolutionary and democratic movement. For poor settlers suffering from the attention of the rich and the powerful, Allen was a potent weapon in an otherwise hopeless situation. He came to represent the resistance of independent agricultural communities against the machinations of distant governments under the control of wealthy speculators intent on stealing the land of the poor. Allen symbolized Vermont, the one great victory of the powerless against vested interest.[15]

We believe that the only way to save America from itself — from its big government, big military, big corporations, and big cities — is by empowering millions of powerless Americans. Downsizing the USA is about empowering states, regions, small towns, villages, community schools, colleges, and religious congregations, as well as individual citizens.

The Breakup of Canada

Few Americans realize that Canada is coming unglued at the seams. Viewing Canadian politics each evening through the eyes of the Canadian Broadcasting Corporation's flagship news program "The National" makes it clear that Canada is facing a major constitutional crisis — much broader and much deeper than Québec separatism alone.

Most of the time most Americans are oblivious to Canada's existence. However, the October 30, 1995, Québec sovereignty referendum got our attention. When French separatists mustered 49.43 percent

---

15. Michael A. Bellesiles, *Revolutionary Outlaws* (Charlottesville: University Press of Virginia, 1993), p. 5.

Ten Decentralist Maxims

1. If you don't know where you are going, no road will get you there.
2. Small is beautiful.
3. Keep it simple — always make molehills out of mountains.
4. Share power — one person, one vote.
5. Might doesn't make right.
6. Reduce tension; don't escalate conflict.
7. There is no daddy or mommy, but if there were a daddy or a mommy, he or she would be you. (Martin Shubik)
8. There is no substitute for personal commitment, responsibility, and hard work.
9. Nothing stimulates a man or woman's mind like the knowledge that he or she may be hanged in the morning.
10. Build small communities, not big empires.

---

of the vote, every major American newspaper expressed editorial outrage against the Québec separatist movement. Our president, our Congress, and the American people all weighed in against the secession of Québec from Canada. A congressional subcommittee has held hearings on the political and economic implications of the breakup of Canada on the U.S.

Even though the French separatists were defeated by the federalists in 1995, Québec separatism is not likely to go away anytime soon under the charismatic leadership of Prime Minister Lucien Bouchard. Known as "St. Lucien" by many of the Quebecois, Bouchard is an articulate, intelligent cross between former Polish leader Lech Walesa and President John F. Kennedy. Himself a victim of leg amputation, Bouchard understands the politics of powerlessness on a very personal level.

The inept response of the Ottawa government to French separatists has not only exacerbated the tension between Québec and the other nine provinces, but has engendered separatist sentiments throughout Canada. Prime Minister Jean Chrétien's decision to ask the Supreme Court for an opinion of the legality of a unilateral declaration of independence by Québec has further enraged Francophones and hardened their anti-Canadian stance.

High unemployment, slow economic growth, large federal and

provincial government deficits, and a deflated Canadian dollar have plagued the Canadian economy in the 1990s. There is increased tension between the more affluent English-speaking provinces — British Columbia, Ontario, and Alberta — and poor provinces like Newfoundland, Nova Scotia, and Manitoba. Prince Edward Island and Newfoundland — hard hit by the demise of the Atlantic Coast fishing industry — are so heavily subsidized by Ottawa that they are like wards of the state.

Newfoundland has its own grievance with Québec. The Newfoundland premier has threatened to cut Québec off from its supply of electricity generated by the Churchill Falls dam unless a new power-export contract is negotiated.

There are even secessionist pressures within Québec. If Québec splits with Canada, Anglophone Montreal might become an independent city-state. The same may be true of the Eastern Townships. The Cree, other Indian tribes, and the Inuits living in Québec all oppose Québec independence, which they believe would further delay eventual self-government for themselves.

Even though Canada enjoys the U.N.'s seal of approval as the best country in the world in which to live, its cradle-to-grave social welfare system also appears to be unraveling. Large government deficits, excess demand for services, and the effects of Reaganism and Thatcherism have taken their toll on the quality of health care and other social services.

The breakup of Canada is the price one pays for a weak central government with very powerful, independent member states. For years

---

Draft Bill on the Sovereignty of Québec

When becoming a sovereign country, Québec will cease to be part of Canada. It will become an independent nation like France, the United States of America and the other members of the United Nations.

Québec will then have full control over all its taxes, and Québec taxpayers will no longer pay income tax or other taxes to Ottawa. But neither will they be represented in the Canadian Parliament.

Current federal laws and existing treaties will remain in force, but all new laws will be passed by the Québec National Assembly and new treaties will be signed by the Québec government.

the Canadian National Railway, the Canadian Pacific Railway, Air Canada, and the Canadian National Broadcasting Corporation were part of the glue which held Canada together. Global privatization has rendered these Canadian icons impotent as integrating forces. Can professional ice hockey alone provide sufficient glue to hold Canada together — particularly after its humiliating World Cup defeat?

Isn't the real reason why Québec separatism makes Americans so uncomfortable that it's too close to home? We encourage secession in far away places like Poland, Lithuania, and South Africa. But Québec reminds us of our own vulnerability — our size and our inflexibility. Just as Ottawa seems powerless to sort out Québec's demand for independence, Washington is impotent to deal with its own combined problems — bigness and diversity.

How strong is the will of the people of Québec to be free and independent? How far is Ottawa prepared to go in imposing its will on Québec?

When the political and economic costs to English-speaking Canada of continued forced federation membership outweigh the benefits, Québec will eventually be set free — which may be sooner than some Americans think.

What if secession fever were to spread over the Canadian border into the United States, where some say it originated over two hundred years ago?

A Nonviolent Secession Paradigm

Thanks largely to Abraham Lincoln, secession has been viewed as a political pariah by most Americans since the Civil War. But suppose the notion that, "Just as a nation or a state has a right to form, so too does it have a right to disband, subdivide itself, or secede from a larger unit," were suddenly to become politically correct? What if secession fever were to become as virulent as Reaganism and Thatcherism? Then what would we do?

One of the biggest obstacles to secession is that no mechanism currently exists in our government to deal with this subject. None of our politicians or government officials have considered the logical possibility of dissolution as a strategy for confronting our immense socioeconomic and political problems.

If secession were no longer viewed as an anathema by our

government, then national guidelines for dealing with U.S. government property, relocation costs, federal debt, and net worth could be formulated to facilitate negotiations with individual states.

The Power to Change the World

Never doubt that a small group of thoughtful, committed citizens can change the world. Indeed, it's the only thing that ever has.

Margaret Mead

Constitutional though it may be, it would be naive of us to prescribe a very specific secession game plan for the United States, since no state has tried secession for over a century. However, we can at least sketch out what we believe to be some of the key elements of a rational, nonviolent secession process.

A critical first step would be convening a statewide convention of democratically elected representatives to consider one and only one issue — secession. Once a majority — better still, a two-thirds majority — of the convention delegates had approved the declaration of secession, the state's governor would be empowered to present the state's secession declaration to the U.S. Secretary of State. This would be followed by a strategy of constructive engagement with the U.S. government modeled closely after those strategies successfully employed by Lech Walesa and Václav Havel in Poland and Czechoslovakia, respectively, to free their countries from Soviet rule. To succeed, such a process would involve a subtle mixture of confrontation, negotiation, and testing of limits spread out over several years. Other factors contributing to the likelihood that a state would be allowed to leave the Union would include the state's size, wealth, and military importance, as well as whether the state was acting alone or in consort with other states.

Ultimately, whether or not a state is allowed to leave is neither a legal question nor a constitutional question, but rather a matter of

---

Size is not grandeur, and territory does not make a nation.

Thomas Henry Huxley

---

political will. How strong is the will of the people in the seceding state to be free and independent? How far is the U.S. government prepared to go in imposing its will on a breakaway state?

Ethan Allen's Politics of Reason

Allen developed his political methodology from a close observation of Native Americans. Historians often note the importance of the Indian style of fighting to America's revolutionary victory, and the American preference for shooting from cover certainly discomfited the British. But Indian methods of war included more than just firing from behind trees. As the weaker party in most military conflicts, several Indian peoples developed an appreciation for the political and diplomatic character of warfare. Allen learned much from the Iroquois practice of constant negotiation with equally powerful enemies. Through most of the eighteenth century the Iroquois manipulated the aggressive designs of France and England, keeping the two nations in suspense over which side they would join, using this tension to preserve their autonomy. The Iroquois began the American Revolution with the same policy but made the fatal error of eventually siding with the British. Ethan Allen avoided that mistake.

Allen learned from the Indians that warfare has a strong psychological component, and that violence can be limited by manipulating an enemy's fears and desires. Allen used these methods to win and preserve Vermont's independence. Like the Iroquois, Allen did not seek conquest but survival in a hostile world.[16]

This is not a call for revolution. We are merely proposing that our government begin planning the process to facilitate the orderly secession of those states that want to assume more responsibility for their own destiny. Such a process will take time. Yugoslavia and the former Soviet Union are good examples of downsizing proceeding too rapidly. To avoid the chaos of Eastern Europe, we need to begin thinking about a New Confederation of American States to replace the old Union.

16. Bellesiles, p. 187.

Such a confederation might combine some features of the European Union and the North Atlantic Treaty Organization.

One could envisage free trade and free travel among states sharing a single currency and a common economic system. Member states might form a mutual defense alliance. However, as independent political units, the former American states would have complete responsibility for and total control of their own taxes, schools, social welfare, health care, law enforcement, highways, airports, housing, and physical environment.

New Nation-States

In many ways Vermont might be an ideal state to test the limits of how far the United States government would be prepared to go to preserve the Union. Vermont is tiny, nonthreatening, and lacks any resources of strategic importance to the rest of the United States. There is not a single military base in Vermont. Some have suggested that Vermont should join forces with New Hampshire and Maine and possibly the Maritime Provinces of Canada as well. The combined population of Maine, New Hampshire, Vermont, New Brunswick, Nova Scotia, and Prince Edward Island is less than 5 million people, making it about the size of Denmark.

Connecticut, Massachusetts, and Rhode Island might also form a small nation. If states were allowed to leave the Union, upstate New York and New York City would no doubt split, since they have little or nothing in common.

One could envision a Mid-Atlantic alliance consisting of southern Virginia, North Carolina, and South Carolina. Northern Virginia, the District of Columbia, and Maryland might unite. Maybe not.

Miami and South Florida would probably become an Hispanic nation, as would parts of South Texas and Los Angeles County. California would most likely split into at least three independent nations. Surely the independent-minded Lone Star State would go it alone.

Illinois, Indiana, Michigan, and Ohio might become the Rust Belt Nation. Pennsylvania might be invited to join them, if it did not opt to travel alone.

The handful of predominantly African American counties in northwest Mississippi known as the Mississippi Delta would probably become the first black nation in America. Parts of Alabama, Georgia,

> ## Florida
>
> Florida lacks a sense of "community." Though we are a state 150 years old in 1995, our citizenry does not exhibit the signatures of an identifiable, unified society, in the manner, say, of Pennsylvania, where 80 percent of the population is native-born. Florida is simply too fractured in its geography, its population centers and its multi-faceted citizenry to permit discovery of a statewide coherence, either political or cultural.[17]

and northern Florida might be candidates for the same. South Louisiana might be reconstituted as Acadia South.

Few ethnic groups in the United States would have a stronger claim for independence than Native Americans. In principle, there is no reason why there could not be several independent Native American nations. In practice, the existing Indian reservations are sparsely populated, extremely poor, highly dependent on the U.S. government, and widely dispersed throughout the United States. However, Indian nations might be sustainable in Arizona, California, and Oklahoma, each of which has over two hundred thousand Indians living mostly on reservations. There are fewer than 2 million Indians left in the United States today.

> ## New American Territories
>
> Spin off the sparsely settled stretches of both Dakotas and Nebraska and Kansas, along with the equally empty eastern stretches of Montana, Wyoming and Colorado, and let it all revert to territorial status. Now there's a step that would neatly symbolize the victory of the new frontier and the inversion of the winning of the West — decommission a state or two and make some of the continental United States a territory again.[18]

17. Michael Gannon, *The New History of Florida* (Gainesville: University of Florida Press, 1996).

18. Charles Harbutt, "The Reopening of the Frontier," *New York Times Magazine*, October 15, 1995, p. 54.

What the Muslims Believe

We recognize and respect American citizens as independent people and we respect their laws which govern this nation.

We believe that the offer of integration is hypocritical and is made by those who are trying to deceive the Black peoples into believing that their 400-year-old open enemies of freedom, justice and equality are, all of a sudden, their "friends." Furthermore, we believe that such deception is intended to prevent Black people from realizing that the time in history has arrived for the separation from the whites of this nation.

If the white people are truthful about their professed friendship toward the so-called Negro, they can prove it by dividing up America with their slaves.

We do not believe that America will ever be able to furnish enough jobs for her own millions of unemployed, in addition to jobs for the 20,000,000 Black people as well.

What the Muslims Want

We want equality of opportunity. We want equal membership in society with the best in civilized society.

We want our people in America whose parents or grandparents were descendants from slaves, to be allowed to establish a separate state or territory of their own — either on this continent or elsewhere. We believe that our former slave masters are obligated to maintain and supply our needs in this separate territory for the next 20 to 25 years — until we are able to produce and supply our own needs.[19]

Washington and Oregon might link up with British Columbia and possibly Alaska. However, both Alaska and Hawaii would encounter tough resistance from the Pentagon if they try to secede, because of their strategic military importance. There could be a Rocky Mountain Nation and possibly a Great Plains Republic as well.

When one begins to speculate about alternative subdivisions of

19. "The Muslim Program," *Final Call*, March 27, 1994.

states and alliances among states, one realizes that most of our states have far less in common than our politicians pretend. If Palestine could be divided into a Jewish state and an Arab state, why can't independent African American, Hispanic, and Native American states be carved out of the United States? The fighting between the Arabs and the Israelis would have ended years ago if we had cut off all U.S. military and financial aid to *both* sides.

Empowering Small Communities

The modern consciousness is dependent in great part on the thought of Friedrich Hegel, who, in the early nineteenth century, taught that the history of humanity is a history of inexorable progression from smaller to larger forms, from simpler to more complex organisms, from irrationality to rationality. Every realm of thought, from theology to economics, from physics to politics was influenced by Hegel's notion of progress. Marxism, for example, with its theory of economic progress from feudalism to bourgeois to communism is Hegelian in origin.

Few today would agree that Marxism represented human progress. Yet many still cling to the Hegelian belief that newer, bigger, and more complex are better. Hegelianism is a hard habit to break. It may be the peculiar gift of life in this century to see the lie in the Hegelian idea of human progression, to have experienced the downside of complex bureaucratic institutions. We predict it shall be the task of the next century to dismantle and dissolve many of the institutions which have dominated us in this century.

Small is Beautiful said E. F. Schumacher in 1973 — small communities, small towns, small businesses, small farms, small schools, small colleges, small churches, and small nations. The only way to empower Americans is to make America and all of its giant institutions inordinately smaller. Big-name politicians, big political parties, big study commissions, big consulting projects, big conferences, big books, big technology, and big computer networks are all part of the problem — not the solution.

One thing is for sure: Neither the Democrats nor the Republicans will be much help in decentralizing and downsizing the USA and all of its major institutions. Both political parties are firmly entrenched in the centralist camp. The Democrats like big cities, big public works

The Cloning of America

Long before Dolly the Scottish sheep was cloned through genetic engineering, millions of Americans were effectively being cloned by our government, our politicians, our large corporations, our universities, and our public schools without altering a single DNA molecule. Furthermore, no one seemed to care.

Even though we all have quite different genetic maps, most of us think the same way, behave the same way, vote the same, watch the same TV programs, buy the same consumer goods, and raise our children the same way.

Multiple political parties are a fact of life throughout Europe and most of the West. Today the only countries without strong multi-party political systems are the United States and a number of third world military dictatorships.

Alabama Governor George Wallace once said, "There is not a dime's worth of difference between the Democratic and Republican parties." He was right. As the 1996 elections reconfirmed, the United States has a single political party masked as a two-party system. Minority parties are impotent.

During the Cold War we accused the Soviets of endless human rights abuses ranging from political manipulation and mind control to the denial of basic rights — freedom of speech, freedom of the press, freedom of religion, and freedom of assembly. Refuseniks were often jailed. We don't imprison political dissidents in this country. It's not necessary. So powerful is the message from the center that those few who disagree are effectively marginalized and relegated to the political sidelines.

(continued on page 283)

projects, and big social welfare programs; the Republicans, big business, big military, and big prisons.

There are no serious external threats to the United States. Both communism and the former Soviet Union are dead in the water. Today's enemies lie entirely within our own borders — excessive centralization and bigness.

(continued from page 282)

In no institution is the pressure for conformity greater than in our colleges and universities. If an undergraduate degree has any meaning anymore, it is to certify that recipients are no different from thousands of other like-minded graduates. This is known as *academic freedom*.

The dumbing down of our over-centralized, over-regulated, values-free public schools is nothing new. Above all, what one learns at school is what it means to be "cool." What is cool determines how you dress, how you behave, how you speak, whether you have sex, and whether you take drugs and abuse alcohol. Our public schools are among our nation's most effective cloning agents.

The Internet is more of the same. For millions, it has become not only their primary source of information, communication, and entertainment, but also a wellspring from which they hope meaning, community, and human connectedness will flow. President Bill Clinton, who loves the Internet, calls it "our new town square." And as if this were not enough, we are bombarded by the silver-tongued messages of countless televangelists offering to clone us right on the spot in front of our own TV.

So why is human cloning such a big deal? We have already been cloned, and don't even know it.[20]

Thomas H. Naylor
The Baltimore Sun

The terms "liberal" and "conservative" are Cold War relics with no meaning anymore, other than the election of lamebrain politicians whom we allow to jerk us around with the same old divisive rhetoric which has worked so well for so long. What American liberals and conservatives share in common is a preoccupation with individualism and individual rights at the expense of group rights and community rights. Our interest in this book in downsizing and decentralization

20. Thomas H. Naylor, "Cloning Is Nothing New in U.S.," *The Baltimore Sun,* March 23, 1997.

stems primarily from a concern for the rights and responsibilities of small local communities.

We have no grand scheme for downsizing America, for such a plan would be antithetical to what we are trying to accomplish. If nothing else, we hope we have better equipped the reader to confront bigness in every form, shape, and variety.

What we are proposing is decentralizing, downsizing, and dissolving virtually every major institution in America and replacing these obsolete monoliths with collections of small, voluntary, cooperative communities, developed entirely through bottom-up participatory means.

For years conservatives have complained that what's wrong with America is that our government is too big, too powerful, and too intrusive. Today few liberals would disagree. But the size of our government is only one piece of the political puzzle. Our government is too big because our country and nearly every other social and political institution contained therein is also too big. Fine tuning or patching our unmanageable meganation and all of its turgid institutions are pretend solutions. To conservatives and liberals alike we say, "It's time to fish, or cut bait."

There are no quick-fix solutions to our joint problems of bigness and lack of connectedness. Ultimately there is but one solution — empowering, nurturing, and supporting small communities. But as we all know, community building is a slow and arduous process. And from the story of the Tower of Babel we learned that not all communities and unification schemes are good. We have to learn to ask the right questions about the underlying purposes of community.

About life after Babel, what can be said? Will it be more of the same? We hope not. But do we possess the political will to rebuild a smaller, more beautiful, sustainable America? Is the meltdown of America a threat to be avoided or an opportunity to be grasped? The options are all too clear — the choices, our very own.

Index of Names

285